CW00403524

East of the Moon, West of the Sun

A Journey to the Antipodes

Sam Donegan

For my parents and grandparents.

CONTENTS

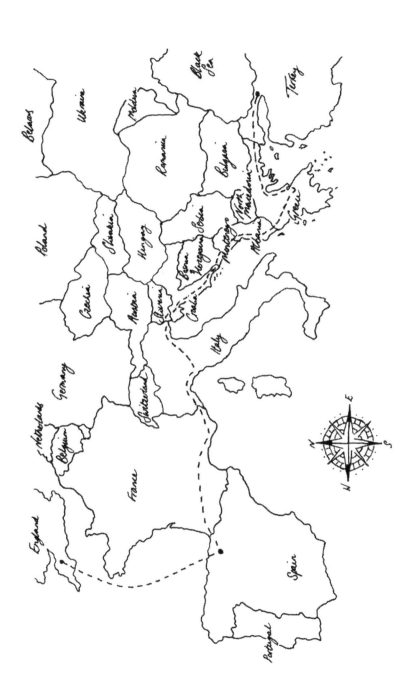

Chapter One

We are sailed, I hope,
Beyond the line of madness.

– Richard Brome, *The Antipodes*

A journey is something made in the mind. It is a time in our lives bookended by two pillars, a beginning and an end, which are boundaries of our own invention. These pillars prevent a journey from collapsing in on itself, keep it from spilling over its edges, and bracket it off as something special, as something distinct from the rest of our memories.

When journeys are undertaken alone, almost everyone leaves home a hero, at least in their own mind. More than any other species of traveller, it is the solitary kind who are most prone to fictions, who are most likely to have spent the months prior to their departure wrapped in daydream and reverie, guessing at what wonders the world might hold.

By the time a departure comes around, it has already featured in so many of a traveller's imaginings that it has grown to critical status. It is the beginning of their journey, that crucial first pillar, and must encompass both a grave goodbye to the safe harbour of home and a celebration of auspicious times ahead. It is a melancholy moment, steeped in hope, which feels incomplete without a sombre crowd of family and friends, gathered together to witness the exit of a brave, intrepid soul out into the world.

Such an atmosphere prevailed at the dawn of my own journey, but only for a brief time. It began to disintegrate after the third failed attempt to start my motorcycle engine, and then evaporated altogether on the fifth try, when an overly zealous pump of the kick-stand on my part caused a piece of my headlight to fall off. A few more unsuccessful starts and some of the neighbours who had come to wave goodbye began to peel away into the morning mist, whispering to each other of my imminent jeopardy. It was not the beginning I had imagined.

However, it probably was the beginning I deserved. The motorcycle I was sat upon had been bought in a dark, abandoned car-park one winter night from a suspicious man who had told me his name was Neil Diamond. It was wretchedly cheap, falling to pieces, and I highly suspected had been stolen. When Neil handed me the keys, I knew nothing about motorcycles, and by the time of my departure, I knew nothing more, apart from how it felt to crash them, following one unfortunate collision with a Wiltshire hedge. But a few months after my meeting with Mr Diamond, I did gain my legal motorcycle license. And just five days after passing my test, I had packed my bags, thrown them onto the back of the machine, and announced that I was leaving for the other side of the world. Uninitiated is an understatement; I was irremediably clueless.

From where I was stuck atop my driveway in Somerset, there were only seventy-five miles between myself and a ship, named *Pont-Aven*, which was due to sail for Santander in a matter of hours. The frustrating thing was that I knew the way to the harbour, having undertaken countless rehearsals in my head, and could conjure every mile of it in my mind. I knew I had only to turn left from my house, make the climb up onto the Blackdown Hills, twist right at the first scent of scorched honey and shock of yellow that announced the fields of rapeseed, and then follow the bright, perfumed cloak of that crop down the spine of Somerset and Devon, until the road reached Plymouth, where it would meet the sea. But until the motorcycle would start, I was captive to my street.

After muttering several strings of profanities, I managed to cloak the visor of my helmet entirely with fog, which meant my family could no longer see my face. This proved to be a mercy when I discovered that I had not yet turned the silver lever on the side of the motorcycle that allowed fuel to flow through the machine, which was why it would not start. With my cheeks flushing scarlet, I feigned the adjustment of a shoelace, bent down and gave the switch a discrete flick, and to the astonishment of everyone present, the next time I kicked the engine to life it whimpered but did not die.

After a few triumphant twists of the throttle, just to let the neighbours who had vanished know that I was finally leaving, I clunked out onto the road and set off for the hills, one valedictory leather-clad arm raised high, and my gaze so affectionately fixed on the image of my family in my left mirror that I very nearly ran into a post box one hundred metres from my house. It took only another hundred metres for me to realise I had never ridden a motorcycle with luggage on before, and I suddenly feared that with the extra weight the pitiful machine might never make it over the Blackdowns. Nevertheless, in under half an hour, I had gone over the hills and come down onto the Devon Expressway, where with the aid of a gently sloping road, the cycle managed its top speed of fifty west-country miles per hour.

I had been told by real motorcyclists that rolling along at fifty should not feel particularly perilous, but included amongst my machine's imperfections was a tendency for both mirrors to collapse in winds above *forty* miles per hour, which made changing between the three lanes of the caravan-clogged road to Plymouth a near-lethal task. Added to the mirrors, my speedometer was broken, my alarm would sound spontaneously whilst I was riding, and changing into fourth gear rendered all electrics on the motorcycle impotent. Before my ride to the ferry-port, I had known the cycle was a weak creature, with failing organs and arthritic parts, but only afterwards did I realise the full extent of its feebleness.

And even then, I only learnt of the motorcycle's favourite trick several hours into the *Pont-Aven*'s crossing of the Bay of Biscay, when a strongly accented voice crackled out of the French ferry company's loudspeakers and announced:

'Can the owner of motorcycle registration plate WG15 BHF please report to the information desk immediately.'

At hearing the characters of my license plate read aloud, my heart dropped like an anchor. Walking down seven flights of stairs to the information centre in the belly of the ship, I wondered what calamity could have possibly befallen the motorcycle only a few hours from

English shores. I braced myself for news that the machine had been ripped from the hold and had fallen prey to a rare Atlantic whirlpool, or had spontaneously combusted and started a small fire below decks, or had perhaps come loose from its fixtures and flown through the windscreen of a Ferrari.

'Hello, I'm the motorcyclist you're looking for,' I said, speaking to a uniformed lady sat behind the desk.

'WG15 BHF?' she asked in a grave tone.

I gulped and nodded.

'Hm, please follow me, monsieur. There is a problem.'

Wordlessly, ominously, I was led deeper into the ship, through a slippery riddle of wire cables and winches, past lines of trucks and buses, until we finally arrived at the vast huddle of motorcycles where I had earlier deposited mine. It was still there, looking impish and fraudulent amongst a far brighter, more capable crowd, but beneath it, and stretching out a metre either side of the wheels, a greasy puddle of oil was creeping further with each pitch of the ship.

'What would you like to do about this?' said the uniformed lady, tipping her head towards the broadening blemish.

'Do you have any paper towels?' I faltered.

'Paper towels? You do not want to fix it, monsieur?' she asked, her eyebrows convening in a sceptical frown.

'I would very much like to fix it, but I'm afraid that you probably possess more mechanical knowledge than I do. Are any of the ship's engineers familiar with motorcycles?' I joked.

'You can find some paper towels over there,' she replied, staring blankly back at me whilst pointing to a nearby stairwell. Shaking her head, she made to leave, but after a few steps, she turned and asked:

'Monsieur, where are you taking this motorcycle?'

'New Zealand,' I said with a grin, as the dark arches of her eyebrows rose once again, propped up by a condescending smile, which was a silent confirmation that in this young lady's opinion I was, without a shadow of a doubt, something akin to a lunatic.

***

I did not know it then, but my motorcycle's incontinence would become something of its trademark - a roughish signature that it would produce everywhere I left it over the following months, like a mutt marking its territory. It meant that replenishing the oil became a daily necessity as the leak was never fixed, but nor did the engine ever succumb to it. In time, I even came to look upon the greasy dribble as useful because as long as the engine was leaking oil, I at least knew that it still had some oil within it. And more than that, the leak proved an effective security measure. No self-respecting motorcycle thief stumbles across a machine resting in a puddle of its own liquids and decides it to be worth the effort of stealing.

In the end, the motorcycle proved charming in its wretchedness and revealed a talent for turning its many flaws into virtues, but this knowledge had not yet dawned on me as I knelt on the steel floor of the *Pont-Aven's* second deck and built a small pyramid of soiled towels between its wheels. By the time I was done mopping, it was nearing midnight, and after leaving the under-decks, I went in search of the passenger lounge. At the summit of the ship, I eventually found a dark room, cluttered with ranks of uncomfortable chairs, which was the place reserved for passengers unwilling to pay the price of a cabin.

Groping through the darkness, I searched for an empty chair, noticing on my way that the walls were trembling. At first, I thought this was just the rumble of the ship's engines, but as I sat down I felt my chair quaking violently, and looking along the row of seats, I spotted a vast creature, embalmed in blankets, drawing monstrous breaths nearby. Shutting my eyes, I hoped for sleep, but alongside the leviathan's heaves, more noises and murmurs began to grow out of the dark. From two rows forward, I could hear the sound of fangs gnashing, from elsewhere came the click of a porpoise's tongue, and the back of the room echoed with deep, sonorous mumbles. I drifted for a while, unable to sleep, imagining myself at the bottom of the ocean and shuddering at the thought of how much water lay beneath me. And when I opened my eyes later in the night, glows and flashes were lighting up the room, glinting amidst the darkness like the lanterns of those crumpled fish that live so deep underwater no light ever reaches them.

As well as the residents of the passenger lounge, there were another two thousand people aboard the *Pont-Aven,* all sleeping soundly in every direction around me. It is a strange sensation being surrounded on every side by thousands of lives, all for a brief time sharing the same fate, confined for twenty-four hours on a single floating raft charting a passage across the ocean. Great ships are the most collective mode of travel ever invented, and yet, thanks to the silly solipsism that accompanies the start of most journeys, I imagined myself to be distinct from everyone else on board. In my mind, I was the only person awake to each roll of the ship, the only person fully attuned to the marine. Distinct from everyone else except the captain of course, who I hoped was awake, and who I pictured standing alone on the bridge, scanning the black Atlantic with a pair of heroic eyes, watching for the white wake of other vessels or the distant lights of land.

In reality, the true reason for my insomnia was that I was worrying about my infernal machine spilling its bits all over the hold, whilst also trying to estimate the magnitude of embarrassment that would ensue if I could not even get the motorcycle down the gangplank and onto Spanish soil. I admit that a motorcycle was a strange choice of transport for someone who did not know a single thing about motorcycle maintenance, and who had never ridden more than one hundred miles on one of the machines. Perhaps my insomnia was deserved. But for a poor writer with a long way to go, the motorcycle offered the richest ratio of freedom to cost, which was vital for someone with my agenda.

That agenda, though simple, was vast. I had decided to try and travel overland from England to New Zealand, despite not having much of a plan, and with no appropriate experience. And at the root of this scheme, like almost all decisions made in my life, lay a book.

It was two years earlier, whilst sat in the musty chill of my university library, that I first took down from the bookshelf a slim volume titled *The Antipodes.* A seventeenth-century comedy, written by the playwright Richard Brome, *The Antipodes* follows the plight of a young man named Peregrine - an avid reader who suffers from an acute addiction to travel literature and an ardent desire to see the world. To cure Peregrine's obsession, his family seek the help of an apothecary named Doctor Hughball, known for his unorthodox treatments. After administering a sleeping drug, the doctor whisks his patient away to the countryside, and when Peregrine wakes, he is convinced by a troupe of actors that he has been taken to the Antipodes, a land on the other side of the earth, geographically opposite to England, where society is the inverse of all that Peregrine has known. After spending time amongst the 'Antipodeans', Peregrine is eventually cured of his travel mania and returns to his normal life, a happy and satisfied man.

When I first read the play, I was a pale and withered student, long confined to the library, who yearned to see the light of day just once more before I fully metamorphosed into parchment. And as I read *The*

Antipodes, I found my own desires to match those of the restless Peregrine. All my life I had been reading travel books, but I barely knew the world. Certain that I would not be satiated by theatrics like Brome's protagonist, and with the beastly responsibilities of adulthood beginning to bay, I decided that once my degree was finished, I would set out for the Antipodes of my home in Somerset, which, when I checked on a map, turned out to be a remote square of the Southern Ocean.

Not in possession of a boat, and coming to the conclusion that an isolated patch of the Southern Ocean might be difficult to reach and not especially interesting, I settled for Slope Point, the southern tip of New Zealand's South Island, and decided that rather than fly – a mode of transport that I felt resembled Peregrine's anaesthesia – I would try and arrive there by travelling across the face of the earth, at least as far as was possible.

That said, I have never been a purist, and I knew from the start that the motorcycle would only take me so far. Due to the unfortunate fact that there are always wars being fought somewhere in the world, and with great ribbons of ocean in my way, planes, boats, and other means of transport were inevitable from the start. But in my dusty university library, I decided that within reason I would try and cross the earth alone from one side to the other, and two years later, thanks to that scheme, I was aboard the *Pont-Aven*, struggling to sleep, stuck in a torture chamber of gurgles and whimpers, wishing I only had some of Doctor Hughball's potion to hand.

***

To say that I was pleased the following morning when my oil-starved motorcycle started in the ship's hold would be an understatement. When I then managed to make it off the *Pont-Aven* without slipping into the docks on my oiled tyres or crashing into any of the sinister-looking motorcyclists surrounding me, I was so elated that I misread the signs, took a wrong turn, and ended up on the Spanish motorway. I had never driven on a motorway before, in a car or on a motorcycle, and all I thought to do was panic, put on my hazard lights, and ride for ten miles up the hard shoulder. It did not feel like a promising start to my time on European roads.

Coming off the highway, with nowhere at all to go, and surrounded by signs written in an indecipherable language, I simply chose one direction and kept riding. A short while later, after several close encounters with Spanish motorists, I found myself ascending a hill, riding along a road that ran parallel to a curving stretch of parkland. Mercifully, the road was quiet, and the further I went, the emptier it became. Eventually, it tapered to a single track, which I followed right to its end, stopping at the foot of a tall, white lighthouse which looked out over the Bay of Santander.

Leaving my motorcycle in the shadow of the lighthouse, I took my first steps on continental soil and walked out into a field of thick grass. From the edges of the park before me, sharp grey cliffs buried themselves at steep angles into the sea and conspired at one point to form the face of a man. As I walked a little further along the promontory, I felt as if the face in the cliff was watching me. Every time I turned back he was there, looking at me through stony eyes, with his brow supporting the white lantern, his nose facing straight out to the Atlantic, and his long granite neck barbered with sea-foam.

All along the cliff-edge surrounding the face, a steady assault of waves ricocheted off the land, glowing white as they struck against the rocks, then gradually fading back to translucent blue. But a few pale flecks survived and floated out to sea - little white rebellions that drifted atop the ocean, wobbling in the swell for a while, before finally unfolding their wings and stepping up out of the surf to join the helix of chattering gulls spiralling above the cliffs. I walked out to the edge until I could walk no further and then turned my back to the water. From where I stopped, the rock rolled backwards into grassland, and from the fields of grass sprouted forest. Beyond the pine trees, the whole of Spain lay before me, and beyond that, all the rest of Europe and Asia unfurled in one unbroken, billowing skin, hitched there to the Atlantic by the pale stake towering beside me, and not meeting the sea again until the Straits of Singapore. I stood and breathed in the salt-sodden air, listened to the cries of the gulls behind, and grew giddy at the thought of all the earth before me.

***

Waking on my first morning in Spain, I looked out from my tent and found myself stuck in the damp heart of a cloud. In the night, an armada of Atlantic fogs had converged upon Santander and buried the city in vapour, gathering in greatest number about the Cabo Mayor lighthouse, which rose beside me cocooned in mist, like a stick swaddled in flossed silk.

Stumbling about, half-blind, I found my motorcycle and made my slow way down from the promontory, following a road that was little more than a clipped strip of asphalt floating between invisible streets. As I continued east across the city, the fog persisted, until it began to feel like Santander was punishing me, as if the city had decided that if I was only going to stay one night then I didn't deserve to see its features, and so had petulantly erased itself. It was a loss that I lamented, and though I longed to spend a week wandering the town, the distance I had to travel and the slim profile of my purse instilled in me a fear that I could only satiate with speed.

Following a small, neglected road, I kept to the coast, catching glimpses of tattered cliff-tops breaching through the fog. The only traces of life on the road were signs announcing the cities of Bilbao and San Sebastián, which brought with them visions of old Sagardotegi firesides, and thoughts of sheep's cheese, fresh bread, and sweet Basque cider. I would have liked to spend a week in either city, but I felt compelled to press on through the gloom, beating my way through a steady curtain of brine blown up by the waves onto the road.

Inciting my haste was a swollen sense of nervousness inspired by the difficulties of my route. When it was not skirting the waves, the road I followed tracked the edges of precarious cliffs, curled around wind-stricken headlands, and tunnelled through wet walls of stone. My first full day of riding took more from me more than I was willing to give, and at its end, all I had gained was a jacket patterned with sea-salt, damp hands wrinkled with cold, and a meagre line drawn on my map, one hundred miles across.

The next morning brought more fog and another ride through unknown country, but by midday, bars of sunshine began to break through the cloud, and in their light, I realised that the road-signs had slipped from Spanish into French. I had not known what to anticipate at the border, but I had expected some signal, even if only a damp tricolour hanging limp in the sky. Instead, there had been nothing to announce the first border-crossing of my journey, and I had completed it that morning unwittingly. Before I even had time to process that I was there, Spain had passed me by, little more than a phantom wrapped up in bleak weather.

As I turned inland, the country changed countenance, and France gradually made itself known. The jagged coastline gave way to flat fields of vines, white farmhouses, duck-sheds, and straight Roman roads, banked by mottled elm trees which cast tattoos of shade about their feet. Avoiding highways, I went from commune to commune, passing through eerily vacant villages, their inhabitants busy tending the fields or taking refuge indoors from the sun.

I went on like this for three days, passing through silent towns, sheltering from rainstorms in ancient churches, and feasting on fresh baguettes. I rode beside meadows and fields redolent of Romances, past towns baked red by the sun, and over hills smothered in blue wildflowers, stitched together with seams of navy. As the days grew hotter, warm blizzards of black poplar seeds choked the air, and I glimpsed signposts for places like Montpellier, Nîmes, Arles, and Marseille. Then, as I steered towards the Rhône-Alpes, the air turned cool again, and down the steep roads, each leading an avalanche of sound, came trains of French motorcyclists, every one of them with a hand raised high in a sign of fraternal welcome.

Save for the rocking noise of my engine and the whistle of the wind, that first week passed in silence. I rode all day, every day, and discovered a peacefulness on the road that I had not expected. Riding for hours without pause on the motorcycle, piloting the machine through crooked mountain passes and down slender country lanes, felt like a glorious way to be spending my days. The road was total: there was nothing beyond it, no time to focus on anything but the black maw of a looming tunnel, the blind hump of a bridge, or the dancing shower of sparks left behind by my foot-pegs on the tight mountain bends.

At first, those days bred a lightness in me that I had never felt before, but following close behind that lightness came a score of ugly anxieties. As my journey progressed, the novelty of riding the motorcycle slowly began to fade, and I realised that I was passing through parts of France that I had never known existed, placing my faith in signs and maps, without ever speaking to another human to confirm my location. In the mad imaginings of a lonely brain, I began to wonder if maps could be trusted. Never having travelled alone, and unsure of the world, I thought of Peregrine in Brome's play and considered if I might also have been the victim of a cunning trick. Though the *Pont-Aven* had promised to drop me in Santander, I wondered if the ship could have been diverted to the edge of an elaborate stage, leaving me to disembark onto the map of a cruel fiction. Fertilised by silence and solitude, my sense of dislocation grew, and after several days of ceaseless riding, I had never been more uncertain of my place in the world.

But then one morning, a week after leaving Santander, I came down from the Esterel Massif towards the Côte d'Azur, and for the first time on my journey, I recognised my surroundings. Ahead of me, round the next bend in the road, I could see an old stone town built on top of a steep hillside. Standing seven miles back from the sea, the town was one of those rare places that possess the kind of prettiness not usually found beyond the bounds of fantasy. At its centre, a cluster of ancient, ochre towers stood above a swathe of green woodland, which rolled down from the feet of the town towards the Mediterranean, striking the sea at Nice, where the jewelled fringe of the Riviera unfurled against a backdrop of brilliant blue.

The little town was named Tourettes-sur-Loup, and after parking my motorcycle in its main square, I found a seat in a familiar café and ordered a carafe of wine. Across the road, beneath the shade of an aisle of trees, a group of old men stood in a gravel pit tossing little silver spheres which gleamed like comets as they flew through the air. A thin film of drizzle began to fall as I sipped my wine, and I watched the rain gild the yellow towers of the town, with all their wild angles, sunken rooftops, and crooked edges exactly as I remembered them.

I knew Tourettes-sur-Loup because a friend of mine, a man named Jake Donald, had a family home there. Only a few months before, I had sat with Jake in the same café, sipping the same wine, and watching the same old men play pétanque in the town square. The sense of familiarity was intoxicating, and it brought a new validity to my journey. For the first time since leaving England, I was certain of where I was and no longer feared that the universe was lying to me. Over the past seven days, I had blundered my way along six hundred miles of road, barely conscious of the world, spurred into a mad panic by thoughts of how vast my plans were. But that afternoon, as the fine rain fell outside the café, I let myself rest for a while and had time to take note of everything around me. Later in my journey, I would look back upon Tourettes-sur-Loup as something like an anchor, as a fixed point of familiarity to which all subsequent places, however strange and unexpected, could be tethered. I buried my anxieties there, felt my journey vindicated, and realised that if I did not slow down then I risked passing over the world without seeing any part of it.

For the first time since my departure, my thoughts turned towards home. I thought particularly of Jake, who I knew would be finishing his final stretch at Oxford, the place where we had spent several years cementing our friendship. More than anything else, Jake was known to be a man who made things happen, endowed with an extraordinary knack for bringing plans to fruition. A week before my departure, I had mentioned to him that I would be passing along the southern coast of France and might even ride through his village. True to form, Jake had passed this information on to his parents, Emma and Charles, and with incredible timing, an hour after my arrival at the café, I received a call from Emma letting me know that I was expected for dinner.

The Donalds' hospitality was famous, and more than anything else, the prospect of a whole evening of conversation fell upon me like a gift. As I made my way to their beautiful home, at the very top of the hill overlooking Tourettes-sur-Loup, I thought of all the times that I had worried my family by stating my intention to travel in the manner of a tramp. I was sure that back home, my parents were imagining me pitching my tent beside wild and dusty roads, in places where ugly bandits roamed and wild carnivores congregated. Yet here I was, less than one week into my journey, trading my damp tent and camp-stove dinners for the warmest welcome I could have wished for and a room overlooking the whole of the Riviera.

'Welcome!' beamed Emma, as she opened the door to the house, releasing a wave of delicious smells from the kitchen. 'We're roasting a leg of lamb for dinner. I hope that's alright?'

I thought of all the miserable pasta I had eaten over the previous week and smiled.

'Lamb sounds perfect. It's very kind of you to invite me.'

'It's good to see you, Sam. Would you like some wine?' asked Charles, having already poured me a glass of something rich from the southern Rhône. 'Tell us, how's it gone so far?'

'Well, there's already been a few mishaps...' I said, marvelling at the unfamiliar tone of my voice which sounded alien and strange as I began to describe the oil spill on the ferry.

Poor Emma and Charles probably did not realise what they were letting themselves into by inviting me to dinner. Starved of conversation, from the moment I walked into their kitchen, I began babbling like it was the last evening of free speech I would ever be granted. As we sat down around the table, they graciously tolerated my monologues, listening with interest throughout it all, never once questioning or doubting my plans. Their optimism meant more to me than they realised, and as in the café that afternoon, I felt my journey affirmed, and believed there and then that I really might reach the Antipodes. After a week of solitude, every word of conversation was like a banquet to me, and when Charles made the fatal error of producing a map, I was furnished with an excuse to unload a rough itinerary of my entire journey, talking long streams of gibberish about countries I might never even see.

'That was wonderful,' I said, eventually putting down my cutlery, amazed that I had found time to eat amid so much rambling.

'Shall we sit on the terrace for a while?' suggested Emma, steering me out onto the patio, wisely leaving the map behind on the dinner table.

Outside, the sky was just beginning to darken, and from the terrace, the whole of the Riviera was visible, from Cannes to Nice to Monte Carlo and beyond. We went out just as twilight was falling, and in the first throes of dusk, a handful of lights flickered tentatively into being far below us. Then, within minutes, the entire coast was aflame, the lights glowing brightest along the curved beaches, before steadily thinning as the towns trickled back into the hills.

From above, the golden towns of the Riveria seemed to hang off the coast like a crescent of gems draped upon a woman's throat - the jewellery of a supine giantess, still and invisible, who lay with her head buried beneath the Mediterranean and her heels sunk into the channel at Normandy. I sat and admired the view for a while, but weary from riding, and feeling the wine's gentle lullaby, I soon said goodnight to Charles and Emma, just as rainclouds began to appear above the house. Once in my room, I opened the shutters, expecting to hear the patter of drizzle, but in a matter of minutes, the weather had cleared. In its wake, all that remained was immaculate darkness, spread in thick folds about the hills of Provence, and a silent sky, laden with the scent of damp pine needles and all the fresh fumes of sleep.

Chapter Two

Wine is sunlight, held together by water.

- Galileo Galilei

Unlike its French neighbour, the Italian Riviera was not half as enchanting as I expected it to be. Riding eastwards from Nice, Monaco passed in a gasp, and then came Ventimiglia, the first in a long, pale crust of small towns and cities lining the Ligurian coast. Some of the towns were not unattractive, built of dusty streets framing glimpses of cobalt-coloured sea, but they came in such quick succession, so stiflingly close, that I could see no real distinction between them. The apartment blocks and villas might have thinned for a little while, but they never fully disappeared before another signpost announced another little town and the concrete began to thicken again.

But things changed as I neared Cinque Terre, a pretty little ellipsis of five hamlets separated from one another and the rest of Liguria by cliffs so viciously steep that cars have never been able to reach them. For me to even get close to the hamlets meant having to pass through the earth, along tunnels dripping with brine, guided by sporadic gashes in the rock which let in shafts of sunlight and white jets of sea-spray.

Barely able to see beneath the dark tint of my visor, I splashed my way southwards through these tunnels, chased by impatient Italian drivers and the monstrous sounds of my engine melding in the darkness behind me.

When I finally emerged in daylight, I found myself in Cinque Terre National Park, where the coastline grew bolder, more rugged, and too sheer for concrete to cling to. From Levanto, where I parked my motorcycle, the 'five lands' of Monterosso, Vernazza, Corniglia, Manarola, and Riomaggiore unpacked themselves down the coastline, a guillotine blade of green hillside severing each from its neighbours. I learnt that the only way to move between the five villages was by boat, or by a railway built into the cliffs behind them, so after buying myself a ticket, I caught the next train out of Levanto and was soon speeding through another tunnel, heading for Riomaggiore, the largest of the lands.

Stepping out from Riomaggiore's station, I found myself walking along cool alleyways, shaded by knots of balconies, buttresses, and washing lines that clung to one another overhead. Underfoot, smooth flagstones, polished by centuries of footsteps, glimmered in the little light that reached them. Following a square of sunshine down through the hamlet's narrow streets, I emerged in an opening that looked out onto a tiny clutter of pastel-coloured houses, stopped from sliding into the sea by a miniature harbour, coloured every shade of chalk, cream, amber, mauve, periwinkle, and pink. Aside for a few grey blemishes, where a jealous sea had licked patches of bright paint off the walls, the morning sun was busy teasing every colour it could from out of the town and the green cliffs surrounding it. Meanwhile, all along the harbour wall, the tourists and their cameras were waiting.

But in Cinque Terre, the tourists were palatable, the beauty of the place remaining inviolate despite the crowds. The absence of motor vehicles helped, but crucial were the huge cliffs rising between the towns, with walking trails snaking up their sides, which allowed for an easy escape whenever the next group of tourists came looming. These trails, connecting all five of the hamlets, wound through terraces of grapevines and were marked out by rough arrows, painted on stones by farmers tired of finding heat-stricken hikers lost amongst their olive trees. Late in the day, the hills were full of flabby limbs, cargo shorts, and the smell of sunscreen. But when I arrived early in the morning, the trails were quiet, the views staggering, and I had the terraces all to myself.

Of the five hamlets, I thought Manarola the prettiest, and whilst searching for a better view of its harbour, I stumbled into a graveyard overlooking the sea. The ominous stone gates and concrete tombs deterred any other tourists from entering, as did the deathly portraits of Lorenzos, Marios, and Giusseppes affixed to each gravestone, slowly fading to ghosts under the strong Mediterranean sun. I sat alone amongst the stones for a while, admiring the view and thinking that there are few better ways to learn about a community than to find where they keep their dead. Of all the villagers buried there, not one of them looked to be young in their graveside portraits. The faces were all bronze and well-wrinkled, still glowing from a diet of sunshine and wine, looking out with laughing eyes at the crowds below who had travelled halfway around the world to take pictures of a view which the villagers had admired every day of their lives, and which they were still able to gaze upon, even in death.

After stomping from Manarola to Corniglia through the midday heat, it was time for some rest of my own. Falling into the chair of a restaurant in the centre of the third hamlet, I asked a waitress to bring me some water and whatever else was good. She forgot the water, but that did not matter, because when she returned she was carrying a glass of cold wine, the colour of straw, with condensation falling in cataracts down its curved sides. I grabbed it, gulped at it, and was taken back up onto the terraces, to a cool patch of shadow, tucked tight beneath an olive tree, close to where the old vines grew thickest. The wine was slightly sweet, like a pocket of summer air laced with pollen, and I tasted at its very end a subtle trace of sea-salt - a memory of the sea blown up onto the cliff-top by an unexpected storm, one dark afternoon three summers ago.

'You like the wine?' asked the waitress, in reply to my widening eyes.

'It's delicious. Where does it come from?'

'From here. The vines are grown on the cliffs of Cinque Terre. The slopes are so steep that every grape has to be picked by hand. I shall bring you some more, Signor,' she said, before disappearing with a smile.

Ten minutes later, the waitress returned with a half-litre carafe of wine and a plate of thin lasagne sheets, brushed with green pesto.

'Some pasta for you too, Signor. The pesto is also made nearby. It is the most famous dish of Liguria.'

Picking up my fork, I was glad that I had done most of my walking for the day. Halfway through my lunch, I realised that it was the first meal I had ever eaten alone in a restaurant. This might not seem momentous to many, but to my twenty-two-year-old self, dining alone was a novelty, and that simple lunch proved to be one of the greatest of my journey. I had no company, no distractions, not even a book - just myself, the wine, the pasta, a little plate of bitter purple olives, and uninhibited delight. The simplicity was perfect, and after an espresso, I was about to order another carafe of wine and wait there until the dinner service, but the waitress arrived with my bill and the sad news that her restaurant was open only for lunch.

Slowly, I walked on from Corniglia to Vernazza, arriving there just as the sun was setting. Atop the grey harbour wall, a choir stood singing to a crowd, and people lay tanning everywhere on the hot rocks. In the water, a gilt-skinned fisherman was mending his nets, flirting with ladies near to his boat as he listed all the ports he had visited in his life. A single fish was tattooed upon his brawny forearm, whilst a string of others lay bloodied at his feet. He reminded me of a mural I had seen painted on a house in Riomaggiore that morning picturing a weathered seaman, smiling in his boat, tending to his gear. Reaching down, the fisherman picked up a fish, wrapped it in paper, and then offered it to one of the women. She took it gladly, expressing her gratitude by laying the most tender of kisses upon his golden cheek.

Along one edge of the harbour, there was a little church which was empty like the graveyard in Manarola. Inside, it smelt of cold stone and incense, and the walls rang with my footsteps as I walked along the nave. Tired from a day of hiking, I lay down upon a pew and looked up at the ceiling where the evening light, after vaulting off the waves in the harbour, was playing across the roof-beams of the temple. As the watermark danced up and down the ceiling, I imagined myself encased in a vast stone submarine, slowly sinking to the seabed. Outside, I could still hear the choir singing and the faint voice of the fisherman, but the sounds seemed to be fading. Lying atop the pew, I stayed and watched the light for a little longer, enjoying the cool touch of the wood against my skin, until gradually I felt myself drifting away, buoyed by the happy memory of my lunchtime wine, ushered towards sleep by the muted music of the falling tide.

***

I am not sure at what point during my journey I gained enough confidence to start riding the motorcycle at speeds above a modest dribble, but it must have been around the time I left Cinque Terre because half a year later, the Italian Police sent me a letter explaining that I had been photographed riding at fifty-three kilometres per hour just outside Levanto, on a road where the limit was thirty. How they found me, I do not know, and from rural Vietnam (where I received the news), I told my father that he should re-post the fifty euro fine to the Tian Shan Mountains, addressed to the Kyrgyz farmer who had become the illegal owner of the motorcycle. Dad was unimpressed.

On the day that I incurred the fine, I left Cinque Terre, rode over the Apennines, and crossed the flat back of Italy in a single day, from the Adriatic to the Mediterranean, arriving in Venice at dusk. Nine hours of riding across hot country left me exhausted, and by the time I reached the edge of Veneto, the sun had burnt deep purple circles onto the parts of my hands not covered by my riding gloves. These dark emblems would stay with me for the next five months as I chased summer around the globe, each of them a testament to all the hours I spent in the saddle: two scars of which I would come to be proud.

The only time to visit a place as infamously popular as Venice is early in the morning, so after arriving in Veneto, I camped five miles from the city centre and bedded down early. At dawn the next day, I took a bus across the lagoon and started walking in the direction of the Piazza San Marco, expecting the city to be clogged with walking tours and museum queues. But at seven o'clock in the morning, aside from a handful of old matrons hanging washing from their windows, Venice's streets were still and quiet. Apart from a single barge laden with fruit and vegetables making its way to market, the canals that I had expected to be choked with boats and gondolas were also empty. In any other city, such details might have been trivial, but in Venice, they seemed vital. I took them as proof that the city's heart had not yet entirely succumbed to the canker of modern tourism.

I had chosen to walk to the Piazza San Marco simply because the huge russet campanile of St Mark's Basilica made for a convenient way-point. From the famous square, I turned and crossed over the Ponte Dell'Accademia into Dorsoduro, before walking to the old custom's point at the tip of the sestiere. It was only there, looking out across a wide stretch of water, with San Marco to my left and Giudecca to my right, that I came to appreciate Venice's true relationship with the sea. The sun-studded waves, a lurid aquamarine, came up to the doorstep of every house and palace along the city's edge, and those buildings, though impressive, were furrowed with signs of strain. The truth is that Venice is a sunken city, not a floating one - a place which battles against the waves, rather than resting freely upon their surface. Edged by decadent walls, and propped up by wooden supports fastened with hubris, the beautiful town is built upon land stolen from the Adriatic, and it wears, at its elegant fringes, the unutterable knowledge that it will one day slip back into the sea.

'Beautiful, isn't it?' said a voice beside me as I stood looking out across the lagoon.

'Peaceful too,' I replied, turning around to the dark-haired Italian man, standing there with a little dog on a lead, who had stopped to speak to me.

'It is this morning, but did you not see it a few days ago during the vogalonga? It was anything but peaceful then.'

'The vogalonga?' I questioned.

'You did not see it?' asked the man. 'That is a pity. Every year Venice hosts a regatta known as the vogalonga. Only rowing boats are allowed to enter, but it's still chaos on the water. It took place only a few days ago. Most tourists like you come to Venice at this time of year just for the event.'

'It is an old tradition?' I asked.

'At least fifty years old. It started in protest against the number of motorboats in the canals. Their engines destroy our buildings by turning the lake acidic. The vogalonga gets bigger every year, but the number of motorboats is still rising.'

As the man spoke, a speedboat came barrelling past, its black lacquer belly shining insidiously in the sunlight.

'Enjoy our city whilst you can,' said the pensive Venetian. 'It won't be here forever.'

Despite the damage they inflicted, I could understand why motorboats were so prolific: Venice is a perilous city to wander on foot. All day I watched trains of people walking aimlessly around, blindly following unwitting leaders who sweated over crumpled maps. I confess that I was no better navigator myself. All day I trudged across the islands, walking back and forth between San Marco, Santa Croce, San Polo, Dorsoduro, and Cannaregio. On my travels, I saw a city given over to indulgence, lined with bars, restaurants, hotels, and shops selling all manner of glittering things. I stood looking into windows, wondering who came to Venice to spend a few hundred dollars on a quill or a wine glass, or a few hundred thousand on a painting. But then a lady would walk past drenched in diamonds, or I would catch sight of a perfectly cut suit floating into the gilt lobby of a hotel, and I came to realise that Venice is not one city but three. It has an exterior, open to all; an interior, accessible only to a privileged few; and a hidden part, lying beneath the waterline, which remains the secret of its builders.

Several hours later, as I padded my way back to the Piazza San Marco once again, the sun was low in the sky and the crowds of tourists had begun to thicken. Walking amongst them, I thought of how the first inhabitants of the lagoon had fled there in the fifth century to escape the barbarian hordes spreading across Europe after the fall of the Roman Empire. The irony of Venice is that over the centuries, the measures taken by Venetians to isolate themselves from the rest of the world – namely, building a city in the sea – are now the very reason Venice attracts so many outsiders. It may have taken them over a millennium, but the hordes made it into the republic eventually.

Yet, I still spied groups of Venetians amongst the crowds. They could be told apart from the tourists by the rolling music of their speech and their impeccable dress. And as the evening deepened and sunlight became a coveted commodity, it was the Venetians who knew where best to catch it, congregating at the few bars and coffee shops which looked far out enough over the water to see something like a sunset. There they stood, drinking espressos and blood-red glasses of Aperol, decked in floral dresses and adorned with silk pocket squares, stuck in patches of sunlight like petals trapped in amber.

Hoping for a quiet place to write, I found a little wine bar which was decorated along one wall with thousands of empty bottles, each wearing a paper label around its neck with the names of those who had drunk the wine scribbled upon it. Taking a seat, I opened my notebook and ordered myself a glass of Amarone, a wine that I had first tasted many years before when my best friend opened a bottle one howling winter night. It had been the first wine to make me realise just how magnificent wine could be, and after we had finished the bottle, my friend told me of a great poet who had once explained the importance of drinking red wine every day after dark, because it is the only thing that can be trusted to fight off the night in our souls. Since then, Amarone - a rich wine from the hills north-east of Verona - has long been a favourite of mine.

Sat near the bar, I watched as a waiter poured out a glass for me, the wine falling from the bottle like a stream of rubies. The first sip brought the taste of dark grapes, harvested long ago, and every day of sunshine which first nurtured and later withered them. The second brought a rich, pleasant woodiness that made me think of old oak doors, smoothed with age and stained with varnish. Bold, potent, and elegant, it was the best Amarone I had ever drunk, a bottle so good that it could only have been taken from the cellar of a Venetian possessed of impeccable taste.

I was so engrossed in the wine that by the time I picked up my pen again to write, the bar was close to closing. Most of the waiters had gone home, leaving one old man to close down. After writing a dozen more pages, I finished my glass and looked up again to find that all the other customers had left and the bar was now empty. The old man alone remained, and upon catching my eye, he walked over and sat down at my table.

'You enjoyed the Amarone?' he asked, a warm smile spreading beneath his glimmering eyes as he spoke.

'One of the best I've ever had,' I replied.

'Amarone,' he explained, 'comes from the Italian word amaro, which means bitter. The house which first made Amarone produced sweet wine, but one vintage, when they left their stock in barrel for too long, the wine changed. It grew stronger, more powerful, and though it was not sour, it did not taste sweet like they expected. Hence the name Amarone.'

'I take it you like Amarone too?' I asked.

'For me, it is the king of wines. Amarone can be made from any blend of three grapes, and because the winemaker does not have to list the proportions of each grape on their label, every bottle is a mystery.'

When I asked if he could write the names of the grapes in my notebook, the old man faltered for a moment.

'I warn you, my writing is not so good,' he said, as he picked up my pen and began to scratch the words - *Corvina, Rondinella, Molinara* - in my book, with a hand that was rough and ill-practised, and which I suspected had never been properly taught.

'How long have you worked in the wine industry?' I asked.

"All my life. This wine bar is mine,' he said, looking around affectionately. 'But I have not always lived and worked in Venice. When I was young, I did not go to school. I spent my youth in the fields, cutting the vines and picking the grapes. I've seen many sides to the wine trade.'

'I was in Cinque Terre just yesterday and had a beautiful wine with my lunch. I can't imagine how difficult it would be to work in the fields there,' I said, watching the old man break into a wide grin.

'Ah, Cinque Terre - I know those slopes well.'

That simple sentence was all that it took to throw him out of his Venetian bar and send him back, salt-stained and sun-baked, to the terraces of Liguria. He never said for certain that those vine-covered cliffs were where he learnt his craft, but in my mind, that was the past I invented for him. Travel is a wonderful way to disrupt the fictions by which we are bound, but it also provides no end of opportunities for invention. There seemed no place on earth better suited for the beginning of this man's long career than the harsh hills of Cinque Terre, so I asked no more questions, in case his answers spoiled the myth I wanted to weave around him. Instead, I sat and listened to his lessons as he poured us both some more wine, scribbling notes in my book about the different grapes of Italy, and raising my glass to chink against his every time he declared another toast to his beloved Amarone.

Chapter Three

And still, a ship upon her seas,
Went sailing on without the gale:
And still there moved the moon so pale,
A crescent ship without a sail!

　　- James Elroy Flecker, 'A Ship, An Isle, A Sickle Moon'

I am one of the unfortunate few people on earth who suffer from a very real fear of lightning, though this was not always the case. When I was a boy, getting caught in storms was a favourite pastime of mine, and whenever dark clouds gathered over the hills of Somerset, I would slip on my trainers and run out into the rain, giddy to meet the tumult. But then one afternoon, several years before my journey to the Antipodes, I was swimming in a river in China when a lightning bolt hit the water and sent a current flying through my body. I was not hurt, and thankfully neither was anyone else in the group I was swimming with, but the shock was enough to leave us rigid and speechless, paralysed for a moment atop the water, before panic set in and sent us kicking towards the riverbank. The celebrations that night (in honour of our close encounter with death) featured lightning bolt tattoos, gallons of rice wine, and the eating of a still-beating snake's heart. Though my memory of the day was marred by the debauchery which followed it, I left China with a permanent respect for lightning. Whereas electric storms had once called to me with a beauty that was mythical and enthralling, after my swim in the Li river, I could not help but view them as lethal agents in possession of a very credible weapon.

So when I was riding down the Dalmatian coast on my second day in Croatia and saw thunderclouds gathering over the Dinaric Alps, I set to studying them with a wary eye. Since that morning, what had begun as a few dark clouds had grown in number and deepened in shade until a second set of peaks towered above the Dinarics, fat with water and fizzing with charge, impatient to split apart and unleash their black bladder of rain. By the afternoon, more storm than I had ever seen hung above the mountains, so much that it looked powerful enough to cut the alps into pebbles and carry them piecemeal out to sea. Then, as the first violet vein opened in the sky to my left, followed a moment later by another lance of light which buried itself in the Adriatic, I felt the return of a very familiar fear. As the storm tightened around me, rolls of thunder began to sound, and I realised I had nowhere to go.

Leaving Venice, the weather had been perfect. A steady sun followed me as I rode past Trieste and turned right into Slovenia, where the countryside passed by in the form of thick forests, neat little hills, and whole pigs roasting on the road-side. Within a few hours, I was in the north of Croatia, still subject to unrelenting sunshine and doing my best to make sense of the Slavic road signs. Entering Croatia had meant crossing the first physical land border of my journey, and just getting past the guards felt like a minor victory. Not that they had been attentive at all – the guard took half a glimpse at my passport, muttered an uninspired 'Dobar Dan', and waved me through without even asking to see under my motorcycle helmet. But for the first time on my journey, I was in a country I had never visited before, where they used a currency I had never held, and spoke a language which, after Italian's hospitable roll, seemed to drop its heavy syllables like hammer-blows.

I camped for one night near a town named Kraljevica, before continuing southwards down a coastal road the next morning, heading in the direction of Split. Three hours later, I was riding through water as deep as my shin-blades, battling to keep my rear wheel from slipping in the corners, and watching with dismay as my oil leak left a ribbon of colour behind me on the road. Despite the gathering weather, I never thought to stop, feeling a strange compulsion to drive deeper into the storm, in part because the mounting clouds were the first real difficulty to present itself on my journey, and I had long been waiting for an excuse to test my mettle.

Riding on, I passed small towns and villages, waving at other motorcyclists who were sensibly sheltering in shepherd huts. The rain was unremitting, and I was soon damp enough to feel my fingers crinkling with wrinkles. As I passed the old town of Senj, the road began to climb higher into the mountains, and the first bright bolt of lightning hit one of the peaks ahead. It was then that I realised the full extent of my vulnerability: riding alone on the road, having seen no traffic for hours, moving fast through half a metre of water on a metal machine wearing a helmet studded with steel pins. Another flash lit the sky, followed closely by a volley of thunder. Then another and another, left and right, as well as a slip of my back wheel which nearly threw me onto the wet road. I realised that even if I did survive a lightning strike, the cycle would never stay upright and the ensuing crash would kill me. And if by some miracle I survived a strike and a wreck, it would be hours before anyone found me on the road, by that time with lungs full of rain. I was alone and afraid, stranded on a mountain surrounded by a sky woven with my greatest fear, and the thunder was getting louder.

I would have stopped riding and sought shelter, but for miles there had been nothing but empty road and bare landscape. My exposure seemed unsolvable, and with nowhere to hide, I kept on, suffocated by fear. But just as I reached the centre of the storm and the lightning reached the summit of its power, I saw a large tree and a house to one side of the road. I stopped, left my motorcycle under the tree, and made for the door, desperately hammering its steel panels, despite the fact it looked long deserted. I hit the windows, shaking the glass and shouting to be let in, manic, frantic, and sodden. Then there was another strike, so close this time that it left an imprint of lavender glowing behind my eyes and a ringing in my ears that banished all other sound.

Running away from the steel door, I fled towards a half-ruined outhouse and crouched down behind the remnants of a wall, hoping that if lightning struck it might hit the tall tree, or the metal rafters of the house, or even my motorcycle, anything but me. With the centre of the storm directly overhead, I could feel each crack of thunder deep in my bones. All I could taste was rain, all I could smell was wet earth, but I could hear the horror in everything. Every raindrop on the road, every loosed mountain stone, and every toppling tree was calling out in concert - an orchestra of chaos, playing a wild lament, as all around me the mountains of Dalmatia were being ripped to pieces and set alight with electric fire.

***

The storm near Senj left me damp for days, and it was not until I reached Split, two hundred miles further down the coast, that I felt fully dry again. Arriving at the city, I hoped it would provide me with an opportunity to recuperate for a little while. It was, after all, the place where the Roman Emperor Diocletian chose to spend his retirement, growing cabbages in the lavish palace he built for himself there. When the messy tetrarchy Diocletian left behind in 305 AD began to disintegrate, the Roman populace begged for the old emperor's return, but he refused, explaining that he would never give up his beloved gardens or the nourishing Adriatic air. As a place fit for an emperor's retreat, I had high hopes for my own time in Split, and as soon as I arrived, I made straight for Diocletian's palace.

Walking around the white stone complex at the centre of the city, I was pleased to find that it was still the bastion of leisure and pleasure that its builder had intended it to be. Everywhere near the palace, there were restaurants, cafés, bars, and shops built into the fabric of the Emperor's old residence, which was thronged with summer tourists from end to end. I thought about sitting outside a café and writing in the sunshine for a while, but then a dark cloud appeared in the sky, and I decided to step inside to wait out the looming weather.

Without thinking where I was going, I entered the palace, walked down a long flight of stone steps, and found myself in the underground vaults where Diocletian once stored the best wines in all the empire. At the entrance to the vaults, a woman stood beside a table of empty glassware.

'Welcome to Split Wine Festival,' she said as I approached, before beckoning me over and handing me a glass in exchange for a fifty kuna note.

'Thank you,' I said, feeling lucky to have stumbled upon the event. 'Is it a large festival?' I asked, trying to peer into the gloom beyond.

'Croatia is home to over one hundred and seventy different types of wine, and almost every kind is waiting inside for you to try,' said the lady, pointing towards the cellars and smiling mischievously.

Inside the dark underground chamber, I found a crowd of vintners to whom pouring a glass of wine and spending half an hour in idle chatter were the greatest possible pleasures in life. The moment I stepped inside, I was confronted with a dozen handshakes and as many offers to fill my glass. Selflessly, I offered myself up to the crowd and began to be passed from table to table, barely able to keep up with the flurry of white, red, and rosé that seemed to spontaneously appear in my glass. I met old vintners and young vintners, some starting in wine for the first time, and some who were descended from many generations of growers. Most followed traditional methods, but others boasted of their inventions and experiments, like wine aged in clay cases sunk to the bottom of the sea. I met young men fresh from school who had poured everything into their businesses, and I met old grandmothers for whom wine had been a life-long vocation. The whole crowd was riddled with a deep and unshakable love for grapes and their juice, and most passionate of them all was Antonio Lipanović.

Antonio, a giant of a man, had spotted me tottering unsteadily near his table an hour after I arrived and graciously decided to bring over a plate of smoked meat and cheese.

'Do you know why Croatia has more types of wine than any other nation?' boomed a great voice, as I turned around and found my eyes level with the tip of Antonio's beard.

'I'm afraid not,' was my feeble reply.

'Because of our islands!' growled Antonio, uncorking a bottle as he introduced himself. Sensing that my new acquaintance was inclined to give me a lesson in Croatian wine, I steadied myself against the table, accepted his offer of a glass, and made ready for a lecture.

'At one time, Croatian wine was famous all over the world, but our industry was ravaged during the communist regime. The people you see here today are all trying to give new life to the trade, but it is a difficult task,' said Antonio, looking around at the crowd and nodding his head proudly, before taking a deep gulp from his glass.

'More than anything else, wine needs time. It took me eleven years just to make my first hundred bottles. What is so special about Croatian wine is that each of Dalmatia's islands are made of different soil, and each has a special relationship with the sun. This means that there is more variety in Croatian wine than anywhere else on the planet. We're all here today to try and help the rest of the world realise that.'

'Eleven years to make one hundred bottles?' I said disbelievingly.

'It is a labour of love. Though it was difficult at first, my winery is doing well now. You should visit for a tasting. My cellar is something quite special,' he said, pressing a business card into my palm.

Thanking the giant winemaker, I received a heavy farewell clap on the shoulder, and then I walked back through the vaults with visions of his bright white grin floating before me in the dark. Once out into the evening sunshine, I was glad to find my crumpled bus ticket still in my pocket. I started to make my way back to my campsite, but I must have drunk more than I realised, because I awoke on the bus at the end of the line, five miles past my stop. At first, I was dismayed, but the walk back along a white sand beach hardly seemed such a labour. And as I trudged back through the twilight, letting the surf wash over my ankles, I watched as a lone sailboat left Split harbour, sailing out towards the Adriatic, slipping away quietly at dusk.

***

Words, over time, if used too often, can lose some of their potency. Serendipity is one example of a word which has been abused, misused, and put in all sorts of situations it was not meant for. Few people know that the term derives from a Persian fairy-tale about a trio of brothers from Serendip (the classical Persian name for Sri Lanka) and their lucky adventures abroad. This means that despite all its misuses, serendipity is an apt word for the traveller, and the further I ventured around the world, the more my journey seemed to be defined by a string of happy coincidences, my time in Split being no exception. Only the day after I glimpsed the sailboat leaving the city at sunset, I received a surprise call from my cousin Jennifer. She had just arrived in Croatia with some friends to charter a yacht for a week, and if I could get myself to a marina by the following morning, then there was a spare berth aboard for me.

I met Jen and the rest of the crew - Steve, Tish, Tom, and Greg - at Kaštela marina where the forty-two-foot *Antares* was waiting. I had never sailed before in my life, and having only just become familiar with motorcycles, I was nervous when presented with the intricacies of a boat. Every line, winch, and fender looked so pristine and ordered that I did not want to be responsible for anything, not even a single rope. It felt criminal just to step aboard and risk disrupting the harmony of it all.

When we cast off the next morning, there was a murmur of wind, but not enough to sail by. Heading out from Split, we had been steaming for half an hour when a bolder breeze began to stir. Looking across the water, I watched a score of yachts bloom on either side of us, mainsails rising and genoas blossoming as a dozen wooden masts put on their leaves again. No sooner had the wind started to blow than Greg, our appointed skipper, let fly a volley of commands:

'Turn her into the wind, bring in the mainsheet, ready on the halyard!' he cried, putting me to work pulling on a heavy line, though which part of the boat it was connected to remained a mystery to me.

One glance at Greg as he was standing in the cockpit, gripping the helm with his fingerless gloves, and it was plain to see that he was a man who took his sailing seriously. In between issuing orders, he spoke to me in an alien language about his love of 'goose-winging on a dead run', his longing to see 'St Elmo's fire', and how he once met a man who had 'pitch-poled in a gale'. As the week went on, I came to understand our captain better and found him to be possessed of two distinct characters. Half the time, Greg would seem stern and severe as he paced around the boat, fiddling with ropes, arranging the deck, and mumbling curses, looking serious in his work. But at other moments, a jolly madness would descend upon him, and in an instant, he would rig up a plank and make us all walk it, or tie a fender to a halyard and catapult himself out into the waves. True to the character of the mariner, he also possessed a talent for the consumption of liquor and knew by heart an ancient recipe for a potent rum punch which earned him the name Captain Grog, a sobriquet to which our crew adhered devotedly. It took me only a single morning on the boat to realise that there could be no finer captain to teach me the ways of the sea.

The first night out of Split, we moored off the island of Šolta, and all the crew sat together in the saloon in the evening to plan the next few days of our voyage. When Greg suggested we make for an island named Vis, a glimmer of memory loosed in my mind and began a slow ascent to the surface. The name Vis was undoubtedly familiar to me, and I was sure I had heard it somewhere before. Then I remembered the business card Antonio had given me in Diocletian's vaults. Pulling it from my wallet, I held it up to the light and read the address of Antonio's winery. Of all the islands in Dalmatia, it just happened to be located on Vis.

The next day, after mooring in a tiny harbour, we went ashore to seek out Antonio's cellar. Leaving the main town of Vis behind, we followed a road that grew gradually more rugged and wild, and with each step, it seemed less and less probable we would find a winery at its end. But then, just as the first murmurs of scepticism began to sound amongst the crew, the road stopped before the entrance of a wide concrete tunnel built into the hillside. In front of the tunnel, a dog with a mouth full of menacing teeth stood chained to a pole, and fixed atop the pole was a little sign announcing the Lipanović winery.

Edging past the dog, which strained against its rusty chain, I gingerly entered the darkness of the tunnel, calling out Antonio's name. It seemed impossible that wine could be made in such a place, but as my eyes adjusted, I noticed crates of glasses stacked against the walls, and in the distance, I could see the silver gleam of a huge steel barrel. Then, a short way down the tunnel, a door creaked open, spilling electric light, and a huge figure stepped out into the gloom.

Half-worried that we had just entered the lair of an evil villain, or perhaps had discovered the secret laboratory of a nefarious scientist, I was relieved when the silhouette materialised into the form of Antonio and his wide, familiar grin.

'Welcome!' he bellowed, motioning for us to step inside and follow him deeper into the cavern.

'What is this place, Antonio?' I asked.

'Old army tunnels,' he said, his monstrous voice echoing in the darkness. 'During the rule of Tito, Vis was an important base for the Yugoslav National Army. After deciding that the island was of extreme military importance, Tito ordered fifteen miles of tunnels and underground barracks to be built on Vis. When Yugoslavia fell in 1992, some of the tunnels came up for sale. Dark, cool, and dry - they are a winemaker's dream.'

Here, the giant man gave one of the curving concrete walls an affectionate pat.

'I bought this little piece of history and have been making my wine down here ever since, storing my bottles between the same walls that once housed Yugoslavian soldiers.'

It was clear that Antonio saw a romance in the tunnels, and as we walked down the main corridor of his sprawling winery, he pointed excitedly to side-passages and antechambers, home to bulging steel vats and long rows of bottles which glinted like green eyes in the beam of his torch. Aside from the noise of our footsteps and the shine of Antonio's light, the musty tunnels were dark and silent. But when we arrived at the door to the tasting room, Antonio led us into a small, white chamber furnished with wooden benches and decorated with rows of photographs of his family. On the tables, white candlesticks stood half-melted in empty bottles, and in one corner of the room, a colossal Balthazar stood as a testament to the lavish dinners Antonio sometimes hosted down there in the dark.

'Please, take a seat, imagine yourselves at home,' said the winemaker, uncorking three bottles for us to try.

After pouring the wine, Antonio disappeared, returning a minute later with a tray of toasted bread, topped with pieces of white fish and tart green capers. The image of a good host, he was perfectly at home in Tito's old tunnels, having adapted with ease to the subterranean lifestyle. The wines he poured - a white, a rosé, and a red - were all delicious, and the white, in particular, seemed to bring back memories of my last underground encounter with Antonio in Diocletian's vaults.

'This white wine seems familiar,' I said. 'Is it the one we drank in Split?'

'Ah, the Vugava! You are right to remember it. This wine is quite special,' said the vintner, re-filling all our glasses. 'Vugava means song in Croatian, and it is a wine that we usually keep for important occasions. Made only on Vis, the best Vugavas are the colour of gold, with the bitterness of almonds, the sweetness of honey, and the perfume of peach blossoms. And they always taste better when accompanied by the loud celebratory songs of a traditional Croatian wedding.'

Antonio was a giant who lived in a cave, but he could speak about wine with the most feminine delicacy. It was easy to picture him in his dark communist tunnels at midnight, loping from barrel to barrel with his thief in hand, checking his wine with religious devotion. It was a happy irony that the communist regime which had brought the Croatian wine trade to its knees had also been responsible for the creation of Antonio's cellar. And as we sat there in the cool tasting chamber, sipping some of Croatia's best wines, we all raised a toast to the dead dictator Tito and the mad plans of his paranoid brain, without whom the tunnels of Vis might never have been dug and Antonio's Vugava never made.

***

The next day, as soon as we were clear of Vis harbour, the wind began gusting at thirty knots, which to me felt like a minor hurricane. Springing to action, we quickly raised the mainsail, unfurled the genoa, and the *Antares* began to heel so far over that our mast looked like it was about to kiss the horizon. Cruising along at a speed of eight knots, it felt like we were flying, and I was just beginning to wonder where the lifejackets were stowed when I spotted a dark bank of water moving rapidly towards us. The black waves came closer and closer as I searched for the cloud that might make such a shadow, but as I was looking upwards, a vicious gust took our sail between its teeth and dragged the boat so far over to one side that I found myself looking up not at the sky but at the sea.

We hung there for several seconds, as if on a precipice, with the whole hull balancing on a wave's edge. From where he was studying some charts in the cabin below, Greg roared out to the crew:

'Everybody to Starboard!'

Needing no further encouragement, everyone on deck flung themselves across to the edge of the boat that was hanging high in the air and leaned as far out over the side as we dared to try and counterbalance the yacht. Only a few degrees more and she would have tipped and sent the Mediterranean flooding into the cabin, but mercifully the thuggish gust abated, and the *Antares* fell back into balance.

Greg had just got on deck and was making his way to the helm when from somewhere below an ominous beeping began to sound. Muttering a string of curses as old as the sea, he turned back and went below decks to search for the noise. A minute later, the persistent beeping began to grow louder and faster, just as Greg's flame of red hair re-appeared at the gangway.

'THE DEPTH METRE!' he screamed, pointing to a little screen by my ankles. 'What does it say?' he asked, panic rising in his voice.

'Two point five metres!' I shouted, as Greg sprinted towards the helm, ordering me to put the boat in reverse.

1.7m. 1.5m. The number on the depth metre kept falling as I realised I did not even know how to start the engine, let alone make the boat travel backwards. A second later, Greg reached the helm and his practised hands began dancing over a small collection of buttons and levers. But by the time the engine started, the reading on the metre had changed, and we had returned to deeper water.

Everyone let out a long sigh of relief, relieved that we had not run aground, and as the crew gathered, suggestions were made as to what might have caused the drama.

'Perhaps it was a school of fish?' said Jen.

'An errant whale?' I ventured.

'A trapped pocket of air from the wake of the ferry ahead of us?' said Steve, which seemed by far the most sensible suggestion. Meanwhile, Greg was silent until we had exhausted our thoughts, then looked at us with superstitious eyes and said:

'I'd put my money on a monster...' before climbing back into the cabin, grumbling of krakens and sirens and ship-eating squid.

After a morning fraught with fear, we pointed the Antares in the direction of the island of Brač, looking for a secluded cove to call our own for the night. The rest of the way there, the sea and wind were tamer, and I lay at the front of the boat, watching waves being built and unbuilt, each little blue world riding on a white bank of foam. Alone on the bow, I had one of those moments peculiar to travelling where I wondered what everyone I knew might think if there was a lens suspended above my head and they could all spy me through it. I had many moments like this on my journey, always at times when I was experiencing something far from what I expected when I set off on my tramp across the world. Sometimes I simply felt that the life I was living had become too improbable for it to be my own any more, and it seemed as if I were looking down through a lens and watching somebody else's journey rather than my own.

I knew when I left home where I wanted to go - the end aim of my travels was always clear. But already in the few weeks since my departure, I had experienced so many things I never could have fathomed. And as I lay slowly bronzing on the deck of the Antares, I was suddenly shaken by the thought of how many possible forms my future journey might take. Looking out across the Adriatic, each wave in sight seemed a possible future, each one a unique formula of experiences, many of them similar, but no two the same. Some waves were running towards me, whilst others fled from the boat, and some sank away into nothing. I could see a thousand shifting possibilities, any one of which might come true, but I could have one and only one, with no way of knowing which it was to be, and that prospect was as enthralling as it was melancholy.

Eventually, we found a solitary cove on one side of Brač just big enough for our boat to anchor in. It was a narrow slice of water, coloured navy at its deepest, then changing to turquoise, before becoming completely clear as it grew shallower. At its middle lay a white pebble beach, peppered with pine-cones, banked by two steep sides of fragrant trees. Swimming in the cove was like being suspended in crystal, and though metres above the bottom, from the edge of the boat, I could count the dark sea cucumbers sleeping on the seabed, nestled beside fat purple urchins and schools of silver fish.

That evening, as the sun went down, I swam to the little beach holding rolls of paper on a stick above my head to build a fire by the shore. Back on board, Greg whispered spells over an array of spirit bottles, mixing some more of his grog. At nightfall, we all sat on the stones and watched as the salt in the timber burned with green flames and the pebbles underneath glowed red. Then, when the punch ran out, Greg scuttled back to the *Antares* and returned a minute later with another barrel he had kept hidden in the galley, alongside two more bottles of Antonio's wine.

We stayed on the beach and drank and sang till the fire burned out. Later, as I lay in the saloon, drowsy and half-dreaming, I lay awake listening to the sound of the waves washing against the boat. I thought that everyone else had gone to their cabins and were sleeping peacefully, but just as I began to fall asleep myself, a mighty splash sounded, followed by drunken warbling. I smiled, realising that our captain, merry on his grog, had just back-flipped off the gangplank, and I watched through the moonlit porthole as he slowly drifted away, gurgling old sailor's songs as he floated on his back in the warm, black sea.

Chapter Four

Great Tsernogora! never since thine own
Black ridges drew the cloud and brake the storm
Has breathed a race of mightier mountaineers.

   - Alfred, Lord Tennyson, 'Montenegro'

When I returned to my motorcycle after a week aboard the *Antares*, the kind Croat who had let me leave my machine in his garden - a man named Jayco - caught my arm as I was packing my bags.

'You are heading south?' he asked, a worried look upon his face.

'Yes, to Montenegro,' I said, my reply causing Jayco to draw a sharp intake of breath.

'Be careful, my friend. The roads in Montenegro are very bad.'

'They are in poor condition?'

'It is not so much the condition of the roads. It is the drivers. A few years ago, I had another motorcyclist come this way. He left me one morning, heading south. A few hours later, he returned covered in blood. The accident was so bad that doctors had to remove one of his arms.'

'What happened?' I asked, suddenly unnerved by the gruesome story.

'In Croatia, many weddings involve a motor parade, where the couple and all their guests drive from town to town celebrating. He was hit by one of these parades and left for dead on the side of the road.'

'Accidents like that are common here?'

'Sometimes. But they are even more common in Montenegro, where the driving is more dangerous. If you ever see a car with ribbons on it, with a bride in the passenger seat, you should get off the road as fast as you can.'

I had thought Jayco's warning ridiculous until a day later when a string of twenty cars appeared in my wing mirror, looming large behind me, swerving across both lanes with their horns blasting aggressively. When the first car missed me by an inch, I pulled over to let the others pass and watched as a train of shining saloons flew by, piloted by groomsmen in dinner jackets who tossed empty wine bottles out onto the road. In the fifth car sat the bride, wearing a long white gown and a white satin headdress which streamed out behind her and twined with the pink ribbons tied to her car, forming a vicious tail that snapped loudly in the wind.

The wedding party, I guessed, was headed for Dubrovnik - the mighty walled city stamped onto the bottom of Croatia which I could just see in the distance. From the road I was following, the city had first appeared as nothing more than a dark ring of stone framed on three sides by the sea. But now that I was closer, I began to appreciate the true size of the fortifications which wrapped around the old town and kept half of the city hidden from view. Those massive walls were once the most famous battlements in all of Christendom, and in the city's long and tumultuous medieval history, Dubrovnik's fortifications were famous for never once having been breached.

As I continued along the road, more details began to form, and the precious centre which the walls protected slowly took the shape of cathedrals, halls, markets, and rows of townhouses clad in the red terracotta roof tiles for which Dubrovnik is famous. But in the pattern of those tiles - some bright red, others more faded - lay the tragic story of the one fight Dubrovnik's walls could not protect its citizens against.

That fight was fought in 1991 when the Yugoslavian National Army besieged Dubrovnik. Like many before them, the Yugoslavian military found Dubrovnik's battlements insurmountable. Their alternative tactic was to send a barrage of mortar rounds raining down upon the city and its civilians. Every shell that fell destroyed a home, business, school, or church, and when the battle was over, the damaged rooftops were repaired with fresh garnet tiles. Less than thirty years on, the restorations still stand out like angry red scars beside the pale old scales of their neighbours: a glowing trail of young wounds shining brightly in the sun.

I had arrived in Dubrovnik at the height of summer, which meant that everywhere tourists were stood in great lines, three hundred deep, waiting to climb up onto the city walls. If the crowds were not enough to deter me, the fact that the cost of gaining entrance to the battlements dwarfed the few notes left in my wallet decided the matter, and I resolved to try and find an alternative way up. So with the shameless bravado of a young man abroad, after parking my motorcycle, I began to skirt the city's edges, testing gates and tugging on door handles, hoping to discover a secret passage leading up to one of the turrets.

After half an hour of trying, all I had to show for my efforts was a hand stained red by rust and a healthy respect for Croatian locksmiths. But then I came to the base of Minčeta tower, the squat fortress standing at the highest point in the city, where I discovered a gate hanging slightly ajar. Unable to quell my curiosity, I pushed the gate open, finding behind it an empty basketball court, which from its far edge offered a view over the entire city.

Spines of terracotta rooftops ran away from the court, swaddling grey church towers, basilicas, and belfries - stone limbs which sprouted like pale shoots between rows of red townhouses. Blanched by the hot sun, the city looked old and agelessly still. And all around the quiet centre the staggering walls bristled with tourists holding sun umbrellas and hand-fans where soldiers might once have raised spears and pikes and ancient instruments of war.

Alone above the city, hidden in a secret corner and free to let my fictions play out in peace, I imagined the tourists as an army hurrying along, making ready to defend Dubrovnik from an attack. I was about to open the armoury, summon the siege engines, and was ready to stage an entire battle in my head, but my reverie lasted only a moment. My mistake was to have left the gate to the basketball court wide open, which meant that only a few minutes after my arrival, a tour group dashed inside, letting out gasps as they arrived beside me and discovered the view. They were soon pressed up against the fence, trying to force their wide-angle lenses through the narrow gaps in the wire, fighting for the best angle. I struggled through the crush and left them there, like creatures clinging to the side of a cage, whilst far below in the city a cathedral's bells began to ring. I watched as a wedding procession made its slow way out onto the street, amidst a flurry of white petals, and then I went in search of my motorcycle, eager to leave Dubrovnik before the groomsmen took to their cars again.

***

From the Montenegrin border, I followed a single road around handprints of the sea, overlooked on all sides by black mountains shadow-patterned with silhouettes of clouds. A breeze licked across the water, chopping the blue into white ridges, but surrounded by such high mountains, the bays I circled looked more like alpine lakes than inlets of the Mediterranean. All the while, the road was cast in permanent shadow, and high above it, the rock-face wore a restless countenance, morphing under the passage of the sky from one mountain into many, with strange peaks rising and false gullies gaping wide each time a change in the wind brought a new scheme of clouds scudding across the sky.

Montenegro is a tiny country, and I was soon in Kotor, a small town set beside a bay with a tapestry of walls and battlements crawling up the mountain-face behind it. By the time that I arrived, it was growing dark, and after finding myself a bed for the night, I settled in a bar to scribble. By this stage in my journey, sending postcards had become something of a ritual, and I had a list of regular recipients. At the top of that list was the landlord of my local pub in Taunton who I had promised to send a card from each country I visited. I had been reliably informed that some of them had already arrived and had been nailed into one of the old oak roof-beams, beside the pewter pots and brass horseshoes hanging above the beer engines, to allow my neighbours to track my progress towards the Antipodes.

As I finished my first beer and asked the waiter for another, an old man on the table beside me turned around and caught my attention.

'It's nice to hear English being spoken,' he said, offering his hand. 'My name's John. I'm an Englishman myself, but I've been away from home for a very long time. In fact, I'm slowly making my way back there now for the first time in twenty years.'

'Nice to meet you, John. Where have you been?' I asked, setting down my pen and shaking the old man's hand.

'Living in Japan for the last decade. I work there as a sailing instructor. Before that, well, I've spent a little bit of time everywhere.'

When he spoke, his heavy northern accent had a peculiar inflection, a slight brightness which tempered the dark, industrial syllables, and I wondered which part of England he was from.

'So where is home in England?' I asked. 'I don't suppose you know the west country at all?'

'Somerset is where I'm headed,' he chuckled. 'To a little town called Taunton. Are you familiar with it?'

'I know Taunton very well,' I laughed, amazed at the extraordinary stroke of coincidence.

'I have a reunion lunch there in a couple of weeks at a pub called *The Vivary Arms*. Don't tell me you know that too?' he said.

I looked down at the postcard on the table in front of me in disbelief. The address in the top corner read:

The Vivary Arms
Wilton
Taunton
Somerset

At eighty-two, John had spent much of his life travelling and was no stranger to the power of chance, but even he recognised that such a coincidence as our meeting deserved a celebratory drink. Pulling his chair up alongside mine, he ordered two more beers, and then began telling me about his life.

'For the most part, I live in Japan now because I am in involved with a woman there. I stay for the summer, but in winter I go to a tiny island off the coast of Vietnam. I return to Osaka every spring, just as the cherry blossoms begin to bloom.

'Like yourself, I undertook a journey by motorcycle when I was young, over half a century ago now, during the days of national service when I was posted to Germany. I borrowed an old Vespa and with a fistful of military fuel coupons I spent all summer riding down the Rhine carrying nothing but a girlfriend for luggage.

'After that, I joined the merchant navy for a decade and sailed all around the world. I spent quite a bit of time in South America, and one year I agreed to lead a Raleigh International expedition across Patagonia. It was a great trip, but a little too cold for my liking, so I spent a few years afterwards warming up in the Laotian jungle. Then I discovered Japan, the only place that has ever managed to cast anything like a permanent hold over me.'

Noticing my black notebook on the table, he produced his own from his jacket pocket.

'I see you are also a scribbler. This book is my life's work. It's got eighty years of memories and observations scrawled inside it. All my life I've been trying to figure out a list of the essential needs of man, and I believe I'm finally getting there.'

I looked inquisitively across at the slim volume, but John quickly tucked it back into his pocket.

'It's not quite ready yet though. I think you'll find a book takes a long time, young man.'

John still sailed, though not as often as he would have liked, which meant that his adventures were now largely confined to land. It was clear that age, for a man like him, was both a burden and boon. In his later life, John had found time to reflect on his richly decorated years, but he was also frustrated by the fact that his travels had understandably tempered since he entered his ninth decade.

The course of almost every story John told ran along the lines of love, and even now, despite his girlfriend in Japan, he was making his way to England through Serbia because there was a woman he had promised to visit in Belgrade. Of all his tales, my favourite featured a close encounter with a jealous Chinese butcher who had caught John flirting with his wife. To escape the cleaver-wielding husband, John had fled the town and dived into the nearest river he could find. When I asked him where in China this had happened, he explained that he had been in a town named Yangshuo and that it was the Li river which had been his means of escape – the very same stretch of water where I had received a shock from a lightning bolt many years later.

Our shared experience of near-death in the Far East was cause for another beer, as was our fondness for improbable motorcycles, as was our common knowledge of Somerset pubs, and before long I was stumbling home through the dark streets of Kotor, propping up a wobbling old man, with him propping me up too, the pair of us hopelessly lost. But for John, being lost was nothing new. In fact, in his eyes, getting lost was a very valuable use of one's time, and it was an experience that at eighty-two, he was thankfully still young enough to enjoy.

***

The ancient walls of Kotor were built bit by bit over the centuries, finally being perfected by the Venetians, before an earthquake rumbled through the valley in 1979 and brought the walls to ruin. But as I stood in the old town late the following afternoon, I could still trace their outline clinging to the side of the mountain. It seemed an unlikely place for battlements, the sheer side of a perilous rockface, but the Montenegrins are mountain people, just as comfortable high up amongst the peaks as down in the valleys below.

Like in Dubrovnik, the privilege of walking on the walls of Kotor came at a cost, but John had told me of a secret passage around the rear of the mountain and had drawn me a map on the back of a napkin. It led me to the edge of the town, to the foot of a rocky serpentine which ran up the steepest side of the valley. Beside the start of the track, scrawled in red paint on a rock at head height was a sign that read: 'DANGER, WOLVES', and I wondered if at John's age there was much left in the world to scare a man.

My legs felt strong, and as the day was growing cooler, I decided to press on up the track, sending little rock-falls streaming down the mountain with every step I took. It was a tough climb, steep enough to leave me gasping for air, and aside from a lone goatherd who was leading his flock to roost on a distant slope, I seemed to be alone on the mountain. But after an hour of climbing, I reached a house at the top of the trail where I discovered a donkey in a shaded garden nibbling grass beside the feet of a sleeping man.

Without meaning to wake the sleeper, I sat down on his wall to rest, but he must have sensed that I was there because a moment later he leapt up from the ground, pulled out two chairs, and invited me to sit with him. As he attempted to speak to me in Montenegrin, only his left eye opened, revealing a crazed orb of opalescent blue shining out from under the overhang of a bedraggled white eyebrow.

'Franovic Spilare!' he said, pointing to his chest by way of introduction, and as far as I could tell from his mimes and gestures, he had lived atop the mountain all of his life.

From Franovic's garden, the bay of Kotor shone far below, and we sat in silence and watched as a vast cruise ship made a slow pirouette, turning around to sail back out to sea. When the wind gusted hard enough, I was sure I could hear drafts of music, blown up from a band playing upon her deck, and perhaps even the ring of wine glasses touching.

Franovic must have heard it too because he disappeared into his house, returning a moment later with a bottle of bitter black wine which smelt of burnt herbs as he poured it into two goblets. Raising his glass to offer a toast, he pointed with his other hand down towards the town of Kotor where Montenegrin flags were flying from every lamppost. Franovic smiled at me with five yellow teeth and said:

'Birthday! Birthday!'

At first, I thought it might have been his birthday, but then I remembered that the flags were flying in Kotor because it was Independence Day. Although the origins of Montenegro stretch back centuries into the past, the modern nation had just turned twelve, and Franovic could not have been more proud.

I sat in the garden for a while, toasting to Montenegro, watching the cruise ship slip out of the bay, and doing my best to drink down the glass of acrid wine. But I was determined to catch the sunset from the top of the mountain, so when dusk began its final approach, I bade farewell to Franovic and his donkey and set off back up the path, wondering if the wolves were waiting until dark to begin their hunting.

In Montenegro, the sun sets twice - once at the moment it first dips below the ring of black peaks surrounding every valley, and a second time when it finally falls below the faraway horizon hidden behind the mountains. In the half-hour between the two, the towelled sky glows and fades, whilst the dark mountains grow taller, menace building upon menace, until their black forms bleed into the night and vanish altogether.

Thankfully, the sun was still up when I found the hole in the wall that John had promised and pulled myself up onto the battlements where I stayed to watch the twilight fade, which meant picking my way down the walls of Kotor in the dark. Letting the lights of the town below guide me, I stepped carefully over the cracked stones, nearly falling down the mountain when a startled goat bolted out from behind a rock. Eventually, I reached the town and made my way back to my hostel, where the receptionist handed me a scrap of yellow paper, covered in an elegant hand, which read:

Sam,

I left this morning for Serbia – sorry to not have caught you. Postcard safely stowed in luggage. I will deliver it personally to the Vivary, assuming I make it that far. Expect we'll meet again, hopefully in a pub. Our conversation last night left me thinking of a line a very wise woman once wrote, and I'm sure given time you'll come to realise yourself that:

'Writing is a complex art, much infected by life.'

Good luck with it all,

J

Chapter Five

The quick Argjiro
with her baby
leapt into the air like a bird
plunging from the castle into the abyss.
She fell like a star,
but her light shone on.

- Ismail Kadare, *'Princesha Argjiro'*

In almost every country I visited, when I reeled off the list of places that my journey would encompass, there was one nation whose mention never failed to induce anxious frowns and words of warning. Yet, of all the places I journeyed through, nowhere defied the prejudices surrounding it quite like Albania, and the characters I met there proved to be some of the most hospitable people I have ever encountered.

Admittedly, crossing the border was not without its trials. My insurance covered me in every country in Europe except for Albania, where due to the wild driving habits and rotten roads, my policy was categorically invalid. But the first piece of Albanian traffic to pass me by was far from ominous. I had been in the country for less than a minute when a horse-drawn cart came clattering down the road, looking like it might fall to pieces at any moment. It held together just long enough to disappear around the next bend, rattling away at five miles an hour, guided by the thick fist of an old farmer bouncing above his crooked wooden wheels.

Letting the cart pass, I walked across to a wooden hut. Stepping through the door, I was met with a quizzical stare from a man sat smoking behind a desk. When I asked for insurance, he vanished outside for five minutes, and from the other side of the thin wooden wall, I heard the sloshing of liquid, followed by the noise of grinding metal, and then a long string of grumblings. There was a crack, a bang, and a whistle, then suddenly a loud petrol generator shuddered into life, just as the man returned.

'For computer,' he said, pointing to an ancient, dust-covered screen.

Ten minutes later, I had a crudely printed piece of paper that insured me on Albanian roads, and I was chasing after the farmer. I never caught his cart, but I soon saw something else which took me by surprise. A mile past the border, standing on a low hill, was the pale dome of a mosque, straddled by two tall minarets, looking from a distance like the blanched body of a vast spider with its forelegs raised in salute. It was the first of many mosques I would encounter across the Albanian countryside, built by rich donors from the Middle East in the hope of bolstering the nation's Islamic identity, despite the fact that the temples are rarely visited by native Albanians.

I followed the road to the northern town of Shkodër and quickly understood why my insurers refused to offer me protection in Albania. On my journey to the Antipodes, I encountered many passionate drivers, but Albanian motorists were by far the most spirited. Whether piloting a horse and cart, a creaking sedan, a rusting tractor, or a sleek Mercedes, they had a habit of waiting until the most inappropriate moment and then overtaking with reckless abandon. And as a motorcyclist, my status on the road was nil, which meant that more than once I was driven off the edge of the asphalt into knee-deep weeds and a blizzard of choking dust.

Circumstances were not helped by the potholes, two metres wide and half a metre deep, that would suddenly open in the road and swallow my front wheel whole. On that first day in Albania, I hit one crater at such speed that my front headlight fell off, requiring the artful deployment of half a roll of duct tape and a few dozen cable ties to fix it back in place. Alongside the potholes, speed bumps kept appearing unannounced in the middle of fast roads, and each time I ploughed blindly into their sides, I winced as I felt my wheel rims striking the asphalt. An hour into the country, I remembered one seasoned motorcyclist on the ferry to Spain who had told me that if my motorcycle survived the roads in Albania, then it would survive anything.

It was late afternoon by the time I arrived in Shkodër, just as the city was slipping into its evening routine. As I searched for a room, café owners and restaurateurs were stepping out of their doorways, throwing buckets of water onto the streets to settle the dust. The first people to step outside were old men, shuffling along in the dwindling heat, spitting sunflower seeds onto the damp pavement as they went. Following close on the heels of their husbands were lines of plump grandmothers, walking along arm in arm, gossiping loudly with each other. After dropping my bags in a hostel, I joined the crowds, just as young children began to arrive riding bicycles, scooters, and anything else they could find with wheels, speeding down the wide boulevards, practising for when they were old enough to drive. Last to appear were the pairs of young lovers who strolled hand in hand, slinking stealthily between the shaded trees.

The city itself was not handsome, but half the population of Shkodër seemed to have emerged into the twilight, and intrigued by the crowds, I sat down outside a café to watch as they passed. Everyone moved slowly around for hours, greeting, kissing, embracing, and shaking hands in the crepuscular light. As it grew darker, electric torches went on, and the old men sat down to play chess at little tables, each game drawing an audience of boys. Elsewhere, people gathered at cafés, balancing little cups of espresso upon their knees and smoking cigarette after cigarette. And when people were not drinking coffee or smoking, they would take to walking again, slowly ambling up and down the city, stopping to greet friends and plant a million kisses on the wrinkled cheeks of their grandparents.

After a coffee, I walked around the city centre, intrigued by the new aspect that Europe wore. Finding a seat beside a gurgling fountain, I sat down in a park just as a speaker crackled into life and sent an Adhan drifting through the air from the minaret of a nearby mosque. Sonorous, melancholy, and hauntingly beautiful, the call to prayer sounded like it had come from very far away, as if it had been born deep in an Arabian desert, before being blown by a hot wind halfway around the world just so that it could hover elegantly above the streets of Shkodër. Stretching across the evening, it drifted lazily amongst the fountains, filling the city with noise, and then as quickly as it came, the song melted away. Nobody paid it any attention. Nobody walked towards the mosque. The crowd were utterly indifferent to its command.

Then, opposite me, a bright neon sign flickered into life announcing the Hotel Europa and lighting up the image of a European flag. Below the sign, hanging from a slanted pole, the national ensign also flickered in the breeze. The Albanian flag had no patterns or stripes, no ornate geometry, just two colours – blood and black – painted into the ancient, terrifying emblem of the double-headed eagle. It was a symbol which made me think of stern-faced men, wrapped in fur, walking in ranks through the snow: a standard made for winter battles, but instead flying here in Shkodër on a warm, lazy evening, beneath a European hotel, in the shadow of a mosque. The world suddenly seemed quite strange to me then, suffused with different light and strung to new music, and I sensed that Albania would prove to be a far more complicated country than I had expected it to be.

***

As soon as I arrived in Krujë, a city which lies a few hours south of Shkodër, I spotted a bust of Skanderbeg, the great warlord of Albania who once had his capital there. Though he has been forgotten by much of the modern world, statues of Skanderbeg stand in great cities across Europe. His face can be seen in Tirana, London, Brussels, Geneva, Skopje, Pristina, and half the towns in Italy. The statues almost always look the same, featuring a body decked in chainmail, a large head sheltered beneath a goat-skull helmet, a strongly hooked nose, a broad beard, and a fierce pair of eyes staring down the hills of Krujë at the Ottoman hordes massing below. At one time, all of western Europe was indebted to Skanderbeg, and though his legend may have faded elsewhere, in Krujë, he is remembered as if he had been a god.

I was doing my best to recall what I knew of the warlord as I strolled through the grass-covered alleyways of Krujë's old ruins. Twenty miles north of Tirana, the city sits halfway up the side of a mountain, a wall of rock to its east and a wide Mediterranean plain to its west. It was a hot day when I arrived there and Krujë's dilapidated streets were deserted. As I walked through the city alone, butterflies bobbed drunkenly beside me, whilst grasshoppers the size of sparrows lay panting on tufts of grass, and frogs croaked from the few strips of shadow that clung to the crumbling walls. In the afternoon heat, the pale stones of the city conspired to make a dizzying maze, and with only insects and amphibians for company, I might have been lost there for hours had I not stumbled upon a house belonging to a man named Irvin Murcai.

'Hello, my friend,' he called, rising from a wooden chair at the walled entrance to a dilapidated property. 'You look lost.'

Before I could confess that I was, the man took me by the shoulder and began guiding me inside.

'My name is Irvin,' he said, as we strolled into his garden. 'I used to be a film-maker in Tirana, but after the financial crisis in Albania, I could no longer make films. Instead, I bought this place, which I am slowly turning into a cultural centre dedicated to the old Albanian way of life. Please, let me show you around. Unfortunately, we do not get many visitors.'

On our way to the small white house standing in the centre of the complex, I noticed a clutter of metal equipment heaped in one corner of Irvin's garden.

'What is all this for?' I asked.

Here, Irvin grinned and ran his hand over the collection of stills and pipes.

'It is for making rakia, my friend.'

'Rakia?'

'You do not know rakia?' he gasped. 'And how long have you been in Albania?'

'Two days,' I said, at which point Irvin nearly imploded with shock.

'Two days? And no-one has offered you a drink of rakia? Please, sit, I will go and fetch some,' he said, leading me over to a small table.

Beside the table, I noticed that an entire wall of Irvin's house had been decorated with a mural of Krujë, imitating a painting that Edward Lear, the man who taught Queen Victoria to draw, had once made of the city. I was still admiring the mural when Irvin returned a moment later carrying two glasses, a bottle of clear liquid, and a plate piled high with plum-sized olives and thick slabs of white sheep's cheese.

'This is rakia, my friend,' he announced, pouring a large measure and handing it to me.

We clinked our two glasses together, and I was about to tip the whole thing down my throat when Irvin cried out:

'No, No! Don't do that,' getting up out of his seat to stop me. 'Rakia is homemade and very strong.'

Heeding Irvin's warning, I put the glass to my lips and took the smallest of sips, but despite my caution, a second after swallowing, my whole throat burst into flame and I found myself battling to stifle a throbbing cough. Placing a fat olive into my mouth, I sucked it desperately, wiping tears from my cheeks as Irvin drained off half his glass and let out a long, satisfied sigh.

'Every family makes rakia in Albania, from whatever fruit they can gather,' he explained. 'Mine is made from the very grapes you see around you. I think it quite smooth by Albanian standards.'

Spluttering something like an agreement, I reached out to grab another olive.

'The olives are grown here too. You will find that Krujë is surrounded by thousands of olive trees. Many of them date back to the time when Skanderbeg passed a law commanding every married couple to plant twenty-five trees to celebrate their wedding.'

'It seems to me that Skanderbeg is very important to the people of Krujë,' I said. 'Earlier, when I was walking through the ruins, I passed a sign for Skanderbeg's tree. Do you know this tree?' I asked, eager to learn more about the old warlord.

'The tree is very famous,' said Irvin, taking another sip of rakia. 'It is where Skanderbeg used to go to think over his battle plans. Did you notice the little fountain beside the tree? It is one of many in Krujë, which in Albanian means *spring*. In the days of Skanderbeg, the fountain and the tree stood outside the city walls, and each time the Ottomans besieged the city, Skanderbeg had to send a man through a secret tunnel to block up the spring to limit the water available to the enemy and increase the flow of the fountains within the city. Three times the Ottomans attacked Krujë, and three times Skanderbeg beat them. They only succeeded in their fourth siege because by then he had died of malaria.'

'Was Skanderbeg the king of Albania?' I asked.

'No. The pope died on his way to Albania to coronate him, and so Skanderbeg was never made king, but he had the genius of a great ruler. You have seen the horned goat's skull attached to his helmet in the statues? Skanderbeg earned that symbol because his favourite tactic was to tie candles to the horns of goats and have them roam around the hills surrounding Krujë to trick the enemy into thinking he possessed far more soldiers than he actually did.'

'Your knowledge of history is very impressive,' I said. 'I don't think many people in my country would take such an interest in the history of England.'

'Yes, but in Albania, we live our history,' explained Irvin. 'We are such an impressionable people, and we have seen such violent times. We speak a language with no linguistic relatives. Our country is covered with mosques, but nobody prays. We were ruled by the Venetians, then the Ottomans, then the Communists, but we have always been Albanian. We're European, but the Union will not have us, and we don't care for it either. We are a complicated country, my friend, with many different pasts.'

In the end, I stayed and spoke with Irvin in his garden for hours, drinking rakia and working my way through the plate of olives. As the afternoon drew on, our conversation meandered from subject to subject, covering history, music, philosophy, politics, and even the merits of travel. Throughout it all, Irvin's impeccable English never faltered, and later in the afternoon, I asked where he had learnt it.

'I have never been to England. I have never had a lesson. I learnt it all from music,' he said, pointing to a speaker above his head, and I realised that whilst we had been speaking, English songs had been playing the entire time.

'But listening to foreign music meant seven years of prison at one time,' he said, wincing. 'And once you were in, you never came out.'

'What do you mean?' I asked.

'During the communist regime, under the leadership of Hoxha, it was illegal to listen to foreign music of any kind in Albania. I wanted to learn English, but the only way to do it was to buy records on the black market and listen to them in my cellar. If I had been caught, even though I was young, I might have been sent to prison for a very long time.'

Irvin's intellect was astonishing, as was his innate generosity and his courage. But after what must have been the seventh glass of rakia, I finally bade him goodbye and walked back through the city to the guest-house where I was staying. Set amongst the castle ruins, the guest-house had been in the same family for five generations. Built of huge stones and dark wood, it looked strong and impenetrable, as the broken castle surrounding it might also once have seemed. But it was too fine a night to stay inside, so I wandered out into the grounds to sit beside a kulla – an old stone fire-tower, one of many that form a long chain running up and down the length of Albania. In the time of Skanderbeg, great bonfires were lit inside the kullas at the first sight of invading Ottomans, warning the rest of Europe of the advancing hordes.

As I sat down at a table out on the terrace, one of my hosts brought me my dinner, and in between mouthfuls I scribbled down all the history that Irvin had told me, fearful that if I left it till morning, it might vanish from my head. By the time I looked up from the page and gazed out across the ruins, the sun was just beginning to set to the left of the kulla, shining in the distance like a glowing lump of timber fallen from the warning torch centuries before. In the dying light, a spectral cat swung between the legs of my table whilst a lone bat flew mad loops around the silhouette of the fire-tower, dancing to the sound of the goat bells tinkling in the nearby hills. Away over the Mediterranean, the hot, falling sun slipped through ribbons of cloud, dying them bloody bronze, slowly dwindling until all that remained was a crescent-shaped ember of light, floating delicately on the surface of the sea. When the sun finally sank below the horizon a minute later, shade fell upon the castle's broken stones, and with the arrival of twilight, a cooler wind began to blow, as one by one the lights of Tirana came on in the distance, lighting the dark valley below.

***

The towns and villages that I passed on my way south from Krujë often looked far bigger as words on a map, and as I rode through their dusty streets, many seemed abjectly poor. Supermarkets stood bare and empty, whilst petrol stations, selling fuel at prices people could not afford, were left unmanned. Usually, the only signs of life were a handful of old men in the fields, guiding rusty ploughs pulled by thin horses. The poverty was undeniable; compared to the rest of Europe, Albania seemed half a century behind.

After Krujë, I passed through Berat, the city of a thousand windows, a place which takes its name from the streets of Ottoman townhouses which hang atop one another in two beetling walls on either side of a yellow river. Spilling out onto the flatlands, I turned east out of Berat and found myself on a coastal road, leaning into impeccable corners as Albania's pristine beaches passed by in stitches of blue and gold. Further down the coast, away in the distance, lay the smoky green hulk of Corfu, but before I continued southwards, I spent a week sleeping on beaches, dreaming on hot sands beside waves of rippling glass and reading books in the shallows.

Albania's coast was bewitchingly beautiful, and I might have stayed there forever had an earthquake not struck one night whilst I was sleeping on a beach named Gjipe. When I first felt the tremors, I had thought I was dreaming, but as the shudders strengthened, I woke up to find the ground quivering beneath me. Poking my head outside my tent, I watched a dim moon wobble on a distant cliff-top and listened to the loud roar of the surf. Sitting upright, I waited for a minute, expecting a terrible wave to come crashing over the beach, but before long the tremors had died away. Dismissing the episode as the unruly imaginings of a sun-soaked brain, I quickly fell back asleep, and it was only one week later, whilst leafing through a newspaper, that I discovered an earthquake really had struck that night, with its epicentre recorded just fifteen miles from Gjipe.

What I remember most about Albania is not its rugged beauty or its complicated history but its resounding emptiness. Though I was there at midsummer, the beaches were vacant, the ruined castles quiet, and I barely met any other travellers. Even when I reached Butrint, an ancient, immaculately preserved city in the south of the country, I had the ruins almost to myself. For a whole afternoon, I wandered alone amongst the pine trees, basilicas, baptisteries, and acropoleis of a settlement so old that Virgil wrote of it in his Aeneid. Ages of man, like species of moss, clung to Butrint's stones - Hellenic, Roman, Medieval, Venetian, and Ottoman were all present. If the city had been built a few hundred miles to the west or the east, in Italy or Greece, it would have been swarming with tourists at that time of the year. Albania, it seemed, was a forgotten treasure, overlooked by the rest of the world. But such places do not remain overlooked for long, and as I rode through the city of Sarandë, past countless construction sites and half-built hotels, I sensed that fragments of Albania were already on the cusp of great change.

My final stop in the far south of the country was Gjirokastër, colloquially known as the city of stone, a picturesque collection of old stone streets which clings to the western flank of the Drino valley seventy miles north of the border with Greece. A place of literary fame, Gjirokastër was used by the Albanian writer Ismail Kadare as inspiration for his book *Chronicle of Stone,* and Kadare's words serve as a better description of Gjirokastër than any I might conjure:

It was a strange city, and seemed to have been cast up in the valley one winter's night like some prehistoric creature that was now clawing its way up the mountainside... Everything in the city was old and made of stone, from the streets and mountains to the roofs of the sprawling age-old houses covered with grey slates like gigantic scales.

I had read that those same grey slates are thought to be the origin of the city's name, deriving from the Greek 'argyos', meaning silver – a reference to the way the city's rooftiles shimmer in the rain. Made from local stone and held together by careful alignment, during storms the tiles are notorious for letting in water, and whenever a leak springs, tradition dictates that it is the youngest child in the house who is sent up onto the rooftop to re-arrange the slates.

On the afternoon that I arrived in Gjirokastër, a light drizzle was falling, but the houses I passed must have all been well built because I could see no children scrambling over their summits. As I reached the centre of the ancient city, the rain grew heavier, so before exploring the castle, I ducked inside a café and ordered myself a coffee and plate of burek - the thinly baked Ottoman pastries beloved by Albanians.

'This is your first time in Gjirokastër?' asked the plump owner of the café as she set the coffee down on my table.

'Yes. It's nice to see it in the rain,' I said.

'You have heard that the city's name comes from the way the wet roof-tiles shine?'

'Is that not true?'

'No, no, no,' she replied, shaking her head and taking a seat at the table next to me. 'Gjirokastër comes from Argjiro, the name of a princess who once lived in the castle. When the Ottoman's invaded, rather than surrender to the enemy, Argjiro jumped from the wall of the castle holding her baby in her arms. The princess died, but her child survived, and beside Argjiro's body, milk began to flow from the mountainside. You can still see the place where the miracle happened below the castle wall - two white streaks of rock mark the spot.'

'So, the city was named after the princess?' I asked, sensing that I had stumbled upon another Albanian with a depthless inventory of local knowledge.

'Yes. It is our most famous myth. Everyone in Gjirokastër knows the story of Argjiro.'

'And what is your name? I asked.

'Klotilda,' she smiled, extending her hand. 'Welcome to our city.'

'Thank you, Klotilda. Can I ask, what happened in Gjirokastër after the princess died?'

'Well, after the Ottomans invaded, they fell in love with Gjirokastër. For centuries, the city's townhouses belonged to the aristocratic families, until the communist regime stripped them of their property.'

'And what about the castle?' I asked, looking out of the window at the vast fortress that loomed over the city, its grey stones glinting in the rain.

'You are English, no?' asked Klotilda.

I nodded in reply.

'In the time of Ali Pasha, your famous poet, Lord Byron, visited Gjirokastër and stayed in the castle. A century later, King Zog, Albania's first and only king, used the castle to keep his political enemies imprisoned there. After him, Enver Hoxha, the communist leader, also used the castle as a prison. Hoxha loved Gjirokastër because he was born here, but he was paranoid of a nuclear attack and he ordered miles of tunnels to be built beneath the castle. One runs directly under this café, though it has never been used.'

Just as with Irvin, Klotilda wore her learning lightly, delivering it effortlessly in impeccable English. I had come to realise that places like Gjirokastër and people like Klotilda are not unusual in Albania. Every town in the country has a dozen different stories and legends attached to its past, and every local is well versed in at least part of their nation's history.

'How is your coffee?' she asked, as I continued to stare distractedly out of the window at the castle.

'Excellent,' I replied, speaking truthfully. 'I've been in Albania for almost two weeks now, and I don't think I've ever seen so many people drink coffee. All Albanian's seem to love it, and I can understand why. Your coffee is very good.'

Here, Klotilda laughed a little, but then a shadow of sadness fell across her face.

'Though you have seen many people drinking coffee, I do not think you have seen many Albanian's eating in restaurants, have you?' she asked.

'Come to think of it, I haven't,' I replied.

'Albanian's love coffee because it's the only thing they can afford. Eating dinner in a restaurant is too expensive for many of my people.

Even in this little café, it's only ever foreign visitors who pay for food. Albania has a lot of history, but no money. Many people don't realise how difficult life is here.'

There was a long pause as she looked thoughtfully out of the window.

'But we must be thankful for what we do have. At least the coffee is good,' she said, with a resigned smile, before clearing my plate and leaving to attend to her other customers.

Over the previous two weeks, as my admiration for the country had grown, I had also become increasingly aware of how poor Albania was as a nation. For so many of its people, life seemed to be a struggle. This undeniable fact was especially sad because the Albanians I met - Irvin and Klotilda amongst them - were some of the most conscientious and generous humans to feature in my entire journey. After I finished my first coffee, Klotilda brought me a second, but she refused to let me pay for it. Our conversation meant that I had been elevated from customer to guest, and as I sat in her café, listening to the wail of the Adhan as it drifted over the damp, old stones of Gjirokastër, I was filled with a profound sense of gratitude. I had passed a golden time in Albania, and though the road to Greece beckoned, I was certain that Gjirokastër, Gjipe, Krujë, and Shkodër were all places that I would long look back upon with fondness.

Chapter Six

But when my will shall be dispos'd to draw you all to me,
Even with the earth itself, and seas, ye shall enforced be.
Then will I to Olympus' top our virtuous engine bind,
And by it everything shall hang, by command inclin'd:
So much I am supreme to gods, to men supreme as much.

- Homer, *The Iliad*, Book VIII, 20-24

From as early as I can remember, every year at Christmas my family has received a battered brown parcel, held together by a web of masking tape and postage stamps, sent from a small town in Greece called Nea Artaki. These brown parcels would always contain five things: a jar of Greek honey, a stale bag of nuts, a lurid red table cloth, a carol-playing Christmas card, and several old Coca-Cola bottles holding litres and litres of foul-tasting brandy. These were our annual presents from Mrs Curry.

It was my father who first discovered Pepita Curry in 1983 when he was sent to install a central heating system in her home. After landing in Greece, Dad realised that the parts which were meant to be waiting for him had not arrived, and so it was impossible to do any work. Instead, he spent two weeks sat on a rooftop drinking gallons of ouzo with Mrs Curry and her husband Taki, and they have been great friends ever since.

For me, growing up, Pepita was a woman of legend. Within my living memory, I had never met her, but there were a few faded photographs of Pepita holding me as a baby. As a young boy, in my mind, she was simply the lady responsible for the huge pots of honey that I would eat a spoonful at a time. As I got older, my interests deviated, and it was not long before I began to respect her as a purveyor of potent spirits. For years, the two-litre bottles of brandy that she sent every Christmas serviced many gatherings of me and my adolescent friends.

The delivery of those bottles was always met with equal parts excitement and trepidation, the liquid inside often tasting of a chemistry experiment gone awry. The smell alone was enough to strip the hairs from your nostrils, and if your vision remained fully intact the morning after drinking the brandy, then it had been a good batch. From what I can remember, Pepita's potions were directly responsible for one small garden-shed fire, two minor bicycle accidents, and a dozen or so impromptu bouts of vomiting in my father's vegetable patch. Needless to say, she was rather famous amongst my friends.

In return for Pepita's gifts, my family would send a parcel to Greece each year, though the contents of our packages were more sober, typically featuring tea bags, marmite, shortbread biscuits, and some photographs of the family. From my older teenage years and onwards, I would also send a post-card with our parcel, letting Pepita know just how well her illicit liquor was received by the youth of Somerset. To me, the woman was a hero, so when my father suggested that whilst in Greece I should visit the ninety-three-year-old lady, I thought it a wonderful idea.

This meant that after visiting the monasteries at Meteora, I found myself on an immaculate highway, rolling across the plain of Thessaly in the general direction of Athens. Helicon, Delphi, Parnassus, and many more names, all familiar to me from Greek mythology, passed beside the road, their presence only casually betrayed by humble signposts pointing to distant pine-clad peaks. I wanted to stop and explore them all, but Greece, with such grand heritage, has a site of cultural significance every half-mile, and stopping at one would have felt traitorous to the rest. Instead, I followed the road onwards, watching hawks tumbling above the tree-tops, on my way to the one living Greek who, for me, was still of mythical status.

Nea Artaki itself was an unpretty little town, popular amongst Greek holidaymakers but otherwise unknown to the world. I did not have Mrs Curry's exact address, just the name of her road, but my father had assured me that I would recognise her house as soon as I saw it. He had told me not to look not for a home, but to look for a jungle.

I had only been walking for a few minutes down a row of crisp apartment blocks when I found it. Though it might once have been a house, by the time I arrived at Mrs Curry's address, I was not sure it could be considered that any longer. The rough shape of a bungalow could just be discerned, but the whole building had been enveloped by a chaotic carpet of greenery which smothered every brick, cloaked every window, and had every species of plant and shrub native to Greece entangled within it. I had been told that two potted palm trees marked the path to the entrance and that once I found them, I had only to keep pushing in a straight line through the foliage and eventually I would reach the door.

Parting the leaves, I found the porch and rang each of Pepita's seven doorbells. A strange collection of electrical chimes sounded within, followed by silence. I rang again, but nothing moved on the other side of the door. Given the state of the garden, I began to doubt the house was even inhabited, but I tried the doorbells again, and this time, a short while after the music stopped playing, I heard somebody shuffling on the other side of the glass. There was a series of loud clanks and scraping sounds as a complicated array of locks and bolts were drawn back, then the door swung open. Suddenly, standing there before me, all five feet of her, was the infamous Mrs Curry. Naturally, she did not have the faintest idea who I was.

Garbling some Greek at me, the frail old lady cast a hostile frown up in my direction. In return, I smiled and thrust a bouquet of flowers at her.

'Hello, Mrs Curry. It's me, Sam,' I said.

Pepita mumbled some more indecipherable Greek, then pushed the flowers back at me and tried to usher me away. As I attempted to explain who I was, she jabbed me in the belly, and she was about to lunge for an umbrella standing beside the door when I had the sense to pull out a recent picture of my father and I. In the last twenty years, Dad had not changed quite as much as I had and at seeing his face, a wave of recognition broke over Pepita.

'Sam? Sam! Billy's Sam!' she cried, pulling me down into a stifling hug and peppering me with kisses. When I finally managed to prise myself out of her arms, tears were running down her wrinkled face.

It took some time for me to explain my journey and for the bewildered Pepita to understand that I had ridden my motorcycle all the way from England to Greece. But as soon as she was sure that I was not an apparition, and that I was the same human she once held as a baby, I was taken by the hand and immediately subject to a full tour of her house, accompanied by a blistering commentary of her life in Greece which ran unbroken for nearly an hour.

Pepita lived alone, her second husband Taki having died decades before. There were pictures of him all over the walls – a stout, handsome man, with slick silver hair and a single black eyebrow. There were also some pictures of me, standing proudly in my various school uniforms, alongside all the postcards I had sent over the years. I soon realised that Pepita's friendship with my father, however remote, might be one of the only relationships she had left. Her health was good, and she suffered no shortage of energy, but Mrs Curry had not escaped the inevitable attrition of family, friends, and acquaintances that affects all people who have lived for nearly a century.

'You must tell your Dad to double the number of teabags he sends each year. One parcel is never enough,' she said, in her thickly accented English, as we entered the kitchen. 'Would you like a cup of tea now, dear?'

'I'd love one, thank you,' I said, taking a seat at the table and watching her slowly shuffle around the kitchen. Five minutes later, Pepita placed two mugs of tea on the table in front of me, but as I reached out to pick one up, she quickly swatted my hand away.

'Wait just a minute. I need to add a special touch,' she said, opening the fridge and taking out a clear plastic bottle labelled 'HOLLY WATER'. Pouring a splash into each mug of tea, she turned to me and explained:

'This water is blessed at a nearby church where they keep the dead body of a saint. I have a glass every day, usually mixed with some brandy. It's the reason I've lived as long as I have. Speaking of brandy, have a splash of this, for your health,' she said, taking down a bottle from an enormous collection stored in one corner of the kitchen, before pouring a healthy glug into my cup. Amongst the bottles, I spotted several plastic containers filled with clear spirits and was glad to see that

Mrs Curry was still producing as much liquor as ever.

By the time we finished our tea, I had been at Pepita's house for nearly an hour, but she had never once been still or sat down. When I told her to take a seat, she adamantly refused. My concern seemed to upset her, and instead of sitting at the table with her tea as I had hoped, Pepita grabbed me by the wrist and pulled me towards the door.

'Come on,' she said. 'It's time for my daily walk around the house.'

Up close, the garden was quite a spectacle. The unruly green mess seemed to be staging a slow, successful invasion of the house, with branches and creepers stretching across the veranda and groping at the edges of the windows. The veranda itself ran around the bungalow, encased by a wall of plant matter that had woven itself into a living conservatory. Underneath the canopy, the white stone floor glowed viridescent beneath our feet, and the air was thick with a perfume of compost, dead fruit, and tree-sap.

It was hot outside, meaning Pepita could only manage a slow stroll. Though the garden seemed a web of chaos to me, she could name every fruit, vine, and blossom, and stopped often to show me her favourites.

'Here's my lavender, for the bees. Here are the herbs that I use when I cook. And see here, don't the hyacinths and anemones look lovely? Oh, and of course there's the fig tree. This is my favourite. It makes for a convenient screen when I take my showers outside on the balcony every morning,' she said, gesturing to a shower-head fixed to the outside wall of the house. I had my suspicions that the neighbours were probably just as grateful for the presence of the tree as Pepita was.

Despite the leisurely pace, we made several spirited circuits of the house, but on our fourth lap, something extraordinary happened. We were ambling slowly along when all of a sudden there was a rustling in the leaves above us and a single fat lemon plopped down through the foliage to land with a thud a few steps ahead. It took me a moment to register exactly what the large, ugly yellow ball was, but before it had even hit the floor, Pepita had let go of my arm and was sprinting straight towards the house.

'RUN SAM!' she shrieked in a shrill, terrified voice.

'Mrs Curry?' I shouted, chasing after her, just as two more lemons fell onto the veranda behind me.

For a ninety-three-year-old, Pepita moved incredibly fast, and she had disappeared by the time I reached the dark doorway. I searched inside the house, checking the kitchen and pantry before I eventually found her in the living room, perched on the arm of her chair, her feet lifted high off the ground as if she was afraid one of the lemons might roll through the hallway and take her by the ankles.

'What's wrong, Pepita?'

'Every day they wait for me to take my walk outside!' she shouted, quivering with fear. 'Then, one by one, they start falling from the trees, aiming for my head. It will be one of those lemons that gets me in the end, Sam, I'm sure of it. Big yellow bastards!'

She was still casting her wild eyes anxiously around the room when there was a loud thump above us as another lemon fell onto the tin roof of the house.

'AAIIEEEEE!' she screamed again, leaping in fright from her perch atop the armchair.

Fortunately, my many years of schoolboy rugby meant that I was not completely unpractised in the art of catching odd-shaped objects as they fell to earth, so when Pepita plummeted back down through the air, I was able to gently set her down on the carpet, where she stood for a while, quietly cooing and grasping my shoulder. Then, once she had got her breath back, she tottered off down the hallway, as if nothing at all had happened. Halfway towards her bedroom, she called casually over her shoulder:

'Well, time for my afternoon sleep, Sam. Come back for dinner at six. I'm going to take you somewhere special. Oh and by the way, help yourself to some brandy on your way out, dear.'

***

When I returned to Pepita's house later that day, she was waiting on the veranda, barefoot in a green and silver dress with her toenails painted glittering gold. A fine drizzle had just begun to fall, which Mrs Curry saw as a good omen brought about by my visit (her flowers were thirsty), and she insisted that for the sake of the dahlias I was to return every spring. Also waiting on the veranda were Theodore and Nikki - neighbours who helped look after Pepita, themselves in their sixties - and their two children, Harry and Georgia, none of whom spoke any English or had any clue who I was.

With everyone assembled, Pepita picked up her car keys and bade us all get into her sedan, announcing that she would drive to the restaurant. I was still trying to assess whether her tiny legs would even reach the pedals when Theodore thankfully took the keys from her and insisted that he would chauffeur, reminding Pepita that she would probably want to enjoy a few glasses of wine with dinner. As I squeezed in beside her, raindrops were streaking down the car windows, but Pepita, pinching my elbow, showed me that whilst walking to the car, she had remained dry.

'That's Taki, Sam. Holding an umbrella for me,' she said, raising one gnarled old knuckle to the sky.

The restaurant was a traditional Greek eatery, with a patio that looked out over the Aegean Sea. Seated at the head of the table, Pepita directed affairs, calling forth waiters with a flick of her wrist, requesting plate after plate of food. The first volley of dishes featured steamed crab meat, battered squid, grilled prawns, potatoes, salad, chicken, and a small mound of little fish fried whole. Soon there were so many plates that another table had to be dragged over to accommodate the baskets of bread, bowls of tzatziki, and bucket-loads of olives that the waiter continually replenished. And alongside the food, nestled amongst the plates were huge pitchers of lemon water, bottles of beer, and litres of fragrant retsina wine, tasting like pine needles, which Pepita drank by the jugful.

Theodore's appetite was vast, as was his wife's and that of their children, but I had never seen anybody eat like Pepita. She was no more than half my size, but whatever was placed in front of her, a moment later had vanished. All manner of fish, fowl, and beast were delivered to her plate and promptly devoured. In all my life, I had never witnessed such an impressive display of digestion, and she managed it all with false teeth.

In between swallowing whitebait a dozen at a time, Pepita maintained a steady stream of conversation, translating back and forth between myself and everybody else at the table. Theodore was particularly interested in my journey, and he wanted to know which direction my route would take after Greece. When Pepita explained to him that I was bound for Turkey, a look of horror came over Theodore's face, and after shaking his head vociferously, he looked me in the eyes, pointed eastwards, and dragged a single finger across his outstretched throat. I did not need Pepita's translation to understand that Theodore did not think too fondly of the Turks.

An hour into the feast, the stream of food being brought to our table mercifully began to slow, just as the first tones of dusk fell over the town. By this stage, after we had single-handedly depleted half the fish stocks in the Aegean, my belly was full to bursting, and I could feel the warm, inviting onset of sleep. But then a waiter appeared carrying a huge silver platter which I took to be an ominous sign. As the platter was set down in front of me, with a profound feeling of dread, I beheld a huge white fish, at least half a metre in length, lying atop a bed of green leaves and lemon slices.

'Pepita, what is that?' I asked, wincing with fear.

'Your fish, Sam,' she said plainly, barely even looking up from her wine.

'That is not a fish, Pepita. That is a whale, and it does not belong to me.'

'Don't be silly, Sam. You're the guest, so of course the fish is for you. Eat up now, dear,' she said, casting me an indomitable gaze.

There was no use arguing; Peptia was not a woman to be refused. With the whole table watching expectantly, I took my fork between my quivering fingers, prised off a piece of the bright white flesh, and ate my first mouthful of the fish.

It was delicious meat, delicate and elegant, cooked simply in olive oil and lemon. The sort of fish I adore, and on any other occasion, I would have relished each forkful. But already bulging after two hours of ceaseless eating, that last course nearly finished me. Every time I closed my eyes and swallowed, I would open them again only to see the fish before me, seemingly replenished. Then, finally, just as I seemed to be making some progress, Pepita turned to me and said:

'Tell me, Sam, does Billy still eat an orange for his dessert every day?'

At the mention of the word dessert, I let out a low moan and shuddered. It took me a moment to realise that rather than suggesting we order another course, Pepita was actually asking a question about my father, William.

Born in an air raid shelter in the middle of the Manchester blitz, Dad had grown up in a working-class family, with his only Christmas present each year as a child being a single ripe orange. In his adulthood, when oranges started to appear in supermarkets, he made a point of eating them whenever he could. Unfailingly, every day after his dinner, Dad would settle down in his arm-chair with the biggest, brightest orange he could find, and for five minutes each evening, it would be Christmas again. Whenever I have been away from home, wherever in the world I might have been, his first question on the phone, without fail, was always: how are the oranges, Sam? But I was puzzled as to how Pepita should know about my father's strange habit.

'As a matter of fact, he does,' I said. 'How do you know he likes oranges so much?'

'When your father first arrived at my house, many years ago, his face lit up the moment he saw my orange trees,' explained Pepita, pouring herself another glass of retsina. 'When I told him that he could pick as many as he liked, he thought about never going back to England. In all my life, I have never seen a man eat so much fruit as Billy did.'

I smiled as Pepita told me more about my father's first visit to Greece and his two blissful weeks spent eating oranges and drinking with Taki on the roof of her house.

'You know, when the time came for Billy to leave at the end of his first visit, he started to act very strangely. I remember, as we loaded the car for the airport, he handed me a suitcase and then a separate bag full of all his clothes.

'It seemed such a stupid way for him to pack his things. I kept asking him why his clothes weren't in his case, but he ignored my questions, telling me to hurry and put the bags in the car. Eventually, Taki helped me to wrestle the suitcase off him, and then we forced it open to see inside. You'll never guess what I found when I lifted the lid, Sam...'

'Forty ripe oranges, plucked from my trees that morning! Oh, you should have seen his guilty face,' giggled Pepita, her eyes wet with laugher. And I could not help but laugh too, thinking of my Dad, aged forty-three, on his first visit to Greece, getting caught red-handed with a suitcase stuffed with stolen fruit.

***

At the beginning of my journey, navigation had not proved too complicated because even though I spoke no other language than English, I could at least follow signposts written in Latin script. But in Greece, I began to struggle for the first time, finding it difficult to decipher the shapes and squiggles of an alphabet that was only familiar to me from half-remembered physics equations. Luckily, my route onwards from Nea Artaki was simple. Once Pepita had sent me packing - with five bags of Greek biscuits and two bottles of brandy – my next destination was Mount Olympus, so I simply arced back up across the plain of Thessaly with my motorcycle pointed in the direction of the tallest mountain I could see.

Waiting for me at the foot of Olympus was a man named Jake Brown. Shaped like a Greek god of war, sickeningly fit, and with a fondness for clambering up tall things, Jake made for the perfect hiking partner, and he also happened to be my best friend. We had been halfway around the world together more than once and had passed our fair share of weekends camping wild on the hills of Somerset, so I knew he was good for an adventure. When he suggested joining me for a little part of my journey, few ideas seemed better than attempting to climb the tallest mountain in Greece together.

'It's good to see you, my friend,' said Jake, as we met outside a café in Litochoro, the nearest town to Olympus.

'Thanks for coming,' I replied, hugging him back as he threw his muscled arms around me.

'Wouldn't have missed it for the world. By the way, is it meant to look like that?' he questioned, pointing to the bandage of black tape and plastic cable ties that now held my motorcycle together.

'The roads in Albanian could have been kinder.'

'Well, at least you won't be needing the bike for the next few days,' he said, giving me a shove in the direction of the mountain and speeding off up the walking trail, shouting for me to try and keep up.

Olympus stands at nearly three thousand metres, and our plan was to make the summit in a day and then descend as far as a mountain refuge halfway down the mountain, where we would spend the night. Hurrying after Jake along a path that snaked its way up the thickly wooded slope, I looked up to try and see the summit above us, but the top of Olympus was lost in pregnant cloud. Though the path was steep, the trail was soft underfoot, and the cool, damp air made for pleasant walking. Nevertheless, Jake set a furious pace, and soon the silent pines were filled with the sound of our laboured breaths. Then, after an hour of walking, another noise was added to the silence as a single peal of thunder barrelled down the rock face above us, setting the pine needles trembling, and warning us that Zeus was not in the mood for company.

As the day wore on, we began to realise that the guidebooks which Jake had been reading were optimistic in regards to how long the trek would take (and I was perhaps a little less fit than he had expected). So when the clouds began to clinch in dark spots and sprout rain, we decided that it would be best to settle at the refuge and to leave early for the summit the next morning. This proved to be a prudent decision because the moment we arrived at the mountain cabin, the rain and thunder began in earnest, and after the storms I had suffered over the past few weeks, I was more than glad to find a log-fire burning within, alongside a kitchen serving steaming heaps of spaghetti and jars of warm brandy.

Though we had seen hardly anyone during our five hours of walking, by evening the refuge was teeming with mountaineers of all creed and commitment. There were crews of jolly old men on their way back down from the summit, gulping wine by the glassful, celebrating their ascent. There were young couples in lycra, gobbling pouches of glucose between stretches, who looked serious and were best left alone. And there were whole companies of frumpy middle-aged women, glowing in neon green sportswear, tottering on their walking poles and looking hopelessly lost. The scene was nothing but wholesome, and I would have been quite happy had winter fallen early and all at once, trapping Jake and I inside that lodge for months, so long as the brandy did not run dry.

For those brave enough, there was an unheated shower fed by glacier water, but most hikers went without, and by ten o'clock everybody was wriggling into bed next to each other on huge padded floors where twenty people were expected to sleep in one long row. I would probably have been more comfortable sleeping outdoors on the stony mountainside, instead of having to choose between cuddling up to Jake's muscular hulk or the bloated belly of one of the jolly old men who lay snoring beside me. Still, as the rain continued to fall outside, I was glad at least for the warmth that twenty closely confined bodies provided in the cold wooden cabin.

Groggy and weak, we left the refuge just after dawn and joined a train of hikers silently trudging up the mountain. We knew that Olympus had several summits, the highest being Mytikas, which was a fraction taller than a second peak named Skala, the recommended option for amateurs. And though we were amateurs – the Quantocks and the Blackdown hills hardly comparing to Olympus – we had our sights firmly set on Mytikas, re-assured by one guidebook which had told us no serious equipment was necessary.

As the sun climbed, we pressed on, soon breaking through the tree line and out onto steep scree slopes, some of which were still clad in grey sheets of snow, unmelted from the previous winter. The trail became steeper and steeper, taking us up into drifting clouds, where the footfalls of hikers higher up the mountain started to send rocks tumbling down towards us. Stripped of its greenery and eerily quiet, Olympus became strange and unearthly, the silence only broken by the noise of falling stones and the creak of clouds pouring down from the summit.

Several hours after leaving the refuge, we reached a small crowd of hikers stood by a neatly piled tower of stones that we presumed marked Skala. Half an hour later, we emerged at the peak of the highest ridge around and found a small flag hammered into the ground. There were gaggles of people hugging and clinking small silver flasks beside it, and others posing for photographs.

'That seemed a little too easy, don't you think?' said Jake with a sceptical frown.

'Don't be ridiculous,' I said, clapping him on the shoulder. 'We've made it to Mytikas! The mighty Olympus, conquered in a morning.'

Hearing this, a small, spidery, tendon of a woman padded over to us, bouncing from foot to foot.

'Sorry boys, this isn't Mytikas. You're only at Skala. Mytikas is up there,' she said, waving her walking pole in the direction of a dense white cloud. 'You're not far from the top. All you have to do to reach Mytikas is cross the evil stairway.'

I was just about to ask how that part of the mountain had earned its name when her wristwatch began to bleep, causing her to shriek and run off, muttering something about setting a record time and warning us to be careful on our way to the summit.

'What's the evil stairway?' I asked Jake, turning to face him. 'You failed to mention that part of the climb.'

Then, just as I spoke, the bank of cloud we had been staring at suddenly shifted, revealing a second summit, far higher and much more menacing than the one we were stood upon, with only a narrow ridge of rock connecting us to it. All along the ridge, climbers with helmets, harnesses, and ropes were crawling their way across the mountain, sporting all manner of sophisticated equipment.

'That's the evil stairway,' said Jake, nonchalantly.

'You know, there would be no shame in settling at Skala,' I said.

'Sam, I didn't come all the way to Greece to climb three-quarters of a mountain.'

More than a little nervous, we crawled down off the safe summit of Skala and out onto a hideously steep slope. Every step we took sent dozens of small stones jolting down into the valley below us, and every few metres we passed a hook hammered into the mountainside where ropes and safety equipment were meant to be attached. Focusing on every footstep, I had little time to look around, but halfway across the slope, Jake pointed up towards a small ledge of rock, jutting out just below the summit above us, where a single chamois stood silhouetted against rolling banks of white cloud, looking out over a deep abyss.

Not long after glimpsing the sheep, we found ourselves at the evil stairway. Nothing more than a wafer of rock, it stretched for fifty metres across a chasm with a two-hundred-metre drop on one side. For the first time on our hike, we found ourselves climbing hand over hand, resting every minute to reassure one another and to try and still our trembling legs.

There was no doubting the peril. If we had fallen over the edge, there would have been enough time on the way down for us to regret our mistake. But it was only after our ascent that we realised just how reckless we had been when we learnt that climbers die every year on Olympus. If we had known that before we started, we might have thought twice about attempting the summit in nothing more than baseball caps and trainers.

Still, having crossed the terrifying ledge, it was only a short scramble up to Mytikas, two thousand nine hundred and eighteen metres above sea level. When Jake pulled me up onto the safe mound of rocks at the very top, I felt elated to have reached the mythical home of the ancient Greek gods, which was humbly marked by a dull silver flag staked into the summit. I clung to the steel pole for some time, not trusting my legs to hold me up, transfixed by the sight of Greece, nearly two miles below us. When I finally formed the courage to stand upright and ask another climber to take a triumphant photograph of Jake and I, he chuckled and asked in a thick Greek accent:

'You two are British, no?'

Surprised, we said that we were and asked how he could tell. He simply grinned and told us that there was another British man on the summit – the only other fool with no helmet on.

Sure enough, perched on top of a lone boulder nearby, looking out over the Aegean Sea, there was a young man dressed in a Panama hat and a freshly pressed linen shirt. Feeling unusually gregarious from the adrenalin of the climb, I scrambled over and decided to say hello.

'Just charming up here, isn't it?' said the dusty-haired twenty-two-year-old, speaking in the kind of drawl only obtained after a decade spent in an expensive British school. 'My name is Rupert,' he said, offering me his hand. 'Pleasure to meet you. What brings you to Olympus?'

'Just out for a hike with a friend,' I said. 'And you?'

'Oh, I'm on a jolly too. I'm a classicist from Edinburgh, but I've spent the last few months studying in Thessaloniki. It really is a delightful city, though it's kept me rather busy. I arrived in January, but I still haven't had the time to memorise the second canto of Childe Harold's Pilgrimage, which, as I'm sure you'll agree, is the first thing any serious visitor to Greece should do.'

'That is a shame, ' I chuckled, 'but I'm sure you'll find time eventually. Poetry aside, Thessaloniki is a nice city?'

'The Byzantine relics are quite thrilling,' he said, getting up from his seat. 'Are you heading down the mountain? Let me tell you all about it.'

On our way down from Olympus, Jake and I stopped for lunch at the refuge and invited Rupert to join us. This proved a fortunate decision because Rupert's rucksack was stuffed with all the makings of a British picnic, even, incredibly, a packet of teacakes and a jar of marmalade. Curious as to how he had managed to produce most of the elements required for a respectable high tea halfway up Greece's tallest mountain, I asked Rupert where the teacakes were from.

'Oh, my good man, one should never be without a teacake. Here, let me show you,' he said, pulling a tattered brown map of Greece out of his bag, covered in ink squiggles and circles which marked the locations of every Marks and Spencer west of Thrace.

'Always good to have, just in case you ever get caught short without any decent linen. The one in Piraeus does a particularly nice shortbread.'

I looked at Jake, and we both could not help but laugh. He had come to Greece on my promises of adventure, hoping to return home furnished with exotic stories of our wild time climbing to the summit of the seat of the gods. But there we were instead, sat with Rupert, nibbling teacakes as if it were a summer's afternoon at home and we had just stopped for lunch in a quiet corner of the English countryside.

***

After listening to Rupert extol the virtues of Thessaloniki, Jake and I arrived in the city expecting an immaculate metropolis brimming with

Byzantine wonders. What we encountered instead was a vast, grey grid of identical apartment blocks, standing in orderly rows, each eight storeys high. The whole city, it seemed, was built from the same building, repeated over and over, punctuated occasionally by the red shells of ruined churches, but otherwise bland and monotonous.

I should have known better than to expect to find a Byzantine relic on every street corner. In 1917, the whole city had been gutted by fire, and much of Thessaloniki's heritage disappeared as ashes in the wind. Only a week before visiting, I had read *Farewell to Salonica* and had been seduced by Leon Sciaky's descriptions of a quaint, cosmopolitan city, steeped in Ottoman, Greek, and Jewish history. The title alone should have been enough to tell me that such descriptions were predicated on the death of old Salonica, but as with most books, I wanted too badly to believe the world within it to be true. To chase after places expecting to find them the same as they were once rendered in ink is a certain path to disenchantment; reality rarely surpasses the literary.

Yet, there were still fragments of Salonica left from Sciaky's day. As Jake and I walked around the city, we passed broken basilicas, Byzantine temples, and the crumbling Galerius Arch which straddled the Via Egnatia, the ancient Roman Road built to join the Adriatic to the Hellespont, which I would follow on my way to Istanbul. And down by the water, looking out across the Thermaic Gulf, Thessaloniki's famous White Tower still stood facing the thin line of Olympus, just visible on the horizon.

The sky over the bay of Thessaloniki is one of those sweeping, expansive skies that seem to go on forever, only possible at the sharp edges of cities where tight streets and tower blocks suddenly give way to vast emptiness. On our first evening in the city, Jake and I went down to the bay where a handful of cargo ships were floating far out in the gulf, lying still on the silver water, waiting to enter the harbour. We stayed to watch the boats switch on their lights, the bulbs on their decks igniting one by one in a chain of tiny conflagrations. Looking at them, I thought of Sciaky and his story of the first steamship that docked in Salonica, and how at the sign of its billowing black smoke half the city had gone running down to the waterfront, expecting to watch a sailboat burn.

Jake and I spent a restful few days in Thessaloniki, pottering around museums and playing chess in coffee shops like two old Greek men. We drank retsina and tsipouro, ate mezze and gyros, and by the end of the week felt like natives. The staff in our favourite café knew our faces, as did the fishmonger at our favourite market stall. And after trying dozens, we even decided which pastry shop sold the best Thessaloniki trigonas – small triangles of syrupy pastry, filled with fresh cream, which alone made our visit worthwhile. Although the city was not charming or pretty, it did possess a certain quality which put us immediately at ease, and after just four days there, Jake and I could not have felt more at home.

Despite our growing sense of familiarity, on our last night in the city, Thessaloniki still managed to surprise us. Jake and I had just sat down to dinner on the little balcony of our apartment when a huge crowd appeared at the end of the street, massing together in what seemed like a protest, with many people sporting flags and banners.

'What on earth is going on?' I wondered aloud, watching nervously as the crowd began to swell.

'I think I know,' said Jake. 'I read about this in the news today. They're protesting against the fact that Macedonia is planning to change its name from the *Former Yugoslav Republic of Macedonia* to simply the *Republic of North Macedonia*.'

'Why would that merit a protest?' I asked.

'I know the names sound similar, but it's a big deal for the Greeks. You see, Greece has its own region known as Macedonia, and ever since the collapse of Yugoslavia, the Greeks have campaigned against their northern neighbours being allowed to use the same name.'

'What's the alternative?'

'I think the Greeks want the country of Macedonia to find a different name altogether.'

Whilst Jake was explaining the situation, the blue-painted crowd had been slowly moving down the street, growing in size at every junction. One minute the city was peaceful and quiet, then suddenly twenty-five years of political frustration boiled out onto the streets amidst the clamour of loud shouts and breaking bottles.

As the crowd continued to expand, the protesters became more feverish, and by the time they were passing beneath us, there was enough venom in their chants to make Jake and I glad that we were several storeys out of reach. A minute later, I saw a single red flare spluttering at the end of our road, and then a convoy of police vans arrived spilling armed officers onto the street. At this, the crowd changed direction, just as the police began to fling tear gas and stun grenades. Then more flares went up, fires were lit, and we watched as police and protesters fought their way through smoke-choked alleyways. Soon our road had cleared, but for a long time afterwards, the city rang with the sound of shattered glass and plumes of grey smoke could be seen rising between the apartment blocks. From where we sat, speechless on our balcony, half the city's streets seemed to be filled with smoke. For all we could tell, Thessaloniki was burning again.

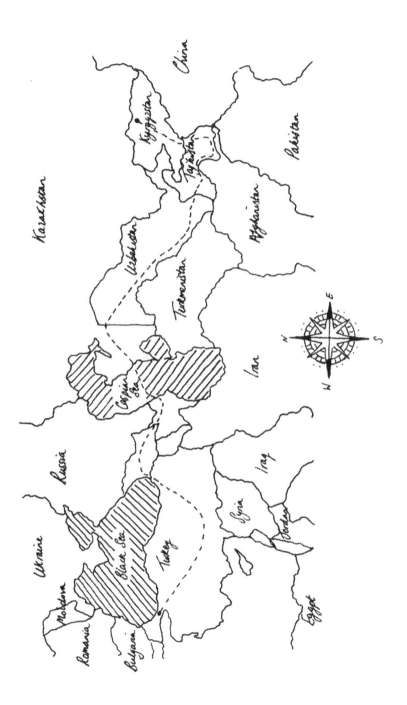

Chapter Seven

The sun himself has sent me like a ray,
To hint that he is coming up this way.

- Lord Byron, *Don Juan,* Canto V

Visiting a city for a second time is not unlike re-reading a book. There is a satisfaction in the feeling of familiarity, a gratification that comes from recognising the characters of the city, anticipating the lines of its body, and finding its precious parts unchanged. Discovering all the pieces as they were left, in a neat little map of memories, gives a traveller the sense that they have some claim over the place. As if being able to take this or that street, with confident knowledge of what lies at its end, means that the city somehow belongs to them.

But in reality, the opposite is true. Re-visiting a city after years of absence and finding all of its parts exactly as remembered only proves how strong a hold the city has over the traveller. The sense of familiarity betrays the fact that despite the passage of time, old roots, laid down long ago, can subsist in our memories for decades. And even after years apart, when a traveller returns to a favourite place, just like when a reader re-visits a beloved book, from the minute they enter the gates, memories begin to stir, and old roots wake, sensing a second bloom.

I arrived in Istanbul, four years after my first visit to the city, on the same day that I left Thessaloniki. I had not planned to travel five hundred miles in a single day, but as I rolled across Thrace, I felt a subtle power pulling me eastwards. It was a gentle journey anyway, on vacant roads across flat land, at least it was until I reached the fringes of the city. Then, as the open country met with the metropolis, the highway that for hours had been quiet and barren was suddenly flush with traffic, and the road only grew more congested as it burrowed through pillars of concrete and steel on its way towards the heart of Istanbul, making for the thick vein of the Bosphorus.

Istanbulars are some of the worst drivers in the world, so I had heard, and the one thing I had been told to remember was that from Istanbul onwards, the horn would be king. I had barely reached the suburbs when the first klaxons began to ring out, beginning sporadically, but soon becoming louder and more venomous. Indiscriminately used to herald danger, voice annoyance, and provide warning, it was impossible to tell if the blast of any single horn signalled salutation, fraternity, rivalry, derision, or some other more ambiguous communication. But after half an hour in heavy traffic, I was still no closer to the centre of the city, and so I felt encouraged to begin liberally sounding my own klaxon, adding one more pathetic note to the swelling chorus of Turkish ire.

Eventually, I came to Sultanahmet, the historic core of the city, where my memories began to ossify back into the streets and buildings I knew from four years before. The first features I recognised were the Blue Mosque's minarets, peeping above the roofline. Then I saw the rose-washed walls of the Hagia Sophia, four summers more faded than when I saw them last. The city's tram tracks glinted in the afternoon sun, Topkapı Palace was where I expected it to be, and the same scent of roasting chestnuts still hung above Sultanahmet square. After nearly twelve hours of riding, I was exhausted, but following the flood of memory, for the second time that day, I felt a peculiar force willing me onwards, drawing me down into a twilight fold of Istanbul's ancient heart.

Almost without meaning to, I began to search for a place that I had visited the last time I was in Turkey. Though I was not sure that I would find it again, I knew I had to try, if only to see how much the city still meant to me. So as the sun started to set, I floated across Sultanahmet, tracking a memory that led me between the Blue Mosque and the Hagia Sophia and onwards in the direction of the Grand Bazaar. The trail I followed was faint but distinct, withered but still alive. I only hoped it would remain intact unto the end.

The entrance to my destination, I remembered, lay to one side of Yeniçeriler road, behind a gateway veiled by gravestones and shadows. But apart from images of tombs, iron bars, twisted pipes, and thick columns of smoke, I could remember little else. Three false starts led me into silent cemeteries to marvel at memorials covered in Kufic script, and several closed wooden doors that I passed might have been the entrance, but each proved incorrect. After half an hour of walking, I began to worry that I was chasing a ghost. Four years is time enough for a city's face to change.

When evening passed to night, I stopped searching in earnest and simply began to stroll. The world had changed aspect once again, and there was a pleasure to be found in its new costume. The busy street, lined with food vendors selling kebabs, sweet baklava, Turkish delight, and ice-creams, wore a new scent, and everywhere lanterns shed their glow over shops selling silver, bags of coffee, mint tea, and incense. As I walked, I passed back and forth between strings of bright shops and strips of silent darkness marking mosques and Madrasas. Light then darkness. Chatter then quiet. I followed the striped hide of the city through its portions of life and silence.

Then I came to a section of the road which was dark and wore the sombre air of a graveyard, but which was just aglow with light. The roadside railings, I noticed, were edged with crimson, and the air was filled with a sweet perfume. Out from the quiet came the muffled sounds of conversation, the ring of metal tinkling against glass, and the gurgle of bubbles ripping through water. I smiled as a sense of recognition settled over me. This was the place I had been looking for: I had arrived at Çorlulu Ali Paşa Medresesi.

Stepping through a crumbling stone gateway, I entered a narrow alley of gravestones, all of them crooked with age. A second stone archway led through to a corridor which was decked on both sides with lines of snaking chimneys, leaking smoke above ovens containing rows of metal pans brimming with hot coals. Beside the ovens, on sunken shelves, a glittering library of glass vases and slender metal sticks stood beneath long carpeted hoses, drooping down from rusted hooks. These were narghiles - Turkish water-pipes - and they had been smoked at Çorlulu Ali Paşa Medresesi for over four hundred years.

Originally a school during the early Ottoman Empire, the courtyard

I entered had, over time, been filled by cafés and narghile houses as they sprouted one by one from each of Çorlulu Ali Paşa Medresesi's little alcoves and pockets. In the centre of the space, a single, ancient vine spread its canopy over the square, its black limbs choked by a steady stream of smoke blown up into its leaves, taunting the plant with the sweet smell of fruit that it would never bear. Around the edges, the walls were strung with tattered carpets and blackened paintings, and light from thousands of hanging lamps tumbled through the smoke. Rubbing my flanks, which had been burnt by the ovens in the entranceway, I stood for a few moments, astonished at finding the place completely unchanged. Then a Turkish man with a heavy brow and thick moustache placed a rough hand on my shoulder, before wordlessly ushering me towards a table.

Everywhere, solitary figures sat puffing meditatively, many of them lost in silent contemplation, completely oblivious as the attendant skilfully slipped me amongst their ranks. On every table, glasses of tawny coloured çay sat steaming, awaiting the inevitable sinking of a sugar lump. A handful of stewards wandered through the crowd of reclining men, serving tea and swinging copper pans full of glowing embers, arriving beside narghiles to replace crumbling coals. In a silent, well-practised ritual, I watched as one steward appeared beside the narghile of my neighbour. After tenderly re-arranging the burning embers with a touch of his silver pincers, the steward slipped away like a spectre, leaving behind a cloud of heat that spilt out from the copper pan swinging by his side, forever swaying to a slow, hypnotic beat.

I was spellbound, but I gathered myself enough to order some çay and ask for a rose and mint Narghile. When it came, the tea was sweet and tasted of cardamom, and the fumes from the pipe were lush and languorous. Behind every table, pale pennants of smoke unravelled out of black beards, curling up into the night. Conversations were begun and then were left to die away, as words were lost to the steady rhythm of slow, deep breaths. It was a fragment of an older time, elegantly preserved, exactly as it had been four years before, and four hundred years before that. I stayed late, drank my tea and smoked my pipe, and then an hour later I stepped back out into the cool darkness, just as the last Muezzin's call began to ring through the streets of the city.

***

With all of its heritage and all of its prettiness, Istanbul attracts tourists in droves, but I never felt oppressed by the crowds there. It is a city which is able to swallow oceans of people and still keep its charm, and as I sat in Sultanahmet square on the second morning of my visit, I had space and privacy enough to rest for a while and study my surroundings.

To one side of me, the six minarets of the Blue mosque sliced the Thracian sky into ribbons, their slender shadows falling across the temple's intricate roof. Below my feet, a cavernous Roman cistern stretched beneath the city, still half-flooded with the reserves that once watered ancient Constantinople. Whilst to my other side, wearing the rugged lines of its history with ageless dignity, rose the Hagia Sophia, massive, solemn, and brooding.

The story of the Hagia Sophia is the history of Istanbul itself: all the city may be read in its symbol. It began life as a Christian cathedral, and when the dome of one of its early iterations collapsed, the emperor Justinian threw down his imperial crown and did not pick it up again for thirty days, so bitter was his grief. Once Justinian's tears had dried and its final form was complete, the Hagia Sophia was hailed as the most precious building in the Byzantine empire. Afterwards, Justinian's successors received their purple robes upon its altar, and under its strong new coronet, the Hagia Sophia remained one of the most sacred sites in Christendom for over one thousand years.

But then in 1453, when Constantinople fell to the Ottomans, the cathedral was transformed into a mosque almost overnight. Despite the conversion, when faced with the beauty of the Christian frescoes painted on the temple's walls, the Ottomans could not bring themselves to wreak total destruction. The Christian symbols and images were simply plastered over and tactfully forgotten, allowed to lay dormant for half a millennium whilst new prayers were whispered inside, destined for a different god.

When modern Turkey's founding father, Ataturk, came to power in the early twentieth century, the building was transformed again, this time into a secular museum, opened to commemorate Istanbul's rich history. When the plaster inside was torn down, the original frescoes were uncovered, and a Turkish sun shone once again upon the Byzantine figures of Christ painted inside the Hagia Sophia. But the story did not end there.

When I had visited Istanbul four years before, I had listened to the wail of the adhan as it floated down from the minarets of the Blue Mosque every morning. At that time, the Hagia Sophia was still solely a museum, and no call to prayer had sounded from its older, more crude minarets. But as I sat in Sultanahmet this time around, shortly after the adhan from the Blue mosque began to sound, I heard a crackle of static, and then a second call to prayer rang out from the towers of the Hagia Sophia.

As I would later learn, within the previous year, a passionate movement had been growing amongst Istanbulars who wanted the museum to be transformed into a mosque again. The previous spring, crowds of thousands had gathered outside the building for an event to celebrate the Ottoman capture of the city. And more recently, a state-sponsored prayer ceremony had taken place inside the Hagia Sophia and had been broadcast on national television, with several prominent government officials present at the event.

This move was typical of President Erdogan's government, which since coming to power had developed an increasingly religious attitude, breaking tradition with previous governments of the officially secular Turkish nation. As I would discover, the potential re-conversion of the museum was a contentious topic in the city. Whilst the number of religionists wanting to worship in the Hagia Sophia was growing, so was the number of business owners who argued that the re-conversion might deter non-Muslim tourists. The government was yet to take an official stance, but it was clear where their loyalty would lie. Meanwhile, art historians all over the world have been given new cause to fear what might become of the exquisite Christian art still preserved inside if the frescoes of the Hagia Sophia are once again confined to the dark by Istanbul's rulers.

After an hour spent ruminating on the history of Sultanahmet, it was time to stretch my legs. I set off walking aimlessly around the city, but before long, I inadvertently found myself outside one of the many entrances to the Grand Bazaar. Like Çorlulu Ali Paşa Medresesi, the bazaar can be an impossible place to find, becoming more elusive the more desperately it is sought. But for the few visitors who do manage to find the bazaar, caution is of the utmost importance, because Istanbul's shopkeepers, wily in business like no other people, possess a charm so potent they are able to persuade any tourist of the vital need to buy a carpet, or samovar, or string of Turkish lights, whether there is room in the suitcase to carry it home or not.

As for the bazaar itself, if there is a commodity which any human in the course of history has traded, and if it will fit through the doors, then it will be sold inside. Every type of clothing, furniture, spice, fruit, tea, coffee, tobacco, and medicine can be found in the market, along with every imaginable gadget and gimmick. The shopkeeper's stalls are filled with equipment for any labour, accessories for any art, and all manner of utterly useless ornament. Never has such a hoard of tat, clutter, and treasure existed in a single space in all the history of mankind.

But the whole entity, the entire frenetic beast, would unravel in an afternoon without its lifeblood: çay. The minute a shopkeeper smacks his lips and feels the first onset of thirst, a boy is there, setting down a saucer with a cup of russet liquid alongside a sugar cube and spoon. These boys dance through the crowds of the bazaar all day long, bearing silver platters of steaming glasses, never placing a foot out of step. And the second a shopkeeper sets down his drained glass, there is a flash of silver, and a çay bearer steps out from behind an archway to retrieve it, before gliding back into the shadows, tinkling as he goes.

Alongside providing sustenance for the shopkeepers, çay is also essential to the conduct of business. Whenever a customer expresses interest in a product in the bazaar, the shop owner need only press a little buzzer hidden beneath his till and the çay is immediately brought, set down upon the table, and then bartering can begin. But as business goes, nowhere is the drinking of çay more essential than in the sale of a Turkish carpet. So when a carpet vendor coaxed me into his shop, it was only a matter of seconds until the seasoned merchant had placed a glowing glass of tea in my hand, before leading me towards a seat in a snug corner of his showroom.

'My name is Huseyin Belli,' he said, vigorously shaking my hand. 'I have been selling carpets in Istanbul all my life, just like my father before me. What is it you do, my friend?'

'I'm a writer from England,' I replied.

At these words, Huseyin's eyes glowed, and the poor merchant mistook me for an established author with a fortune to spend, rather than the penniless scribbler that I really was. But I wasn't going to rush my cup of tea, and as I was interested in Huseyin's business, I decided to indulge his little fiction.

'I shall show you some of the finest pieces in my collection,' he said, turning to a wall of rolled carpets behind him.

The first specimen Huseyin brought down was deep red in colour -

rich and warm like the dry Cappadocian plains in the heart of Turkey where it was spun. Then he produced a luxurious green silk piece, too good for the floor, which shimmered as he unfurled it, rippling in the air as if held together with liquid stitches. The final carpet to appear was a light blue rug, flecked with silver and patterned with peacocks, which changed colour as I walked from one side of the room to the other whilst inspecting it. Seeing my puzzled look, Huseyin explained:

'All my carpets are double woven, in the true Turkish style. Unlike other carpets from Persia or the Far East, only Turkish carpets change colour in the light like this, which is why they fetch high prices.'

'Speaking of price, how much for this piece?' I asked, pointing to the blue rug, which seemed a fairly humble example, little more than the size of a dinner table.

'In sterling, sir, six-thousand pounds. As my father used to say, rich men buy cheap things. Not so rich men buy expensive things.'

Choking on the dregs of my tea, I realised just how mistaken the merchant was regarding my wealth. The cost of that single carpet alone came to over half the budget of my entire journey, and besides, there was little room in my tent for such a luxury. As I mumbled something about having to consult with my wife on such matters, Huseyin smiled and said:

'Do not worry, sir. I understand completely,' pressing a business card into my hand as he spoke, inviting me back any time to look at more carpets, or just to share another glass of tea.

Eventually, I found my way out of the bazaar and walked to Galata bridge, the loud, filthy bond which joins the old European side of the city to its more modern counterpart. Along the underside of the bridge, a row of restaurants and cafés were preparing for the lunch service, whilst along its upper edges, with their backs to the traffic, scores of fishermen were casting their lines out into the Golden Horn. From the ends of their rods, a web of silver swung in the breeze, and every fisherman stood beside a bucket full of shining fish. As I passed, one old man picked a creature from out of his pile, and after whistling a few times, tossed the fish high up into the air. At the sound of the whistle, a gull flew down from a nearby lamppost, arriving above the fisherman a moment later to pluck the fish from the sky, swallowing it on the wing.

After a lunch of river-fish for myself, I followed my usual method of navigation and decided to aim for the tallest object I could see, which in this case was Galata Tower, the tall grey turret which rises sixty metres above the ground close to the bank of the Horn. According to local legend, in the seventeenth century, the famous Ottoman aviator Hezârfen Ahmed Çelebi built himself a pair of wings and leapt from the top of the tower. With Sultan Murad IV watching in astonishment, the pilot soared across the Bosphorus before touching down on the Asian side of the city several miles away. The Sultan was so impressed with this feat that he awarded Çelebi a sack of gold coins, then instantly banished him to Algeria, warning that men of such talent are too dangerous to be allowed to walk freely in the streets.

Once past Galata Tower, I turned down a small, shaded alleyway, eager to avoid the heat of the afternoon. Some way ahead of me, a shoe-shiner was sat resting on a set of steps, but just before I reached him, he stood up and limped away, carrying his box of polish and brushes under his arm. One of the brushes wobbled upon its hook and fell clattering to the street, but the boot polisher walked on, oblivious.

'Excuse me!' I shouted, scooping up the brush and carrying it over to the man.

'Thank you, sir, thank you. I did not see that I had lost it.'

'You're welcome,' I said, walking alongside him up the street. We had gone no more than ten paces when he suddenly stopped and said:

'Please, for thank you, allow me, sir,' before pulling me to a step and starting to unpack his brushes.

'No, it's alright, honestly. I really don't need a polish,' I said, trying to stop the man, but before I had the chance to protest further, my foot was in his lap, and he was scrubbing my trainers with a soapy toothbrush.

I sat there reluctantly, feeling extremely uncomfortable, whilst the shoe-shiner chatted about his life in Istanbul, his wife in Ankara, and the many children she had to care for. Eventually, when he seemed to have finished, I thanked him and had begun to walk away when his hand shot out and grabbed me by the wrist.

'One hundred and fifty lira, sir'.

'What? I thought you said it was in thanks for rescuing your brush?' I said, astonished that the man had just asked for the equivalent of twenty English pounds.

'Yes, sir. Left shoe was in thanks. One hundred and fifty lira is for right shoe. Many hungry babies in Ankara, sir.'

I could see the persistence in his eyes and knew he would not leave empty-handed. Pulling a note from my pocket, I stuffed it into his hand

and stomped off grumbling, whilst the smiling shoe-shiner went on his way, whistling to himself merrily.

Turning around, I eventually reached Galata bridge again, where the fishermen were still casting their lines into the black water. Boats were ploughing up and down the Golden Horn, leaving behind trails of black smoke that blended with the exhaust fumes of five million cars to cast a toxic shimmer over the minarets of Sultanahmet. In the distance, a gorgeous sun was sinking, whilst on the opposite side of the city, a huge moon, the colour of a rose, was rising through the smog. As the last of the light glanced off the water and bounced off my glimmering shoes, I could not help but laugh as I thought about the shoe-shiner and wondered how many times his brush had slipped from under his arm that day, and how many other tourists he had taken for a fool.

From the bridge, I walked back to Sultanahmet, where the crowds were beginning to thin. In the twilight, the vast forms of the Blue Mosque and the Hagia Sophia seemed to grow new features and new mysteries, morphing into incredible shapes. The Hagia Sophia, in particular, with all of its domes, towers, gantries, windows, and buttresses looked more like a citadel than a church, as if entire civilizations were wrapped up in its walls. As I stood there in Sultanahmet looking at the ancient building, a hand came down upon my shoulder, and then a voice said:

'Brother, it is closed now. Open again tomorrow morning.'

I turned to find the kind face of a young Turkish man smiling at me. Seemingly eager to help a visitor, without my asking, he began reeling off a list of all the mosques I should visit the next day, alongside a list of where the best kebabs could be found, and a list of where to catch the cheapest ferries across the Bosphorus. I smiled and nodded to it all before taking my leave a few moments later. I was five steps away when his voice called through the dark:

'Wait, wait, my friend. You know who you look like?' he said, fixing me with a stare of intense curiosity.

'Somebody you know?' I replied.

He flashed me a wide smile, clipped with gold, and held out his hands towards me.

'My friend, you look like a carpet buyer. Let me help you spend your money.'

Laughing loudly, I walked away into the night, thinking that all the vagrants and all the vagabonds in the world could not make me love

Istanbul less.

***

Like a clasp which clutches two continents in its teeth, Istanbul stitches together two portions of the world cut from different cloths. When I left the European side, a brittle dawn was breaking, and twenty million men, women, and children slept soundly around me. When I emerged from the monstrous tunnel which carried me under the Bosphorus, the same city still slept, and the sun was barely a fraction higher, but something momentous had shifted. The sprawling, empty streets looked the same, and the white tower blocks and silver mosques mirrored those across the water, but the city was different. An unspoken fact hung in the dawn, blatant and unabashed: I was in Asia now, Europe had been left behind, and silently, enticingly, Istanbul introduced a vast new continent.

I rode that day to Ankara, but the capital was only a fleeting stop on my path across the belly of Turkey. For days, I raced across wide plains of wheat, leaning sideways into brawny winds and fighting gusts that threatened to spill me onto the road. Just to stay upright, I had to keep one eye watching for the tell-tale ripple of the roadside grass, and another looking for dust devils that rose from the plains and came racing towards me like wind-whipped djinns. Eventually, the parched fields gave way to dry salt lakes, and the lakes melted into an endless horizon that shimmered beneath a gargantuan sky. The earth, the air, and the land were immense, and next to the countries through which I had already passed, Turkey unfurled like a prostrate Goliath.

But after a thousand miles of flat land, the salt lakes gave way to wide rocky plains, before those plains gradually began to crack into valleys. After days of monotony, my eyes were glad of the change and turned inquisitively towards the landscape. At first, the valleys were empty, but I had reached the navel of Anatolia where stone behaves in strange ways. The further I rode, the more alien the country became, and soon I found myself riding along a road that curled between slender pillars of rock, navigating my way past fairy-tale towers that bubbled up above the dark valley walls like fossilized trees encased in stone.

I had reached Cappadocia, a region in the centre of Turkey made famous by the thousands of naturally occurring cones, pillars, towers, turrets, and chimneys, known to geologists as *hoodoos*, which stretch in a string of improbable ornaments from one edge of the province to the other. But more than just ornaments, for thousands of years, the hoodoos have also been used as temples, schools, and shelters, providing dwelling places for entire communities of humans ever since the first hermit arrived in Cappadocia and decided to carve a home for himself inside a pillar of rock.

It was during the early Christian period that human colonies initially flourished in Cappadocia. Some of the founding fathers of the Byzantine church were born and raised in the chambers of Cappadocian caves. But during the Arab-Byzantine wars, which were fought between the eighth and twelfth centuries, living in the stone towers no longer afforded Christian's adequate security, so to protect themselves from the invading Muslims, the Byzantine's also burrowed down into the soft rock beneath Cappadocia, building entire cities under the earth.

In total, over two-hundred underground settlements lie beneath the region, the largest of which is Derinkuyu, a sprawling subterranean complex, large enough to house thirty-thousand people. As well as living quarters, Derinkuyu has its own stables, cellars, wine presses, chapels, and schools, some of which lie as deep as sixty metres beneath the ground. It was a strange world that once existed in Cappadocia, home to entire civilisations who lived above, within, and below the earth, but never simply upon it. As I arrived there, I could only imagine how it must have been a thousand years before my visit, when the tunnels still smelt of the stable, and incense smoke could be seen drifting out from ancient churches, dug into stone towers high above the ground.

Nowadays, Cappadocia attracts millions of visitors every year, and in towns like Göreme, tourists can find bars, restaurants, and entire hotels built within the hoodoos. Preferring the open air, I made my camp in a place called Rose Valley, not far from the centre of Göreme, and set out to spend my first evening in Cappadocia exploring on foot. As I walked down the valley after a long day of riding, the grass crackled with creatures emerging from the day's heat, crawling, creeping, and rattling their way out of shaded leaves into the cool evening. Lizards lay on warm rocks, snakes slithered away at the sound of my footsteps, and I wondered what else lay dormant in the valley. It was Cappadocia, after all, where Saint George was first said to have slain the dragon.

Like the critters at my feet which were dwarfed by the tall grass, as I walked through Rose Valley, I was surrounded on all sides by towering stone stacks - some slender and elegant, others twisted and bloated - that stood in thickets of strange forms, each of them gilded with dusk. The fairy-like chimneys and towers were everywhere, often standing in clusters, like gnarled toadstools sprouting from the ground, with wide canopies dwarfing their delicate stems. It was a land of fantasy, made more surreal by the fact that cut into the sides and feet of the hoodoos were dark windows and entranceways, chiselled into the rock centuries earlier to build homes that had long since been abandoned.

Poking my head through some of the crude archways, I found that many of the towers were empty and bare inside, being the ancient remains of simple living quarters, once home to families of Byzantine Christians. But in some of the hoodoos, faded frescoes were still visible on the walls, tinged with red and gold. And in a precious few, faint figures of Christ were still recognisable, the sacred pictures now left to watch over empty chambers where entire communities once gathered to worship the icons in the half-light of the caverns.

In between exploring the shadowed interiors of the towers and scrambling over mounds of loose boulders, I made steady progress along the valley. Since leaving my tent, I had seen no-one, but I had occasionally heard the sound of distant car engines, which was strange in a territory that otherwise felt old and mythical. Then, as I was walking along, I suddenly noticed the smell of spilt petrol in the air, and turning around a corner, I found an upturned car stuck fast between two stone columns. Beneath the wreck, a dark stain was slowly spreading in the dust, and I could still hear parts whirring in the engine.

Running forward, I half expected to find an injured person in the driver's seat, but the car was empty. A badge on the rear windshield listed the name of a rental company, and I remembered having heard that off-road driving was a popular tourist activity in Cappadocia. Clambering to the top of a nearby hoodoo, I looked out across the valley, and in the distance, I could see a faint trail of dust leading away from the wreck, kicked up by frantic feet. Whoever had crashed the rented car had clearly panicked and fled. Having heard that the local police were not known for their kindness towards tourists, and realising that being found beside the car would make me look culpable, I decided to hurry away myself and quickly disappeared amongst the shadowed canyons.

I slept soundly that night in my tent in Rose Valley, but I was woken before dawn by the sound of short, loud blasts, like sudden gusts of wind blowing above my head. I lay and listened for a while, wondering if the rock formations surrounding my camp shaped the morning breeze in strange ways. But I was puzzled by the fact that whenever the wind blew, the sides of my tent stayed completely still. Curious, I decided to step outside, and just as I did, a tall column of flame shot across the sky, lighting up the swollen template of a huge balloon that was lumbering its way up into the air only a few hundred metres from my tent.

After the livid flame died away, everything went dark again, but now that I was outside, I noticed that lights were flashing all across the sky. Hundreds of tall, elegant flames were burning above me, each illuminating the bulging silhouette of a hot air balloon. Twinkling in and out of existence, the flames were slowly being blown all across the valley, where they hung like a vast net of fire, waiting to drop down upon the stone towers which stood invisible in the darkness below.

Dawn, however, was about to break, and just before the sun appeared, a blanket of potent orange spread across the sky, pockmarked in places by the silhouettes of balloons which hung like dark droplets of dew on the canyon-sides. Then, as the sun rose above the horizon, steady colours began to emerge, and the canopies of the balloons became patterned with stripes, spirals, and inscriptions that stretched and wobbled as their pilots nonchalantly bumped into one another, setting their great baskets swinging high in the air.

Tourists almost always dampen the beauty of a place, but in Cappadocia, the presence of the hot-air balloons only compounded it. Sat outside my tent at dawn, I could barely imagine how impressive the view must have been from two hundred metres above, but it was no less beautiful from below. Resting alone atop a hoodoo, I watched as the walls of Rose Valley were slowly stained red by the rising sun, along with every spire, turret, chimney, and tower, until the entire valley was aflame, lit with a rich scarlet light that dripped down the curving canopies of the balloons, flowed through the ragged canyons, and then spilt out onto the plains of Cappadocia, flooding the tattered landscape with the first fierce heat of the day.

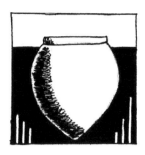

Chapter Eight

To see the eagle's bulk, render'd in mists
Hang of a treble size.

   – Gerard Manley Hopkins, 'I Must Hunt Down the Prize'

'When God had finished making the world, he called all the tribes of mankind together to decide which portions of the earth they would inherit. Everyone gathered, eager to hear his word, except for the Georgians. It was rumoured that they did not appear because they were too busy feasting and drinking.

'Angered, but willing to give the Georgians a second chance, God waited a while before calling another council. Once again, all the peoples of the world gathered. Once again, the Georgians did not appear. But this time, the noise of their banquet was so loud that God could hear their revelry from heaven.

'Deciding that the Georgians had to be confronted, a furious God approached them and asked how they could be so disobedient. The feast fell silent for a moment before the wise Georgian toast-master stood up from the table.

'"God, we are sorry for our absence. We were simply too busy drinking to *your* health and toasting *your* generosity to hear your call for council. Please, all, let us raise our glasses once again to God!" shouted the tamada, casting a sly look amongst his compatriots.

'God was flattered by this cunning speech, and he regretted ever doubting the Georgians. To honour their loyalty and to reward their dedication, he decided to make the tribe a special gift. So when it came to portioning out the world to all of mankind, the Georgians received the part which God had reserved for himself, with all its green fields and snowy mountains, and that is how we Georgians inherited the most beautiful country on earth.'

After finishing his story, Eraklos the wine merchant reverently poured two glasses of chacha and handed one to me. The fact that it had just turned ten o'clock in the morning mattered little to Eraklos: a story about Georgia deserved a fitting toast, whatever the time of day. Besides, chacha was a drink to give you strength, he told me, popular amongst Georgian farmers who take a glass of the clear brandy each day with their breakfast, despite its notorious potency.

'Where have you come from?' asked the merchant, after draining his glass and letting out a satisfied sigh.

'From Turkey,' I replied. 'I followed the coast of the Black Sea around from Trabzon as far as Batumi, then I turned inland and the road led me here to Kutaisi. I wandered down the steps to your cellar looking for a café.'

'A happy accident,' said Eraklos with a grin, pouring out a second brandy. 'By the way, in Georgian tradition, there must always be an even number of toasts,' he explained, raising his glass once again to mine.

I had heard that the Georgians had a fondness for drinking, a fact which made me nervous given that I was due to spend the next few weeks driving on Georgian roads. Naturally curious, after our second toast, I asked Eraklos why alcohol featured so heavily in Georgian culture.

'Georgians are the finest drinkers in the world,' he boomed. 'These little chacha glasses are for children. This is what real Georgian men drink from…' and as he spoke, he turned around, reached up, and pulled a long animal horn off the wall. Only then did I notice that there were rows of similar vessels hung all around the cellar, plucked from the skulls of every mountain beast imaginable. Holding the horn delicately in his hands, Eraklos was about to fill it with liquor when a woman who had been browsing his wines interrupted.

'Excuse me,' she said, in a mixed accent, part English and part Slavic. 'Did you just say that Georgian's are the finest drinkers in the world?'

'You disagree?' said Eraklos, casting a defensive gaze in the young woman's direction.

'My parents in Ukraine might have something to say about that,' she said, turning over a glass for herself and sitting down at the bar next to the huge jar of brandy. 'And where I'm from, tradition states that we must always drink an odd number of toasts.'

'A Georgian host is never one to disappoint his guests,' said Eraklos as he dutifully poured three more glasses of brandy. 'But,' he continued, after swallowing his glass, 'we also expect our guests to honour our traditions,' and to my astonishment, he poured another three measures, handing one expectantly to me.

I realised then the trouble that I was in, stuck in an underground wine cellar, surrounded by bottles of brandy, forced to mediate between a Georgian and a Ukrainian in disagreement over drinking etiquette. The resolve in Eraklos's eyes told me all I needed to know about how important drinking was to Georgians, but Sacha, the Ukrainian woman, gave me no reason to doubt that it was just as sacred to her.

They were two opponents, locked in a stalemate, and I had the unfortunate duties of both umpire and contestant. As Sacha poured another three glasses, in the twilight of the cellar, time began to blur. The last clear memory I have of that day is of Eraklos opening a fresh jar of chacha, and of his unsteady hand pouring out yet another three measures, just as the clocks outside were striking midday in the ancient city of Kutaisi.

***

In my final year at university, I shared my rooms with a man named Tom. Though I consider Tom to be a good friend, to describe him briefly is difficult. Blisteringly intelligent, uniquely charming, and often cryptic beyond comprehension, he is uniquely odd. In all my life, I have only ever known one man whose eccentricity surpasses that of Tom. His name is Alex, and he lived in the room above us.

Every night, just as Tom and I were going to bed, Alex would charge down the stairs and burst into our study, fizzing with energy and jabbering nonsense. Like a Great Dane after an adrenalin shot, he would clatter around, knocking furniture to the floor, vying for our attention.

Then, after twenty minutes of bedlam, he would eventually tire and collapse face down on our carpet, where he would soon be sleeping sweetly, content amidst his nest of chaos. The magnitude of Alex's clumsiness is without limit, but so is the size of his heart, and he has never given me any reason to doubt that there is anything but goodness in his bones.

However, several years of friendship with Tom and Alex might have driven me irretrievably insane if it was not for Emma. For three years, out of some inexplicable sense of duty, Emma took it upon herself to absorb the combined imbecility of Tom, Alex, and I, guiding us out of innumerable muddles, always with unflappable good grace. She also once accompanied me on an erratic jaunt halfway across Europe, which left us wandering the streets of Athens at midnight, lost, alone, and without a penny to spend. There are few others I would have wanted for company in that situation; she is one of the bravest people I know.

I considered myself very lucky to have such good friends, and I felt even more fortunate when they announced their intentions to join me for part of my journey across the world. As Alex could speak Russian and Emma loved the outdoors, the mountains of Georgia seemed a natural choice. So just a few weeks after the plan was hatched, I found myself sat in the centre of Kutaisi, nursing a crippling hangover courtesy of Eraklos, and waiting for their arrival.

That arrival needed no herald: Alex's driving was unmistakable. Several years before, having secured his license after six failed attempts, Alex had spent two months developing his unique sense of road awareness on the wild plains of Kazakhstan as a participant in the Mongol Rally. Behind the wheel, he made even the Georgians seem timid. So when a vast blue jeep came careering through the city centre, I knew instantly that my friends were inside. But just in case I had any doubt, Alex was hanging halfway out the window, steering with one hand, waving emphatically with the other, whilst Emma looked on in horror and Tom giggled in the back.

'Crikey this thing is quick,' shouted Alex, as he brought the car to a stop on the roadside.

'Perhaps a little too quick,' warned Tom.

'It's good to see you three,' I said with a smile, throwing my bags inside and diving into the alien comfort of an air-conditioned car.

'First stop Tbilisi?' suggested Emma.

'Well, about that,' began Alex. 'I was actually thinking of making a little detour. Ever heard of a place called Gori?'

'We haven't even started and you're already making detours. What's at Gori?' asked Tom.

'Just wait and see,' said Alex, as he floored the jeep and sent us barrelling towards the highway.

With an obsessive interest in Soviet history, Alex had long been waiting for the opportunity to make a pilgrimage to Gori, a small town in the centre of the Caucasus which was the birthplace of Georgia's most infamous son: Joseph Stalin. As we approached the town, I was unsure how the life of one of the world's most notorious dictators would be remembered. But as we arrived in the centre of Gori, I spotted a statue of Stalin surrounded by wreaths of red roses, which set a tone of admiration that only strengthened as we stepped inside the nearby museum.

In several large rooms, artefacts and testimonies were arranged in a celebration of Stalin's life, forming a collection closer in nature to a shrine than an archive. There were tables full of his childhood possessions – school books, drawings, and keepsakes - as well as countless portraits of the handsome youth. Framed on the walls were his battle strategies and dictates, alongside images of him broking deals with leaders from across the world. And everywhere, covering every available space, were countless letters penned in the dictator's delicate scrawl.

Georgian script is undeniably pretty, with all of its half-hearts and arcs, but Stalin's hand was positively elvish. As I glanced over the winsome lines of his diaries, I wondered how many arrest warrants and execution orders that same hand had signed. But those documents would have been penned in Russian. Georgian, a language entirely of its own, with no relatives on earth, seemed too pure and elegant a script to have been used for anything so sinister.

After an hour in the museum, we returned to the road, soon reaching the fringes of Tbilisi, where it was up to me to bully our way through the city's dense traffic. Eventually, we dropped down into the cramped brown valley cradling Georgia's capital, passing beneath Narikala fortress which loomed over Tbilisi's skyline from the top of a towering cliff. Beside the fortress, at the summit of Sololaki hill, stood an even more impressive monument: a towering aluminium statue of Mother Georgia, her two hands raised aloft, one clutching a goblet of wine in a gesture of welcome to friends, the other wielding a formidable sword in a warning to prospective enemies.

The city itself, home to four million citizens, was a mesh of modern and old. On our way through its centre, we passed flamboyant steel bridges stretching across the Kura, bent into graceful curves, but we also passed squat terracotta domes, housing Tbilisi's ancient Sulphur baths. There were steel towers and apartment blocks, the hallmarks of a thriving capital, but there were also round spires, capped with golden crosses, crowning medieval churches. And everywhere I looked, filling every available space, there were statues of David the Builder, Georgia's favourite King, who in the twelfth century had restored the country from the Seljuk Turks and established Tbilisi as his capital.

At the end of a long day of driving, all our thoughts turned towards dinner, and it was not long before we were sitting down around a restaurant table in Tbilisi's old town. After a week spent tasting all manner of Georgian food, I was desperate to share some of my favourite dishes with Emma, Alex, and Tom.

'Do you mind if I order?' I asked, and when my friends nodded their assent, I turned to the menu with enthusiasm.

Rich and nourishing, Georgian cuisine has developed through the ages to provide the maximum amount of warmth and sustenance for when the weather turns foul in the mountains. As if sensing that the warm evening was not the right setting for our meal, the moment the waitress left with our order, a tremendous rain-cloud emptied itself over the city, flooding every street in the capital. With no space available inside the restaurant, vast umbrellas were quickly raised, and along with everyone else dining outdoors in Tbilisi that evening, we ate with our feet raised on our chairs as a torrent of water swept the city clean.

Over the previous few days, it was not just Georgian food that I had developed a deep attachment too, but also Georgian wine. Long before the Greeks or the Romans cultivated vines, Caucasian people had become well acquainted with the virtues of fermented grape juice, and archaeological records have proven that wine was being made in the Caucasus over eight thousand years ago, making Georgia one of the oldest wine-producing regions on earth. To celebrate our reunion, I ordered a bottle of red from Kakheti, an area of vineyards to the east of Tbilisi. Like many wines in Georgia, the Kakheti had been aged in qvevri - huge clay amphora, lined with beeswax, which are buried underground and hold the wine until it is ready to be bottled. Deep black, richly spiced, and unabashedly powerful, it was the perfect match for the dozen plates of rich Georgian food that were soon to cover our table.

After the wine, the first dish to arrive was a khachapuri, a Georgian staple that exists in many different forms across the country. The Adjarian khachapuri that we ordered came in the shape of a boat made of baked dough, in the centre of which lay a molten muddle of butter, cheese, and eggs. Tangy, salty, and shamelessly indulgent, it was a dish built to bring warmth in even the bleakest midwinter.

'That looks like a heart attack on a plate,' observed Emma, as Tom, Alex, and I shovelled fistfuls of the dense, golden cheese into our mouths.

To provide some light relief after the khachapuri, the next arrival was a plate of pkhali. The dark green balls, made from minced vegetables and walnut sauce, were served with a coronet of pomegranate seeds, bringing a welcome, delicate freshness which made the khachapuri seem cumbersome in comparison. Continuing with the Georgian love of walnuts, following the pkhali came a plate of badrijani - silken slithers of fried aubergine, stuffed with a mash of spiced walnuts and garlic. The starters closed with a warm pot of blended beans, peppered with scallions and coriander, known to the Georgians as lobio.

As soon as the waitress arrived with the next dish, Alex's eyes lit up from across the table.

'I've certainly heard of these before,' he said, gazing hungrily upon the plate of khinkali that had just been placed before him.

'What on earth are they?' asked Emma.

'Dumplings, but there's a particular way to eat them. Let me show you how,' replied Alex, reaching out and picking up one of the fist-sized balls by the little knuckle of dough that had been moulded into a handle at its summit.

According to tradition, the soft dumplings are meant to be held aloft by their little handles, then punctured with a tooth and gracefully drained of the rich, peppery juice contained inside. Though Alex might have been familiar with this traditional way of eating khinkali, his execution did not quite go to plan, and all that his first inelegant bite achieved was a minor explosion of steam and beef broth, leaving him muttering curses whilst the rest of us laughed at the rivulets of gravy running down his chin.

As a vegetarian, Emma's enthusiasm understandably waned as dinner took a carnivorous turn. But Tom, Alex, and I still had strong appetites and were soon fighting over a clay pot that contained an entire chicken, stewed in garlic and cream, crispy on the outside and glossy within, which the Georgian's call shkmeruli. Given how much we had already eaten, that plate should probably have concluded our supper, but there was still one more dish that I was eager for Alex and Tom to try.

Just as we were coming to our last drop of wine, the waitress brought us our final course, setting down a cast-iron bowl in the middle of the table. The dish inside was not the most sophisticated of recipes, but it was honest and wholesome. To describe it simply, ojakhuri is a mix of marinated pork, onions, and potatoes, unpretentiously fried in pig fat - the sort of food that Georgian mothers feed their boys so that they grow up strong. It was clumsy and brutish, uncomplicated but sincere, and sumptuous enough to put Alex, Tom, and I into a state of comatose bliss that lasted late into the evening.

***

The following morning, still full from our gargantuan meal, the four of us decided to skip breakfast and set out exploring Tbilisi. In a single day, we visited the ancient sulphur baths, wandered across the old town, and stepped inside dozens of dark churches where choirs were singing the haunting polyphonic music that is popular across Georgia. The capital received our unanimous praise, and we might have stayed a little longer, but Georgia's heart, we had been told, lay in her mountains, and the next day we were back on the road, heading north into the Caucasus proper.

The drive from Tbilisi to Stepantsminda, a town at the foot of Mount Kazbek, normally takes half a day, but thanks to Alex's impassioned driving, after just a few hours we reached Gudauri pass, the highest point on the road at two and a half thousand metres. As we emerged from a bank of mist, a spine of tall mountains unravelled on either side of us. Their steep slopes were lurid green to the top, save for the tallest that were capped with snow or had their summits lost in cloud. Wriggling our way through the pass, we watched paragliders spiral their way down the valley, past the skeletons of ski slopes that stood barren and empty, desperately waiting for winter.

Realising we would arrive in Stepantsminda far earlier than expected, we voted on a detour and decided that we would spend the afternoon exploring Truso gorge, a remote portion of the Caucasus lying to the west of Mount Kazbek. We had just left the highway and turned away from Stepantsminda when Alex made an announcement:

'Just so you know, we should be careful because if we follow this road all the way, we might end up in South Ossetia.'

'What's South Ossetia?' asked Tom.

'Not somewhere you want you want to visit,' replied Emma. 'South Ossetia declared independence from Georgia in 1991 and the area has been a mess for the last three decades. Ever since the Russo-Georgian war in 2008, Russian troops have occupied the region, and they don't have a good reputation.'

I knew that Emma was right. Only a few days earlier, a Georgian man had described South Ossetia to me as a stake driven through the heart of his country. Along with Abkhazia, another disputed region in the north-west of the Caucasus, many Georgians felt that South Ossetia was being used by Russia to prevent Georgia from joining the European Union, because Russia knew that as long as there was ongoing conflict within her borders, Georgia would never be granted membership.

'And why don't the troops have a good reputation?' asked Tom.

'Well,' Alex sighed, 'the Russian military aren't known for their high moral standards, and these lot seem to grow bored quite easily. They have a bit of a precedent for kidnapping anyone who crosses the border and demanding petty ransoms for their release.'

'Fantastic. Kidnap and Ransom. The perfect accompaniments to a holiday in the Caucasus.'

Unperturbed by Tom's sarcasm, Alex ploughed on in the direction of Truso gorge, and before long the smooth asphalt gave way to mud and gravel. Ironically, this meant it was time to hand control of the car to the one member of the party who did not have a license. Having grown up on a farm in southern Australia, Tom knew how to handle difficult roads, and he took the slick dirt tracks and pock-marked trails of the Truso valley in his stride, thrilled to finally be behind the wheel.

Snaking between high peaks with shelves of snow still frozen on their sides, the road climbed and climbed, until we were fifty metres above a milk-white river with only six inches of track to spare. Breaking away from the river, the road then passed chemical lakes, hissing with carbon dioxide, which lay pooled at the feet of brilliant orange mineral deposits that oozed out of the sides of the valley. There were crumbling villages too, and the remains of medieval Vainakh towers - tall, svelte structures, some reaching five-storeys in height, that tapered almost to a point and rose like sentinels along the length of the gorge.

Truso felt like an alien world, a place from the distant past, but people did carve out an existence there. After an hour of driving, we fell in behind a rusting Soviet Lada that was slowly ambling its way up the single lane track. Every half mile or so the car would stop in front of a crooked farmhouse and a man would step out to deliver plastic bottles of clear liquid to haggard, bearded farmhands. Whether fuel, or water, or vodka, it was impossible to tell, but whatever the delivery, the poor farmers were grateful to receive it. This was rough country, where life was something to be endured, not enjoyed. Even the damp dogs, chained outside in the rain, looked miserable. I could not even begin to imagine what life would be like during the winter in Truso when for months on end the whole valley would lie buried beneath metres of snow.

Soon, the condition of the road grew worse, and the old Lada in front of us stopped on the side of the trail, defeated. From then on, the only other traffic we saw were boys riding bareback down the valley, their young faces chapped crimson by the cold. It was not long before the road stopped altogether, ending in front of a squat metal hut which had a Georgian flag flying on its roof. Beside the hut, a colossal guard in khaki uniform sat with an assault rifle across his knees. As we approached in the car, the guard stood up, walked two steps, and then commanded we stop by holding up the biggest hand I had ever seen.

Grey, grizzled, and vast, the guard was more than just imposing. It was as if one of the mountains encircling Truso had grown arms and legs, torn a meadow to strips for his uniform, and then had taken his place there, as guardian of Georgia, with all the strength of his nation manifest in him. As we stepped out of the car, the atmosphere was palpably tense, but Alex's ability to speak Russian brought some relief. We learnt that we had reached Zakagori fortress, but the guard made it clear that we could go no further. Northwards, beyond his hut, lay Russia, and the border with South Ossetia was only a few miles to the west. He did, however, say that we could climb the ruins of the fortress that stood atop a nearby hill, as long as we did not take any photographs.

A minute later, Emma, Tom, and I were scrambling up the hill, desperate to catch a glimpse of the border with Russia, whilst Alex bumbled around the car, insisting on changing his shoes. We were halfway to the fortress when he began jumping around, pointing at the car with flailing arms, and shouting up at us with words that were lost on the wind.

'What on earth is he doing?'

'Is he having some sort of episode?'

'I think he just wants the car boot unlocked…'

As I had the electric key to the car in my pocket, I decided to have some fun. Raising my wrist high, I clicked the button and watched as Alex stepped forward to test the doors, as I knew he would. But in the split second that his hand reached towards the door handle, I pressed the button and locked the car again, much to his frustration and my amusement.

I repeated the joke half a dozen times, Alex growing more and more irate, until disaster struck. My fiddling with the key had confused the car to such a degree that it decided, all of a sudden, to set off a cacophony of alarms and to repeatedly flash every headlight and indicator. At the sound of the alarm, the border guard immediately stood up, raised his rifle, and began shouting in Russian. Alex sensibly bolted and dived behind a nearby boulder, helpfully calling up the mountain to inform me that I would have to handle this alone.

I tried frantically pressing buttons on the key, but the car was unresponsive. With no other option, I jogged down the slope, my hands raised in surrender, hoping the border guard would realise the alarm had been set off by an idiot's attempt at humour and did not signal the imminent detonation of a bomb.

By the time I reached the jeep, the guard was still shouting, and the rifle was still at his shoulder. With his free hand, the soldier motioned for the car to be moved down the gorge. At first, I struggled with the door, then I dropped the keys in the mud, and once inside, I could not get the engine to start. But after a few agonising minutes, the car did eventually growl into life. Immediately, I selected reverse and sped back through the valley, staring down the barrel of the guard's assault rifle all the way.

After hiding the car behind a hill, I ran back to the border, half expecting to find my three friends hand-cuffed to a pole and suffering torturous interrogations. Alex, however, with his ineffable charm, had managed to calm the situation, and he was stood laughing with the guard, with one arm around the soldier's back, begging for a forbidden picture.

'Sorry about that. Please offer my apologies,' I said to Alex as I walked closer.

After Alex uttered a few sentences in Russian, the soldier cast me stern look, then held out one of his enormous paws and violently shook my hand. We were all quite relieved that nobody had been shot, and I made a mental note to hold off on practical jokes when close to turbulent borders. Then, as Alex continued to chat with the guard, I turned to Tom and Emma and suggested we tear him away from his new friend, whilst Anglo-Georgian relations remained amicable.

***

The next day, we left the car behind in Stepantsminda and decided to take a hike. This was not a decision made entirely by choice. The previous night, I had accidentally left the headlights on, which had left us with a flat battery. But it was a fine day for walking anyway, and rising before us, standing at over five thousand metres and looking down on the town of Stepantsminda, was Mount Kazbek, one of the tallest mountains in the Caucasus.

There was a steep trail leading away from Stepantsminda in the direction of the mountain, but we were not alone in climbing it. Alongside us, columns of Orthodox monks, clad from head to toe in black, were making their way up the track. Their destination was Gergeti church, a temple which sits alone on a solitary spur of rock at two-and-a-half thousand metres, encircled by frosted summits. A beacon for climbers, halfway between the safety of Stepantsminda and the summit of Kazbek, the rugged stone church has survived for over six hundred years, alone in the vast arena of nature, becoming a national emblem of Georgia over time. It was, without a doubt, one of the most majestic places of worship that I had ever seen.

Pressing on through the morning, we passed Gergeti and reached an area of steeply sloping pastureland where shepherds were guiding their goats down from the mountains towards the valley. One of them shouted at us, flapping his arms and pointing up at the sky. We took this as confirmation of the weather reports that we had seen, warning of a storm that afternoon. Tom and Alex, giving credence to the shepherd's warning, turned back and retreated, but Emma and I decided to continue for a while, climbing higher up steep fields of scrub.

An hour later, and five hundred metres higher in the valley, the clouds began to darken with intent, and Emma and I decided we had reached our limit. In front of us, a few climbers could be seen crossing the snowline. For them, the summit of Kazbek was still at least a day's hike away. They would have to wait out the storm on the mountain.

As Emma began to walk back down the valley, I paused and took one last look at Mount Kazbek. When I turned back around, Emma was skipping down the green slope with her arms spread wide like the wings of a bird. And at that very same moment, in an instance of exquisite coincidence, the shadow of a raptor raced down the mountain, closely followed by the vast brown wings of a golden eagle, gliding just metres above our heads. It passed so close to Emma that I feared she was about to become its prey, but the bird altered course and soared down past Gergeti, the golden feathers of its nape gleaming in the last rays of the afternoon sun, before it disappeared into the misted valley below.

The eagle was prudent to seek sanctuary. As we were clambering back down, the weather began to close, and I could hear the broiling mass of cloud behind me, creaking and groaning as it encircled the surrounding peaks. Looking up, I watched clumps of dark cumulus bubbling up behind Kazbek as the air grew warm with charge. At the first peal of thunder, I was suddenly taken back to the vicious weather I had encountered in Croatia and Greece, and it was all Emma could do to stop me from breaking into a run as I fled down to Stepantsminda.

Back in the town, my three friends decided that after several months living between my tent and the cheapest hostels I could find, I deserved some extravagance. Sprawling across one face of the valley below Mount Kazbek, Stepantsminda had a single luxury hotel - a refurbished holiday resort that had once served as a retreat for prominent Soviet officers. Naturally, Alex had already taken the liberty of booking us several rooms.

Combining the brutal minimalism of a Soviet army barracks with a heavy measure of alpine decadence, the hotel was by far the most luxurious place I stayed on my entire journey. After checking in, we headed straight to the pool, and whilst swimming looked out through a long glass wall at Mount Kazbek, which was swaddled in storm-clouds and glowing with electricity. Wearing nothing but a towel, and watching from the warm glow of a sauna chamber, for once I was able to look on with enjoyment as purple flashes lit up the sky and lightning danced around the darkened mountains.

By evening, the storm had cleared, and the whole valley was glistening as we relaxed on the hotel's terrace and shared another bottle of Kakhetian wine. Kazbek, which an hour before had been wrapped in dark, portentous shades, now looked amicable, even inviting, yet still regal in its vastness. Sat there with my friends, surrounded by the mountains, life suddenly seemed very fine. I drank it in and drank deep, desperate to get my fill, ever conscious of what lay ahead, sensing that such comforts would soon be little more than distant memories.

Chapter Nine

The virtue of travelling is that it purges life before filling it up.

- Nicolas Bouvier, *The Way of the World*

On my way out of Georgia, I encountered a tattered sign that read:

AZERBAIJAN BORDER
GOOD LUCK

Naturally, these words left me a little nervous. As far as I could fathom, there were only two possible reasons why the Georgians might have decided that such a sign was necessary. Either the border at Matsimi was known for arduous delays, or the Georgian's simply felt that in a country like Azerbaijan, every traveller needed fortune on their side.

Twenty minutes later, I was searching through a pile of maroon passports, most of which were embossed with the golden-flamed emblem of Azerbaijan, the self-declared land of fire. But it was not long until I spotted a faded British coat of arms, and plucking my passport from out of the pile, I rode onto Azeri land without a fuss. Having crossed the border with such ease, the Georgian sign returned to mind, and I began to worry.

But I had no reason to be nervous. After the parched plains of Kakheti, which had suffered that year from blistering droughts, the cool, green landscape of Azerbaijan was a welcome tonic. As was the perfect asphalt road I followed, bound by grass verges and hedgerows, which steadily curled its way around the foothills of the Lower Caucasus. Beyond the road, broad meadows and green forests quilted the rolling slopes, and though the land was entirely new to me, it began to seem familiar.

To describe a place through comparison, by weighing its similarities and differences against other parts of the world, generally makes for lazy writing. As a rule, when keeping my daily journals, I always tried to avoid it. But the scribbles in my notebook dating to my first day in Azerbaijan prove that I did not always abide by my own guidelines. For as I rode across the north-western corner of that country, I could not help but draw comparisons between the Azeri landscape and the south-west of England. Few places in the world had ever reminded me so much of home.

As dusk fell in the Lower Caucasus that evening, I brought my motorcycle to a stop on the side of the road and walked towards the flanks of the foothills. Strolling through knee-high grass, I made for a glade of trees in the distance, and I could just as well have been walking through a field in Somerset. As I pushed through the grass, I could hear the thud of apples falling to the ground nearby, and from somewhere further off, I caught the gurgle of a stream. The air was sweet and thick, heavy with the scent of hay, and even the light and the way it caught between the branches of the trees reminded me of the English countryside.

As I entered the glade, I strode through fading sunbeams that twitched and quivered on their way down to the leaf-litter, buffeted by tiny wing-beats. With every few steps I took, golden worlds appeared and disappeared, made and unmade by the cascades of twilight falling through the trees. In my search for a place to camp, it felt like I was like walking through a world trapped in amber, perfectly preserved, three thousand miles from where it should have been.

I slept soundly that night, nestled in the quiet of the Caucasus, on the fringe of a small town named Sheki. As I walked back to my motorcycle the next morning, the dew-decked meadows were flooded with sunlight, and the green fields had changed into plains of shattered crystal. Riding eastwards, I flew through the cold morning, watching startled birds fly up from the hedgerows, awakened by the noise of my engine. The crisp-white dawn and the immaculate road made for perfect riding, and I would have followed the blue foothills forever, but it was not long until the road turned away from the green pastures and the landscape suddenly changed.

Within an hour of leaving the damp meadows, I crossed over a ridge of hills, and once again I found myself riding through a parched, sterile landscape. The trees disappeared, the rivers dried up, and the only plants I could see were fistfuls of dying grass that grew sideways on the edge of the road, folded over by a dry wind. By the time I had processed the change, the heat had already climbed to above forty degrees centigrade, and I found myself looking ahead, desperately searching for the blue waters of the Caspian Sea. But long before the great lake came into sight, the skyscrapers and sand-coloured streets of Baku rose out of the desert plains.

After fighting my way through an hour of busy traffic, I eventually found a hostel in the centre of the capital. As I stepped inside, the manager peered up from his desk and noticed my jacket and helmet with a look of curiosity on his face.

'You have come on a motorcycle?' he said.

'Yes.'

'May I see it?'

'Sure,' I replied, leading him to where I had parked the cycle.

Outside, on a dusty Baku street, amidst the clamour of construction work and car horns, the hostel manager shot one glance at the machine and then turned towards me with a greedy glint in his eyes.

'I have been trying to buy a motorbike for a long time,' he said, pulling a thick brick of notes from out of his pocket. 'I will give you one thousand manat for it.'

Astounded by the offer, I was speechless at first. Ever since leaving Turkey, there had been a nervousness growing within me, inspired by the uncertainty of the road beyond Baku. In my mind, the Azeri capital was the last line hitching me to Europe and western Asia. Severing that line would mean crossing the Caspian Sea, then the Kyzylkum Desert, and after that the Pamir mountains. The desert alone stretched for over six hundred miles through a country where most cars ran on gas and where petrol was barely available. The hostel manager was offering me enough money to cover the cost of trains and buses all the way to India.

'But if I sell the bike here in Azerbaijan, I will have to pay the import duties, and they're several thousand dollars alone,' I said, searching for an excuse to not part with my motorcycle.

'Yes, but no problem. This is Baku, my friend. We can sort the paperwork without the import taxes,' he said, rubbing his thumb and forefinger together, intimating a bribe.

I continued to hesitate.

'Ok, one thousand three hundred manat,' he said, sensing that such an offer would be almost irresistible.

I saw the deserts and the mountains loom and imagined that I was sitting in the cool carriage of a train rather than rattling through them on bone-shaking roads. The man pulled a sheaf of notes from the brick of money and held them out to me. Visions of Kyzylkum sandstorms filled my mind, followed by flashes of lightning in the Pamirs. I thought about how pretty it all might look rolling past an old glass window. But long journeys fall into natural chapters, and my time with the motorcycle was not done yet.

'I'm sorry, but it's not for sale,' I said.

'That's a pity,' he replied, nodding his head in understanding. 'It looks like a machine with some spirit.'

***

Down by the waterfront the next day, Baku seemed to be a city caught between two identities. Women in niqābs and burqas walked beside girls with bloated breasts and swollen lips clad in skin-tight clothes. Old men in thawbs fiddling with prayers beads talked to slick-haired boys who dangled the keys to sports-cars between their manicured fingers. Dark eyes stared at me from behind black veils, or looked out over white plasters covering the wounds of recent rhinoplasties. It was a capital caught between two worlds, rigorously conservative but also shamelessly vapid, struggling to reconcile its traditional Islamic leanings with the growing influence of Western vanity.

The centre of the city, with its expensive shops and elegant boulevards, looked fantastically wealthy, the origin of its riches lying in the limp rainbow of oil that clung to the Caspian shoreline. As I walked down to the edge of the lake, far out on the water, vast ships were waiting to dock, their bows pointing towards the city and its three famous flame towers which glinted in the sun behind me. Below them rose the twelfth-century walls of the capital's old town, which in recent years had been meticulously restored. But the ancient part of the city, filled with hotels and souvenir shops, was little more than a gimmick dressed up in old clothes, designed to appease the few tourists who visit Baku each year.

After crossing the city on foot, I stopped at a shawarma house for lunch. Sitting down at a table, I noticed a husband and wife arguing in the corner, their voices steadily rising. Turning to my book, I tried to ignore the couple, but the argument grew more heated. Just as my food was served, I heard a sharp, loud slap, and I turned round to see the woman clutching the side of her face. As I tried to catch her eye to see if she was hurt, the husband stood up and asked the waiter for some ice. When it arrived, he kept the cup to himself, melting the ice-cubes in his hand to stop it smarting from where he had hit her. Nobody in the restaurant even looked up from their plates. The woman simply sat there in silence, a single tear hanging like a jewel upon her cheek.

Very quickly, Baku began to weigh upon me, and I found myself desperate to depart from the place that I had thought would be a last bastion of comfort and security which I would never want to leave. To console myself, on the way back to my hostel I decided to stop for a beer. It did not take me long to find a street full of sordid bars, patronised by oil and gas expatriates, with names like 'Otto's', 'The Red Lion', 'Finnegan's', and 'Saigon'.

In the first bar I entered, I sat down by the beer pumps next to a greasy middle-aged European man, dressed in a Hawaiian shirt, who gave me a solemn nod. As the barman poured my beer, a young woman, wearing a low-cut top and heavily laden with make-up, came into the bar and sat beside us. The man in the shirt leered at her, and without even saying hello, drunkenly shouted:

'One hundred manat?'

The woman looked away and ignored him.

'One hundred and fifty manat?'

Still silence from her.

'Ok, two-hundred manat. You can't be any more expensive than that, you stupid whore.'

Displeased with such a low valuation, the woman stood up and walked away, sucking air through her teeth, whilst casting a long, inquisitive look in my direction. The man spat after her as she left and ordered another beer. Five minutes later, when a second woman walked in, he began shouting figures again. This time, I was the one who stood up and walked away, leaving my drink untouched on the bar, even more disenchanted with Baku than I had been at lunchtime.

Back at my hostel, the receptionist told me that there was somebody outside on the balcony who thought he might know me. Surprised, I looked up through the glass doors of the dormitory and saw a man with long, black, tightly curled hair, a strong, stern nose, and eyes as green as snake scales. The image of a Persian prince in exile, he was sat fiddling with a guitar, wearing an old pair of cotton shorts, surrounded by a litter of empty beer cans. Curious, I went over to introduce myself.

'Hello,' I said. 'I believe you might know me?'

'You're the motorcyclist from Somerset, are you? My name's Bertie,' he said, holding out his hand. 'I'm from Taunton.'

Bertie's reply took me by surprise, not just because he mentioned Taunton, but also because he spoke in familiar tones, in an accent that belonged to the apple orchard and the farm-house, not to a wretched hostel in Baku. It took only a few minutes for me to learn that he had gone to school near to my house. A little older than I, we had never met, at least not in our memory, but with only a few years between us, and a host of common acquaintances, we were sure that at some point we must have been introduced to one another in a quiet corner of a Somerset pub.

Bertie, like me, was a hopeful writer who had left England recklessly wedded to the idea of a long journey eastwards. Beginning in Istanbul, he had hitchhiked his way to Baku, guided by a vague ambition of heading southwards into Iraqi Kurdistan. The moment I met him, I had a premonition of friendship, and sure enough, over the next few months, Bertie would become something of a lucky talisman, surfacing at the most unexpected moments, whenever coincidence decided to bring our two journeys together.

'Have a beer mate,' he said, tossing a can in my direction. 'I'm celebrating.'

'Thanks. What's the occasion?' I asked.

'Well, this time last night I was headed for an Azeri jail, so we're celebrating my freedom.'

It transpired that only the day before, whilst in a small town in the north, a policeman had caught Bertie kissing a girl in the street and had marched him towards the nearest prison. Thanks to a small bribe, and the adept deployment of a writer's finest flattery, Bertie had persuaded the policeman to let him go, fleeing to Baku the moment the handcuffs were off.

'This is Jan, by the way,' he said, motioning to a deeply tanned Dutchman sat beside him. 'He's on a motorcycle too.'

'Always good to meet another rider,' said Jan, shaking my hand. 'Yours is the little Chinese thing out the front?'

'Yes, that's mine,' I replied proudly.

'Little bikes are the best. I bet you're having more fun on that thing than I am on my heavy Suzuki. If you're heading east, maybe we could ride together for a bit?'

'Sure, that'd be great,' I said, not knowing that such a simple agreement would lead to many weeks spent riding alongside Jan, in which time he would prove himself to be not only an invaluable travelling companion but also a loyal friend.

As I sat drinking a beer with them both on the balcony, Bertie and Jan had no end of stories to tell. Although only in his late twenties, the Dutchman had already been to more countries than I could name. Amongst his rich adventures, he had swum with sharks in the Indian ocean, slept beside hippos in the wetlands of Africa, scaled the Andes, lived wild on a desert island off the coast of Myanmar, and he had an impressive scar on his leg where he had been bitten by a venomous spider in – of all places – Birmingham. Surrounding him was an air of inexorable calm and a quiet contentedness, which was the product of having seen a great portion of the world and remembering all that it had taught him. In the end, we rode nearly one-and-half thousand miles together, through deserts, mountains, and across the borders of five countries, and I learnt more from him than I did from anyone else I met on my journey to the Antipodes.

After becoming better acquainted over a beer, Jan and I resolved to leave for the ferry port the following morning, though we had no way of knowing when the next boat to cross the Caspian would sail. We had both heard reports that the ferry from Alat to Aktau (a port in southern Kazakhstan) could take days, even weeks to arrive, because high winds often left the old ships stranded on the water, unable to dock. The ferry companies were especially cautious after an overcrowded vessel sank several years before, taking all of its passengers to the bottom of the lake.

'Once the ship arrives, it is loaded, and then it departs within the space of a few hours,' warned Jan. 'The only way to guarantee a berth is to go down to the port and wait, however long that might take...'

***

The ride southwards out of Baku to the Port of Alat only took an hour, but a formidable wind blowing off the Caspian bullied us the entire way and made the journey more laborious than it should have been. The wind started to howl just as we left the city, as the road spilt out onto barren land that was littered with pumpjacks which punctured the desert in their thousands, ceaselessly rocking back and forth, pulling gallon after gallon of oil out of the ground. On our way out of Baku, we stopped at Yanar Dag - a small hill that is permanently covered in flames kept alight by an underground reservoir of natural gas. Surrounded by burning hills, mud volcanoes, and underground lakes of oil, it was easy to see why Zoroastrianism had once flourished across Azeri lands.

Continuing towards the docks, I spent most of the ride leaning sideways, battling to stay on the road. Streams of sand flying through the air bit at the paint on my fuel tank and fired dust up into my helmet, forcing me to stop and wait for the wind to calm. At this point, I presumed that Jan, being a much more experienced motorcyclist and in possession of a much larger machine, was probably regretting his pledge to ride with me. But by the time we reached Alat, even he had a new respect for the wind, and we both understood why the ferry might choose to wait out on the open water that night, rather than risk docking in the hot, violent gale that showed no signs of abating.

Once at Alat, it did not take long for us to realise that the industrial port made no allowances for travellers. The sole facilities were a ticket office and a small shop selling biscuits and cigarettes, each housed in an abandoned shipping container. Long lines of trucks filled a vast car park, in one corner of which another container housed four toilets that served several hundred people. A sad collection of tents and mattresses formed a makeshift camp in the shade of an old custom's house where hunched figures could be seen, sat panting in the heat and looking out at the water, hoping for any sign of a ship on the horizon.

Entering the ticket office, Jan and I were rapidly relieved of two-hundred dollars each and told:

'The ship will arrive tonight. *Inshallah.*'

We were jubilant. The winds were forecast to drop and our boat, *Professor Gul,* was expected to be in the dock and ready for boarding early the next morning. Others had been waiting here for weeks, yet it seemed we would only have to spend one night at the port. Having prepared myself for a long wait, I almost felt a little cheated. With our tickets in hand, we walked triumphantly towards the camp, eager to deliver good news to the few travellers we recognised from our hostel in Baku.

'Let me guess, the boat leaves tomorrow, *Inshallah,*' someone shouted, seeing us approach.

Following the comment, a chorus of laughter rang out, whilst Jan and I cast each other a look of dread.

'Every day we are told the boat is sailing tomorrow, *Inshallah.* But it has been weeks since the last ship was here,' explained another traveller.

Inshallah – meaning 'god willing' in Arabic – sounded sincere when spoken by the port officials, but the word rang with irony when pronounced by the travellers in the camp. Over the next few days, I would come to realise that the ticket officers had no idea when the boat would arrive, but ever the optimists, they would announce each night that we could expect a ship to dock the following morning, *Inshallah.* By including the religious invocation, the ferry officials subtly shifted responsibility away from themselves and onto God. If the boat was delayed by a day, a week, or a month, then it must be the will of the Almighty, which meant it was no fault of theirs. And if any prospective passengers had an issue with that, they were free to take it up with Allah.

Accepting our fate, there was little else for us to do other than settle into the camp and prepare for a long wait. Like everybody else, I found a place to put my things beside the wall of the locked customs house and unrolled my sleeping mat into a scrap of shade. Then I sat for a while, looking about me, studying the rich litter of characters that had made the Port of Alat their temporary home.

The largest group were the cyclists, recognisable by their deep tans and unruly beards, many of them bound for China and beyond. Most had been on the road for a long time, measuring their journeys in years rather than months. Travelling, for them, was more than just an enterprise, it represented a decision to live at a slower pace, in a way that was more in touch with the land. Six hundred miles across the desert might have seemed a difficult prospect on a motorcycle, but my task paled in comparison to what lay ahead for those men and women.

As well as Jan and I, there was a handful of other motorcyclists, all older men on expensive machines who were riding east as fast as they could. One group of Spaniards, dressed in matching motorcycle jackets, had ridden to Azerbaijan from Spain in just nine days. The same journey had taken me three months to complete. Each Spaniard wore a homing beacon that could be activated if they met with any danger, and which would send a specialist rescue team to their location anywhere in the world. Our end destinations and means of travel might have been similar, but our approaches could not have been more different. The monthly subscription for their little beacons alone totalled more than the budget for my entire journey.

Lastly, there were the hitch-hikers, the most fatalistic group of all the travellers, who were the least perturbed by the prospect of a long stay at the port. To them, waiting for the ferry was no different from standing on the side of the road thumbing a lift. When it was time, the boat would come.

The group of hitch-hikers included a Russian vet, a young Israeli fresh from national service, and a French girl named Marine who had fractured her foot in Baku. After tracking down a hospital and getting her leg bandaged, she had stolen a pair of crutches and quickly hobbled off, deciding that she was not going to let a broken bone stop her exploring Central Asia. She arrived several hours after Jan and I, with a diligent sherpa carrying her bags beside her, who, on closer inspection, turned out to be Bertie. Having given up on his idea of travelling to Iraq, his new ambition was to enter Afghanistan, or any another suitably nefarious location between Baku and Kabul - anything in the name of adventure.

We made quite a community, all living together on the hot Azeri concrete, and I could tell from the outset that these people were a different breed of traveller to any I had met before. They had faced hardships and were set for many more, but that prospect was a source of joy, not despair. Travel for them was not meant to be comfortable, nor always pleasant. For many, it had no purpose at all beyond the simple satisfaction of curiosity.

But for every curiosity satisfied by travel, another one blooms, and even after years on the road, the travellers at the port of Alat never grew so excited as when talking about what lay ahead. Collectively, over the coming months, we had plans to pass through every desert, mountain range, swamp, and jungle of central and southern Asia. We would all start in the Kyzylkum, but after that we expected our paths to diverge in many different directions. Some planned take to the Fann mountains, then the Pamirs, and perhaps even the Himalaya. Others intended to cross the Gobi and then the wide bulk of China, aiming for Beijing. A few even hoped to go south through the Karakoram, heading for Punjab and the hot, green fang of India. Vietnam, Japan, Korea, Australia – we lived on a diet of latent possibilities, sharing in one another's daydreams.

Beyond the fanciful, we also shared more literal resources, chiefly bread. Miles from any town or village, no-one knew how long the food we had would have to last, which meant that sharing was essential if everyone wanted to eat. Fortunately, that morning, Jan and I had packed our bags with vegetables in Baku, so whilst they were still fresh, we knelt in the dirt and lit our camping stoves, cooking our first communal dinner alongside everybody else. Breaking bread had never felt so poignant, and for Jan and I, that meal marked the first of many we would share over the coming months as we spanned the wildernesses of Central Asia.

After our supper, darkness began to fall, but the dock was lit with bright floodlights that shined all night till morning. The white halo that surrounded our camp attracted a swarm of flies, mosquitoes, and midges, and most of the critters had a particular taste for me. For the first half-hour, I battled with them, swatting and slapping myself until my skin glowed red, much to the amusement of everyone else.

'You must have sweet blood,' diagnosed one of the cyclists. 'We thank you for that. You might just keep them off the rest of us.'

Taking shelter in my sleeping bag was out of the question; even at night-time, it was well over thirty degrees. In the morning, under the strong sun, temperatures would rise to above forty, so as people went to bed, they took shelter alongside the walls of the customs house, seeking places that might grant an extra hour of shade after sunrise. Too preoccupied with how uncomfortable the night would be, I simply lay down on the hard floor, half-naked atop my sleeping bag, and let myself be savaged by the cloud of insects clinging to my bleeding body.

At first, I thought that sleep would be impossible, but I must have drifted off eventually because I remember waking up in the middle of the night after feeling a ghost-like patter upon my chest. Glancing down through swollen eyes, I saw the body of a camel spider camped on my shoulder, looking pale and monstrous, like an alien creature come down from the moon. A few months earlier, such a sight would have horrified me, but under an Azeri sky, the beast seemed trivial. Its presence upon my chest was a natural consequence of sleeping at the port that I had no choice but to accept, and after brushing the spider off my shoulder, I rolled over, shut my eyes, and tried in vain to sleep again.

Alongside heat, daylight brought with it debilitating boredom. From morning till evening, it was too hot to sleep, too hot to read, and too hot to eat. Once every few hours, somebody would go to the ticket office to ask for news, always returning with the same verdict: the boat will arrive tomorrow, *Inshallah*. Apart from that performance, life at the port was one long monotony, an endless pattern of hunger, heat, and false hope. One day grew to two days, and two days grew to three, as idleness slowly corroded the camp, infecting every one of us, till all we could do was lie comatose on the ground, too tired to even attempt idle chatter.

But on the afternoon of the third day, something shifted at the port. Cody, one of the cyclists, had heard that I had a sewing kit and asked if I could help him repair a hole in his shorts. I sat and taught him how to do a running stitch, and in return, he showed me how to clean the jets of my camp-stove. Watching us, other people then began to show each other how to repair inflatable mattresses, or how to adjust the tension of motorcycle chains, and within an hour, a festival of little workshops had appeared, and a crowd was moving around, helping one another in any way they could. At the end of the day, we even managed to coax some Azeri truck drivers out of their air-conditioned cabins to play a game of cricket. Running around in the sun with a group of strangers whilst chanting and cheering in a dozen unintelligible languages seemed to bring some welcome relief for the truckers, who had spent weeks alone in their cabins, gazing out at the black Caspian, where still no lights could be seen.

Things were very different on the morning of the fourth day. We woke to find that a pipe connected to the toilets had ruptured only twenty metres from our camp, spilling a jet of raw sewage out onto the ground. The only attempt at repairing the pipe was made by the truculent owner of the small shop, who simply stood prodding at it with an iron rod for a while, in between bouts of vomiting. The failure of the pipe meant that the water was shut off, and I watched Bertie stand in the midday sun and use a credit card like a strigil to scrape the sweat and dirt from his body. Then the shop unexpectedly closed, shutting us off from biscuits and cigarettes. And though there was still positivity, with people agreeing to share water and discussing the merits of fasting, overnight our pleasant little camp had taken on an undeniable aspect of the apocalyptic. Voices that had until now been nothing but stoic began to ask how long this could go on for.

Our group decided to take a break from the camp, which was growing fouler by the hour. Together, we packed our things and decided to head for a nearby hill-top, which was rumoured to have a chain of mud volcanoes at its summit. Following behind two German motorcyclists on huge BMW's, Jan and I left the port, and after a few miles along a smooth road, we turned onto a gravel track, which half a mile later melted away completely into a field of loose stones and sand.

Having never ridden a motorcycle on difficult terrain before, I was uncertain about continuing. When the two Germans parked their motorcycles at the base of the hill, I was about to do the same, until Jan appeared beside me.

'Come on,' he shouted over the throb of his engine. 'They're just being precious about their bikes. What's the use of a motorcycle if it doesn't give you freedom?'

Then, with a twist of his wrist, Jan shot off up the slope, and not wanting to lose face, I gunned my throttle, hoping to follow him up the steep incline. A second later, I was lying face down in the dirt at the bottom of a huge hole with my motorcycle on top of me, which is exactly what I deserved for trying to scale a volcano on my first attempt at riding off-road.

'Well, that's one under your belt at least,' said Jan, as he helped to stand the bike upright and stem the flow of petrol that was leaking from its fuel tank. The handlebars were a little twisted, but it was nothing that my dependable Dutchman could not fix. Once vertical again, I jumped back on the machine, and on the second attempt, I made it to the top of the volcano, where I received two enthusiastic handshakes from the pair of Germans, who proclaimed me to be equal parts stupid and brave.

Of the one thousand mud volcanoes on earth, four hundred of them lie in Azerbaijan, popping up sporadically across the arid countryside. The volcano we had scaled was the highest around, and at its top, we found a crater full of gurgling grey clay. Following four filthy days at the port, wracked with boredom, just to watch the mud bubble and boil was enchanting. Shortly after we arrived, the cyclists and hitch-hikers also made their way to the summit, and it was not long before Cody turned to the group and said:

'Well it's nice to watch, but I wonder what it'd be like to jump inside?'

'Are you serious?' replied Bertie.

'It might be the only bath we get for months,' said Jan.

A minute later, one by one, we bombed into the grey mud, each of us disappearing for a moment beneath the surface, before rising to the top covered in a silken sheen. In the thick, warm liquid, it was impossible to sink or swim - all we could do was lay back and float atop the dense ooze. As the volcano coughed and spluttered, I felt bubbles of hot gas pop against my feet, and we joked about the prospect of an eruption. I laughed out loud as I imagined a column of half-naked tourists shooting up into the sky atop a geyser of mud. It certainly would have been an unusual sight for the local Azeris.

After sliding down the slick crater on our backs, we found a second aperture, full of fizzing salt-water, which we threw ourselves into to clean off the dirt of the first volcano. People who were only strangers a few days before stood tenderly wiping filth from each other's eyes, whilst those who had refrained from the mud-bath sat down and started making dinner. Somehow, somewhere, one of the cyclists had managed to acquire a few bottles of wine, which alongside the fumes of the volcanoes gave a gentle shimmer to the evening.

Not long after dinner, mats and blankets were unrolled in anticipation of sleep, as people either failed to notice or willingly ignored the little yellow scorpions running around in the sand. High on the hill, it was cooler than by the docks, and the gas of the volcanoes kept the mosquitoes away. Soon after lying down, I fell into a deep and dreamless sleep, the best I had enjoyed for days, but I was woken abruptly at dawn by the sound of frantic motion.

'Hurry, Sam. Time to pack your things,' said Jan, who was folding his tent away nearby.

'What's the rush?' I asked, still groggy with sleep.

'That,' said Jan, as he pointed towards the distant docks, where workers were running across the concrete to a vast blue hulk that had just appeared beside the moorings. At last, our boat had arrived.

Chapter Ten

Through the black Tartar tents he pass'd, which stood
Clustering like bee-hives on the low flat strand
Of Oxus, where the summer-floods o'erflow
When the sun melts the snows in high Pamere.

-Matthew Arnold, 'Sohrab and Rustum'

An hour after boarding the *Professor Gul,* I was challenged to a game of chess in the passenger lounge of the ship by Azat, an old Turkmen carpet dealer with solid gold teeth who took seven sugars in his tea. The stakes, Azat said, were simple. If I won, I would receive a fine Turkmen carpet as wide as his chest. If he won, I had to promise to get his daughter into a British university, or failing that, try to secure him an audience with the Queen.

In between sucking sugar lumps and moving chess pieces, Azat explained that he was on his way to sell carpets in the bazaars of Bukhara, but first, he had some business in Kazakhstan. His knowledge of English was scant, but as I ventured deeper into Central Asia, I would come to appreciate how much meaning can be conveyed through gestures alone. Azat, in particular, was an adept mimic, and through a series of spirited performances, he helped me to understand that his business in Kazakhstan involved clandestine dog fights and illicit gambling - a side venture he had established after his daughter was born in anticipation of her expensive university fees.

A businessman to the bone, Azat was obsessed with the cost of everything. One by one, he asked me the price of my motorcycle, my helmet, my boots, my books, and every item of my clothing. In his country, Turkmenistan, he told me that some things were cheap, whilst other things were wildly expensive. Gas and fuel, for example, were free for Turkmens to use, but matches were considered so precious that Azat's family kept their gas stoves burning day and night. If I could get his daughter into a good university, he promised that he would write me a sponsorship letter so that I could visit his home and see these things for myself.

Turkmenistan, with its empty deserts, its craters of burning gas, and its history of eccentric dictators had certainly caught my curiosity, but as half of all foreign visas are immediately and inexplicably declined, I had chosen an alternative route across Central Asia, meaning my talk with Azat was as close as I would come to his country.

Knowing this, I was eager to document our meeting, and as I spoke with Azat, I scribbled in my notebook, recording scraps of our mimed conversation. At one point, the curious businessman reached out and picked up the book to leaf through its pages, before touching it to his forehead and whispering *Mashallah* - his amazement stemming from the fact that he had never seen so many handwritten lines of a foreign language before.

Sensing his astonishment, I decided to promise Azat a place in my book, and immediately the size of the carpet I was due to receive grew to the dimensions of a dinner table. Then, after we lunched together in the ship's galley and cemented our friendship with a photograph, the size of my carpet grew again, and by the end of the crossing, he had assured me that a rug half as wide as the Caspian would be waiting for me upon my return to England.

There were many passengers aboard the *Professor Gul* like Azat, mostly Turkmen, Kazakh, and Russian traders, on their way to deliver goods to Central Asian cities along the 'New Silk Road'. I had been told that the crossing would feature bad weather, uncomfortable conditions, and rough company, but these reports turned out to be fictions, peddled by mythomaniacs from western Europe who could not travel far from home without having the world believe they had faced immeasurable hardship. Compared to the ferry port, the ship was the pinnacle of luxury. Jan and I had an air-conditioned cabin to ourselves, the galley served three cooked meals a day, and the burly, unshaven, gilt-gummed truck drivers were the most mild-mannered and pleasant travelling companions I could have wished for. It was impossible to walk through the lounge without being offered a seat, a cup of sweet tea, and an invitation to join their conversation. In fact, the only fault I could find with the ferry was that the crossing did not take a little longer.

The second day, I set about exploring in earnest, and I found that the entire ship was open to passengers. Starting in the hold, amidst the reek of ship's fuel, I checked on my motorcycle, which was still balanced precariously next to Jan's. No ropes or cables had been given to us to secure our machines when we boarded, the only reassurance coming from a deck-hand who had promised us that the crossing would be 'short and gentle, *Inshallah*'. At first, I had been sceptical, but the sailor proved to be a man of his word, and thankfully our cycles were still standing when we docked in Kazakhstan.

From the bowels of the ship, I climbed to its summit, emerging on the bridge, where I was greeted by the *Professor Gul's* First Mate, a man named Ali. Courteously, he gave me a guided tour of the bridge, showcasing all of the ship's instrument panels, half of which were dark without power. Stopping before a cracked window that looked down onto the main deck, Ali gave out a low chuckle. Below us, a member of the crew was hanging from the hook of a crane, dangling five decks above the Caspian, whilst a mechanic fiddled with its control panel.

'Crane is broken,' he chortled in his simple English. 'But no worry. Only for lifeboats, and we not have many.'

Under the hot midday sun, aside from the comical crew, the deck had been empty. But as the day began to wane, passengers emerged from the quiet corners of the ship where they had been dozing all afternoon. Truck drivers, dressed in string vests, gathered for an hour of exercise, running loops around the deck and challenging one another to press-up competitions. Meanwhile, a handful of travellers gathered quietly to watch the sunset. As we waited patiently for daylight to dip below the horizon, just before the sun touched the waters of the Caspian, a loud cheer rang out from the Turkmen truckers. Turning around, we discovered that a tiny, wiry man had been proclaimed champion of the sports tournament. Hoisting him aloft, the man's friends paraded him around the deck, throwing him high into the air in honour of his victory, his wide grin flashing brilliant gold in the fading dusk.

Jan and I had gone to bed that night not knowing how much longer the crossing would take, but we both hoped for several more days of idleness. Unfortunately for us, it had just turned midnight when the ship's cook ran down the corridors, banging her pots against the cabin doors and screaming for everybody to wake. An hour later, all the passengers were stood in the lounge in neat rows facing a company of Kazakh soldiers. A huge dog was unleashed to nose our bags and our ankles, while the commanding officer delivered a speech in Russian. Our luggage was searched twice, then we were searched twice, whilst the officer stared for long intervals into our eyes. His voice was stern, his manner severe, and his face, like most of his soldiers, was distinctly Kazakh, signalling our arrival in Central Asia.

Those thorough searches were just the start of an agonising eight-hour introduction to Central Asian bureaucracy. Everything at the port was done with paper and ink - there were no computers or machines - and each stage of the process brought with it another handful of forms requiring another set of stamps from an office on the opposite side of the port. Gradually, we made our way through the Kafkaesque riddle of customs and immigration, saying goodbye along the way to people we now considered close friends, who pedalled, walked, or rode away as soon as they were free, vanishing into the glare of the port's bright floodlights.

Eventually, long after the sun had risen, Jan and I were finally released and found ourselves standing at a petrol station with three hundred miles of road between us and the Uzbek border. Having been awake all night, we should have rested for the day in the nearby town of Aktau, but sleep was inconceivable to us both. For weeks we had wondered about this moment, our first encounter with Central Asia, waiting for it with both excitement and apprehension, and now that it had finally arrived after so many days of waiting, I think we both feared it might suddenly escape us.

So after filling up our fuel tanks, we took a road running north-east through plains of brown scrubland and started slowly making our way across the Ustyurt Plateau. Aside from a few dusty hills on the horizon, and small crowds of striding camels, the vast clay desert was featureless. It would continue this way for over six hundred miles, the same barren, arid country, shifting slightly from clay to sand at the Uzbek border, where the Ustyurt bleeds into the Kyzylkum desert, but otherwise remaining unchanged. Above the land, even the sky was featureless, devoid of clouds, empty of colour - just a vast expanse, blanched by the sun, unfathomably wide.

In forty-five-degree sunshine, standing still was intolerable, so we rode all day, grateful for the small breeze brought by riding our motorcycles. But that breeze was little comfort in a desert so dry that it felt as if the blood in my veins was turning to vapour. The country was one long, unwatered nothingness, endlessly vacant and viciously hostile. And yet, even in that towering wilderness, we did still occasionally pass little steel homes, alone in the desert, walled in on all sides by hundreds of miles of empty space, prison-like in their exile.

Two hundred and fifty miles later, just as evening was beginning to fall, we reached a small settlement named Beyneu, not far from the border. Little more than a handful of gridded streets and an old military outpost, Beyneu was a bleak town, but we were at least able to find fuel, food, and water. Knowing that this would be the last opportunity we would have to supply ourselves before entering the Kyzylkum desert, it was essential that Jan and I acquired enough petrol to last the journey. Running out of fuel was by far our greatest concern: no supply of water we could carry would sustain a three-hundred-mile trek across the desert.

The only vessels Jan and I had to carry additional fuel were a collection of empty plastic bottles which we planned to tape to our motorcycles. With these bottles and a full tank, I calculated that I should have a range of roughly four hundred and fifty miles - fifteen miles more than I needed to reach Khiva, provided the maps were accurate and that I did not suffer any loss or leakage. The margins were about as fine as they could be.

After tracking down a petrol station, we motioned for the attendant to fill both our bikes and our bottles, but he waved us away, gesturing aggressively towards the plastic vessels and letting us know that he was only licensed to fill vehicles. We pleaded with him, but he was adamant. This was the only petrol station in Beyneu, and without a full supply of fuel, we would never make it across Uzbekistan. Desperate, we were contemplating offering a bribe when a military police-car unexpectedly arrived and an officer stepped out, motioning for the attendant to join him at the kiosk.

'Quick, Sam, let's get to it,' said Jan, sensing an opportunity.

Nervously, we began filling our bottles and hiding them in our rucksacks whilst the policeman kept the attendant engaged in a discussion. We had six bottles in total, and the first five we filled successfully, with Jan holding them steady whilst I operated the fuel hose. But on the last attempt, I squeezed the trigger too hard and accidentally sent a spume of gasoline firing back out of the bottle, which flew straight into Jan's open eyes.

'Shit. Are you alright?' I asked, worrying that I had just blinded him. 'Do you need me to get a doctor?'

'I'll be fine,' said Jan, placing a calm hand on my shoulder whilst clutching his face with the other. 'Just get the rest of the fuel.'

Whilst filling our remaining bottle, I watched as Jan staggered over to a small patch of grass which was being watered by a pitiful sprinkler at the edge of the station. Half-blind, he unhooked the hose and let it dribble into his eyes, scrubbing his face with the green water and spitting petrol from out of his mouth. A minute later, he returned, and despite the red band of raw skin stretching from one of his temples to the other, he shot me a big grin.

'I needed a wash anyway,' he laughed, simply happy that we had our petrol, even if it had nearly cost him his eyes.

When the attendant returned, he was astonished that two motorcycle tanks could hold the forty litres of fuel that we paid for, but he let us go without a word of questioning. A little further down the road, we stopped and took the plastic bottles from our bags and taped them to our machines, the pale yellow liquid inside sparkling in the dusk. If a single bottle leaked or fell onto the road and split, we would never reach Khiva - a danger we had no choice but to accept. Then, after checking the bottles were secure, we took one last look at Beyneu, before turning towards the Uzbek border and riding away into the desert.

***

Despite having been awake for two days, I could not sleep that first night in the Kyzylkum. Not far from me, I knew that Jan would be sleeping as soundly as if he were in his bed at home in the Netherlands. His advice to me had been simple: close your eyes and forget the world. But I lay awake, plagued by visions of scorpions slicing their way into my tent and of serpents burrowing up out of the ground. For a time, I tried to be rational, and then I set rationality aside for fatalism. Humbled by all the wilderness around me, in the end, I just lay down and let the desert swallow me whole.

Early the next day, a fierce wind ripped up my tent pegs, collapsing the walls of my bedroom and smothering me in thin folds of nylon. By the time I battled my way out of the jumble of sheets and poles, dawn was breaking, and a light drizzle had begun to fall. The idea of rain in such surroundings seemed an absurdity; only the day before, it had felt as if we were in the driest place on earth. But the morning dew was just the Kyzylkum's way of mocking us. It began, built up our hopes for a cool day of riding, and then ended, rapidly substituted for the old, familiar, debilitating heat, which we were fools to have ever thought could be avoided.

The evening before, it had taken us two hours to ride ten miles from Beyneu to our camp. Shortly after leaving the town, the road had disintegrated into a trail of sand and loose stones, deeply scored by the tracks of heavy trucks. As we rode, several trucks had appeared behind us, each wrapped in an indecipherable cloud of dust. After passing us with a roar, they had disappeared into the distance, still swaddled in sand, their true shape unknowable. Blinded by dust, the drivers did not even notice Jan and I trundling along inches from their wheels. When darkness forced us to stop, I had felt momentary relief, but the knowledge that the Uzbek border was still fifty miles away brought little comfort.

Our dinner and breakfast, which had been tied to the back of my motorcycle, had disappeared somewhere on the shattered road, so we set out that second day on empty stomachs. Having grown up riding motorcycles on his family's farm in the Netherlands, Jan was completely at ease on this difficult terrain, and there was something poetic in the way his machine glided effortlessly from sandbank to sandbank. Whenever he passed, I looked over to see the same unshakeable grin spread across his face. For Jan, riding roughshod for six hours along a broken road was his idea of a perfect morning.

For me, however, desert roads were still a novelty, and my wretched motorcycle protested fiercely as it was thrown from bump to rut and sent sliding sideways through knee-deep sand. I fell off more times than I can remember that morning, steadily collecting an impressive archive of bruises. But the road was so poor I could not travel at speed, and the desert sand made for a soft landing. So long as my fuel bottles remained intact, I was happy to take a few tumbles, and my overheated, dust-choked engine was also glad of the regular chances to rest.

At times, the dust was so thick and the going so rough that it was difficult to know where the road ended and where the desert began. Thankfully, to help guide us, bands of labourers appeared sporadically across the landscape, busily constructing a highway. This project was one of many occurring across Central Asia, funded by the Chinese, who had plans to build a 'New Silk Road' connecting the ancient trading centres of Central Asia with virgin asphalt. Judging by how diligently the labourers were working, if I had undertaken my journey just a year later, it might have been possible to ride on smooth tarmac all the way from Kazakhstan to Beijing.

It was afternoon by the time we reached the border, where we sat down to a breakfast of stale bread and eggs, cross-legged on the floor of a small wooden hut alongside a company of truckers who offered us vodka in between our sips of tea. I find vodka a difficult drink at the best of times, but it is especially quarrelsome when it is the home-brew of a Kazakh trucker served at forty degrees centigrade. Nevertheless, Jan and I raised a glass, partly for courage (the drivers were drinking their liquor like water, and we had to share the road with them), and partly in celebration, because somewhere amid the desert, back along the broken road, my milometer had rolled over and passed the ten thousand kilometre mark.

On the Uzbek side, I took two-hundred US dollars to a currency exchange and received a plastic bag stuffed full of paper notes, totalling one and a half million som. Seeing me load my bag of cash onto my motorcycle, a border guard came across and told me to make sure it was tied down properly.

'The next two hundred kilometres of road are... problematic,' he said. 'But after that, it is as smooth as silk all the way to Samarkand.'

I sincerely hoped he was right.

'Why are you in the Kyzylkum? You two are scientists?' asked the guard, gesturing to our motorcycles.

'He's a madman who crosses deserts just for fun,' I said, pointing at Jan. 'And I'm a writer, chronicling a long journey.'

At this, the guard gave a low hum of approval.

'The desert is a poem, for those who want it to be,' he said, speaking mystically, before clapping us both on the back and wishing us luck on the road.

On the other side of the border, the strong Uzbek sun drained the life out of everything it touched, and the flat road ran like a collapsed vein through bleached and barren country. In Turkic languages, Kyzylkum means red sand, but the desert was not red, or gold, or brown. It was a pale, colourless husk, bled dry and burnt to a crisp, so pallid that even twilight fell in grey-scale.

All-day I had been losing little pieces of my machine each time I collided with an unexpected crater in the road. My tool bag had vanished, one wing mirror had shattered, and an indicator had been lost forever. My motorcycle was slowly fragmenting beneath me, and when I hit a pot-hole so hard that my front fender snapped in two, I decided to put an end to the attrition.

Jan and I stopped in the very middle of the desert, beside an old wattle and daub wall which rose absurdly out of the sand and provided a slither of shelter for our camp. After an hour tending to our motorcycles, healing their wounds and replenishing their fluids, we set about raising our tents. As we chatted, I began to wonder how a wall had come to be built in such a place. In my life, I had never been anywhere so remote. But then, whilst I was fiddling with my guylines, Jan suddenly stood up and said:

'Sam, there's somebody coming.'

'What?' I asked in disbelief.

'There is a man walking toward us,' laughed Jan. 'Where on earth has he come from?'

A minute later, a tired, weather-beaten Uzbek arrived at the edge of our camp and introduced himself in broken Russian as Urig. After pointing to a distant mound, through mimes and gestures, he signalled that he lived nearby, and let us know that we were welcome to stay with him that night if we wished.

At first, I was too astonished to speak. The thought that someone could exist in such a place was incomprehensible. By the look of Urig, standing there in his withered skin and his tattered clothes, his existence was a hard and lonely one. Whilst I speechlessly grappled with this stranger's improbable presence, Jan introduced us using the few Russian phrases he knew. Though we were touched by Urig's offer, we were both exhausted beyond measure, and we knew that an evening in Urig's home would mean hours spent straining to make conversation through hand gestures and pantomime. Urig understood our fatigue, and he accepted our polite declines with equanimity.

'How do you think he survives?' I wondered aloud, whilst Urig sat and watched us finish putting up our tents.

'I can't even begin to imagine,' said Jan, casting his eyes across the desert, which was empty from horizon to horizon.

Urig stayed for a while, shook our hands, and then made ready to leave, but he had a final message for us before his departure. Pulling a necklace out from under his shirt, he was eager to show us both a large canine tooth which he wore as a pendant. Growling and curling his hands into claws, he hopped around like a cat, before cocking an imaginary gun and firing two shots across the landscape. After waving his arm in a wide circle that encompassed all the desert around us, he performed his animal impression again, except this time, it felt like a warning. Pointing at the knife lying by my feet, Urig nodded his approval, then he walked away to his distant home, vanishing into the Uzbek wilderness.

Despite Urig's warning of wildcats, exhaustion meant I slept well that second night in the Kyzylkum, and the desert was the prettier for it in the morning. We left again at dawn when the half-lit landscape was at its most bewitching, continuing along the same straight line we had been following for over three hundred miles. However harsh the environment, at least we did not have to fear taking a wrong turn: there seemed to be only one road in the whole of Uzbekistan, running south-east along the entire length of the country.

This day, though, the scenery did begin to change, and soon small shoots of grass could be seen lining the banks of the desert. As the road dropped down off the dry plateau, the air grew thick and heavy, and without warning, we suddenly found ourselves sharing the road with trains of camels, driven by shepherds who guided their flocks between fields of scrubland. Soon after the camels, I sensed that we were nearing civilisation, and then we passed a remote, sand-coloured cemetery, full of ornate tombs, marking the return of death, which was the return of life, and the end of the desert's dry sterility.

A few hours later, after three days of riding across the desert, Jan and I finally reached Khiva. For hundreds of years, travellers had been arriving at the doors to the city, seeking shelter after arduous journeys. For us, Khiva marked the end of the most difficult part of our Kyzylkum crossing. We entered the city as two proud but broken men, wearied after six hundred miles of riding through despicable heat. Still, we were grateful that our engines had reduced a journey that would have once taken months to just a matter of days. I could not imagine how the traders, adventurers, and imperial agents of old must have felt at their first sight of Khiva, limping towards the oases across the hot sands on their burnt and blistered feet.

Like a pale wave rising out of the desert, a thick wall ran around the edge of the city, protecting the Itchan Kala, Khiva's ancient inner town. Parking our motorcycles beneath the city gates, we ran up the battlements, eager to see the skyline. When we reached the top, we discovered a maze of desert-coloured streets, all built from the same pale stone, as if the whole city had been crafted out of the sands of the Kyzylkum. Every home, shop, school, and marketplace was identical in hue, built from the same dusty bricks, quarried from the surrounding countryside. But amidst the uniform paleness, there were also flashes of colour, precious patches of bright blue tiles that cloaked domes and ran in rings around tall minarets like ribbons of glazed sky.

As we walked further along the wall, other portions of the city were gradually revealed, bringing more and more flashes of brilliant blue. Then, halfway along the battlements, we finally caught a glimpse of Khiva's centre and its famous unfinished minaret, the Kalta Minor. Standing in the middle of a faded square, the squat tower was coated in every imaginable shade of blue and turquoise, its bright teal tiles standing out in rebellion against the pale stones surrounding them. Burning brightly beneath the midday sun, the minaret shone like a beacon, its vast, blue hulk casting a signal across the landscape, drawing caravans in from the desert with enticing promises of shade, shelter, and water.

In need of sustenance ourselves, Jan and I clambered down from the wall and entered the city, where we sat down at a table outside a modest kitchen. Once again reverting to mime, we let a shy girl know that we were hungry, and she went to fetch two servings of lag'mon – a central Asian staple of noodles, meat, and vegetables, served in a tomato broth. On the counter beside our table, I spotted a box of matches fastened to the bar with string and thought of Azat and the Turkmen with their perpetually burning stoves. Just as in Turkmenistan, matches were precious in Khiva, but unlike their neighbours, the Uzbeks did not receive free gas, so when the girl returned with two bowls, our lunch inside them was cold.

Later that day, whilst Jan slept in the dormitory of a home-stay, I returned to the Itchan Kala on foot and walked into the heart of the city. In the cooler afternoon, Khiva was even more enchanting, and it seemed to me that there was not a single street which did not lead to the foot of a towering minaret, or which was not banked by glittering domes. When the narrow alleyways did open into squares, the empty spaces were enclosed on all sides by elegant iwans - the lavishly patterned, paper-thin facades common across Persia and Central Asia. Behind the iwans, the contemplative chambers of mosques and madrasas branched out from silent courtyards, which in their empty serenity gave the inner town an air of unbreakable calm. But Khiva had not always been a peaceful city.

In the middle of the nineteenth century, the khanate of Khiva, along with its close neighbour the emirate of Bukhara, found itself caught between two imperial forces. To the north, the Russian Empire stretched deep into the lands now belonging to Kazakhstan, while to the south, over the mountains of Afghanistan, lay the frontier of British India. The deserts and mountains of Central Asia were, at one time, all that separated the two mighty rivals.

The British knew that the Russians coveted India, and their concern grew in the early 1820s when reports began to circulate that the Tsar had sent imperial agents to assess the viability of an invasion of India by way of Central Asia. In response, the British sent emissaries to the Khan of Khiva and the Emir of Bukhara, hoping to win their loyalty and to persuade them that Russian troops must not be allowed to cross their land at any cost.

For nearly a century, an intricate tournament of espionage and diplomacy played out across the region, with agents from both empires arriving at Khiva unsure whether they would be welcomed or slaughtered by the capricious Khan. To add to the danger, diplomats and soldiers often had to make perilous journeys across the desert, living under the constant threat of being discovered by hostile natives or agents of the enemy. British historians have since dubbed this period of Central Asian history the 'Great Game', but such a title trivialises the sacrifices made by agents of both sides, many of whom lost their lives.

In the end, Khiva fell to the Russians in 1873, but the Tsar never staged his invasion of British India. Khiva's last Khan, Sayid Abdullah, abdicated in 1920, four years before the khanate of Khiva was divided between the Turkmen and Uzbek states of the newly formed USSR. Nearly seventy years later, those states became the modern nations of Turkmenistan and Uzbekistan, and all that remains today of the old Khanate where the fate of empires was once decided is a small, unknown city in the middle of the Uzbek desert.

***

Jan and I recovered well in Khiva, but after a few days, we started to become restless. On our way to the city, we had crossed the wide Amu Darya River - or to use its famed Latin name, the Oxus - which runs down into Uzbekistan from the Afghan and Tajik mountains. We both knew that each day we waited meant that we were a day closer to the Pamiri winter, and we were desperate to cross Tajikistan before the snows started to fall. Ever mindful of what lay ahead, after three days in the city, we left Khiva early in the morning and headed south, skirting the Turkmen border, along a road that ran parallel to the banks of the Amu Darya.

Several hours later, we arrived in Bukhara, an oasis city lying in the delta of the Zeravshan River, at the juncture of two deserts: the red sanded Kyzylkum and the black sanded Karakum. Like Khiva, Bukhara was once a prominent trading centre which for centuries provided shelter and repast for caravans travelling between the Far East and southern Europe along the Silk Road. For Jan and I, it marked the end of our ride across the desert. From Bukhara, we had only to race up the Zeravshan Valley to Samarkand and then turn east and enter the Fann mountains, which would bring new challenges of cold and ice, but at least the days of drought and heat were finally behind us.

Though Bukhara only lies on the fringes of the desert, when we arrived at midday, it was still unbearably hot, and the city's streets were empty. Once again, I left Jan sleeping in a hostel and strolled out towards the city alone. My first destination was the Ark of Bukhara, a vast fortress with bulging walls three times the size of those at Khiva. As I walked towards the stone battlements, I remembered reading of a local legend which told how the first Ark was built by a boy who sought the love of a royal princess. The Emir of Bukhara, who disapproved of the union, gave the boy permission to marry his daughter, but only if he could build a fortress within a bull's skin. Unperturbed by the seemingly impossible challenge, the boy slaughtered a bull, slit its hide into thin strips, and then made a rope from the skin which he lay down in the desert and built a fortress inside. On that same site, over thousands of years, fortresses were built and destroyed, until the Ark reached its current, massive iteration, which after surviving centuries of conflict, looks set to stand forever.

Before the nineteenth century, there was little contact between the Western world and the Emirate of Bukhara, and the Emirs treated foreigners with even deeper suspicion than the Khans of Khiva. In front of the Ark's ceremonial entrance, I walked across a square which was once favoured by the Emirs as a site for public executions. It was there that on the 17th June 1842, Nasrullah Khan ordered the beheading of Colonel Charles Stoddart and Captain Arthur Connolly, two agents of the East India Company who became some of the most famous victims of the Great Game.

Stoddart had arrived in Bukhara first, in 1838, hoping to establish an alliance with Nasrullah. His fatal error was to refuse to bow in the presence of the Emir at their first meeting, an indiscretion which earned Stoddart a place in the city gaol. With no indication that his compatriot would ever be released, Connolly was dispatched to rescue Stoddart, but his mission was another catastrophic failure, and Connolly was also thrown in prison. A short while later, both men were executed on charges of spying for the British Empire, and for years afterwards the British government discouraged all officers and subjects from setting foot in Turkestan.

Quite by accident, on my way to the city-centre after visiting the Ark, I stumbled across Zindon prison, the gaol where the two English officers were held. Walking through a series of small chambers, I passed a pair of shackles chained to the wall, and then I found myself in a low room staring into a hole six metres deep. This was the infamous 'bug pit' of Zindon, a dark, filthy cave, only accessible by rope, which was reserved for the most ill-fated prisoners. Stoddart had spent years in this hole, scraping about in total darkness, whilst the prison guards poured piles of scorpions, snakes, and insects upon his head. A makeshift wooden grill had been placed over its entrance to stop tourists from inadvertently falling in, but no sign explained what had occurred there. It felt as if the bug pit, unhappy with its relegation to the status of an artefact, chose to remain unannounced, patiently waiting for one last victim.

A short walk from the prison, I found myself in the centre of Bukhara, standing beneath a twelfth-century minaret which had a nefarious history of its own. Built to carry the muezzin's call far across the city, the Kalyan minaret was also used by the Emirs of Bukhara as an instrument of justice, with criminals regularly being thrown from its upper gallery to meet their deaths on the city's streets below. This punishment was especially popular during the violent period between

1917 and 1920 when the final Emir battled against the Russian troops of the Red Army. Eventually, the city fell to the Bolsheviks, and upon realising defeat was inevitable, the Emir took the Royal Treasury and fled to Kabul, ordering upon his exit that the Ark be blown to pieces so that its secret chambers, especially the harem, not be desecrated by the Russians.

A century later, it was difficult to imagine the graceful, ageless city ever suffering such unrest. The cries of battle and the song of the executioner's sword were fragments of a distant past. What remained of Bukhara was a city, like Khiva, which had been sculpted from the desert, built from walls of sand and sky-blue tiles that pooled upon glistening domes and ran in waves around narrow towers. In the silent midday heat, I paced across its breathtaking squares, amazed that two beautiful cities had survived for so long so close together, despite being surrounded by the extreme wilderness of the desert and both suffering periods of heavy violence.

But long before the invasion of the Bolsheviks or the turbulent decades of the Great Game, Bukhara was once the cultural capital of the Islamic world, second only in fame to Baghdad. On my way around the city, I caught glimpses of madrasas where the finest scholars in Islam once trained, and beside the madrasas, I encountered mausoleums where the great men of Bukhara's history lay encased in decadent tombs. Walking along empty streets, I passed under the shadow of the Kalyan minaret and entered the adjoining mosque, where eloquent patterns of tiles adorned every inch of its courtyard. Beyond the walls of the temple, the leaning towers and shattered domes of Bhukara re-arranged themselves with every few steps that I took, an endless archive of cities repeatedly re-framed in each of the mosque's many archways. And within the temple itself, all around the ancient walls, blue mosaics curled and coiled in leaps of flawless symmetry, looking as fresh as if they had been hung only days before, the lustre of their youth preserved through the centuries by the dry desert air.

Chapter Eleven

Mirth, Spring, to linger in a garden fair,
What more has earth to give?

- Shams al-Din Hafiz Shirazi, 'To Linger in a Garden Fair'

I had been in Tajikistan for little more than an hour when the first real mechanical calamity of my journey struck. Jan and I had just passed the village of Panjakent and were riding up a steep road in the western Fann mountains when my engine let out a squeal and abruptly lost all power. Coasting to a stop, I got off to inspect the cycle but could see no obvious issue. I was just about to start my engine again when Jan called out:

'Sam, I wouldn't do that if I were you.'

'Why is that Jan?' I asked, as he cast me a look like that of a tutor disappointed in his pupil.

'Because your chain is no longer attached to your sprockets...' he said, pointing to my limp chain which lay sprawled upon the ground. It seemed that four months of riding the motorcycle had not yet imbued me with the level of mechanical proficiency I had hoped it might.

As Jan rolled out his tool bag, I lay down in the dirt on the side of the road and tried to fathom how my chain had detached itself. Whilst I set to work unravelling the tangled links, I soon developed the sense that we were being watched, and a minute after our arrival, amidst a concert of giggles and yelps, a gaggle of Tajik children came bounding down the road from a cluster of houses, carrying bottles of cool water and bags of dried fruit for us. After delivering their gifts, the children stood around watching, weighing our spanners, prodding our backs, and goading each other to jump on the back of the bikes when we were not looking. Dark-haired, amber skinned, with bright green eyes, they had the widest smiles I had ever seen.

Though we managed to put the chain back onto its sprockets, Jan realised that it was severely worn. This meant that at various stages during its revolution, the chain would go from very tight, to very slack, to very tight again. However we adjusted it, riding ran the risk of both snapping the chain and the risk of it flying off due to looseness. Either eventuality could lead to the chain wrapping around the spokes of my rear wheel, which at speed would spell disaster. I desperately needed a replacement, but Dushanbe was over one hundred miles away, and we had only a few hours of daylight left.

Our journey that morning had taken longer than expected because of delays at the border. After four hours of waiting, and a dozen different pieces of paperwork, Jan and I had finally been granted entry into Tajikistan. Leaving the deserts of Uzbekistan behind, we had passed into green countryside, following a gently sloping road up towards the Fann mountains. As the peaks grew in size and stature, it was not long before we found ourselves riding through valleys cast in deep shadow, where small earthen villages clung to the mountain-sides, almost invisible in their camouflage. Through every village we passed, dogs barked their disapproval, old men nodded greetings at us, and children left their games in the mulberry groves to run out onto the road with outstretched hands, begging for high fives at fifty miles an hour.

Sitting in the dirt near Panjakent, I caught sight of myself in my wing-mirror and wondered what the Tajik children surrounding us thought of me. With four months of motor grease under my nails and a black smudge running down one side of my face, I looked half-wild crouching there in the dust. Though I knew I was no mechanic, I certainly wore the pretences of one, with oil stains on my trousers, crusts of Azeri mud on my scuffed jacket, and the unshakable stench of Kazakh petrol clinging to my clothes. I also had two purple patches of burnt skin on the backs of my hands, outlined by the holes in my riding gloves, which had grown several shades deeper under the strong Uzbek sun. As dishevelled and unkempt as I was, I looked upon these marks of the road as badges to be worn with pride, every scuff, stain, and scar testifying to some small portion of my journey.

To the children, Jan and I must have seemed especially strange as we wallowed in the dirt, muttering curses in two different languages, hammering and yanking my stubborn chain into place. But they remained champions of our cause, fetching more water and holding out our tools for us like a company of eager apprentices. When my chain was finally back in place, I restarted my engine to spirited applause and cries of excitement, and as Jan and I tore away along the asphalt road, it was now the children that I saw in my wing-mirrors, racing one another with outstretched arms, riding imaginary motorcycles off into the mountains.

As we climbed eastwards towards Tajikistan's capital, the road followed the curves of the Zeravshan River, growing more impressive at every turn. Meaning 'spreader of gold' in Persian, the Zeravshan's upper reaches are rumoured to be abundant with treasure, and down in the lower Fann, the sluggish waterway gleamed like silver as it meandered between the walls of red rock that bound the valley-sides like colossal jaws. But as the landscape grew steeper and more fierce, the river turned from silver to white, and the road soon began to struggle to find its way through the rocky peaks, curling back and forth upon itself, until eventually, left with no other choice, it turned towards the rock-face and disappeared into the mountainside.

I had been hearing reports of the Anzob tunnel for some time. It was another Central Asian horror that featured prominently in the mythology of most Western tourists who had visited the region. At an altitude of two thousand seven hundred metres, the tunnel stretches for three miles through the belly of a mountain, reducing the travel time to Dushanbe by hours. But because the tunnel had opened prematurely, before any lights or ventilation were installed, it quickly gained a notorious reputation. Cyclists, in particular, loved to whisper of its menace, telling stories of their kind who had emerged from the tunnel retching and bleeding, half-suffocated by the poisonous fumes that collect inside.

Short on time, Jan and I had no choice but to take the route leading to Anzob, and before long I found myself riding towards a crude hole cut into the earth, surrounded on both sides by rock-falls, into which whole cars began to disappear in front of me. Once through the archway, amidst Anzob's reeking fumes, the darkness was enormous. More than merely the absence of light, the gloom seemed like a physical thing - an insidious potion of murk, shadow, and shade which dripped down from the roof of the tunnel and rendered my headlights useless.

Lifting my visor, I could just see the tail lights of a truck in front of me, but exposing my eyes caused them to burn, so I had no choice but to keep my visor down and ride blindly on, trying to feel the camber of the road through the seat of my cycle whilst Jan followed behind me. Several times, holes in the ground sent me dropping unexpectedly through the darkness. Falling off the bike in that tunnel would have been like falling through empty space for eternity. When we finally emerged on the other side into a bright arena of snow-tipped mountains, it was like returning to another world, and we stopped for a while on the side of the road, glad just to be able to breathe and see again.

Several hours later, as darkness was beginning to fall, we arrived in the smog-smothered streets of Dushanbe, and my motorcycle limped to the door of the city's only hostel with its chain miraculously still intact. The following morning, knowing that I could not prolong the motorcycle's neglect any further, I left the hostel with the address of Dushanbe's only motorcycle mechanic scribbled on my hand, and as I rode across the city, I had a horrible presentiment that my time with the cycle was coming to an end. I had been told to go to the garage and ask for Azziz. If he could not help me, the receptionist had said, then nobody in Dushanbe could.

I arrived at the dark, deserted workshop to find a drunk man loudly snoring atop a grubby old sofa. After some heavy prodding, the man rolled over to tell me that he was not Azziz, before aggressively asking that I leave him alone to sleep. With nothing to do but sit and wait, I walked back outside, just as an ancient Vespa petered around the corner, ridden by a debonair man wearing corduroy trousers, brown leather brogues, and a red handkerchief tied around his neck.

'Azziz?' I asked, as he stepped off the Vespa.

'Pah! Azziz!' cried the man in a strong French accent. 'Does such a man exist?'

Ignoring my confused expression, the Frenchman kicked his front wheel and said:

'The clutch. C'est mort. I have been waiting here for two days, but still no Azziz.'

Maxime, as I would later learn, was an engineer who had taken a career break and decided to travel from Paris to Ulaanbaatar on a thirty-year-old Vespa. He, too, was in need of the mysterious Azziz, but Maxime was in no rush. With a cigarette between his teeth, he sat down in the garage to wait and muttered that I should do the same.

Inside the dark workshop, the floor was littered with the remains of old engines, stripped from the carcasses of motorcycles which lined one edge of the room. On the walls, yellowed maps hung beside violent looking tools, charting every mile of the Pamir Highway. Beneath the maps, a rack of tyres ran along the wall - large lumpy things designed for dirt-bikes, very different from my smooth road tyres with seven thousand miles of wear. But then there was Maxime, with his dinner plate Vespa wheels and decades-old engine. For the first time on my journey, I had found a motorcyclist with a machine more pitiful than my own, and I liked its rider immediately.

Eventually, Azziz did appear, three hours after I arrived at the garage. The mechanic mumbled a quiet salaam, offered a limp handshake, and then shuffled past, ignoring the man asleep on his sofa. Azziz, it seemed, was quite accustomed to finding impatient foreigners waiting on his doorstep, and I am sure he would have left us waiting there for another three hours had I not dragged him outside to look at my chain. Crouching down, he took one glance at the links before turning to me and declaring:

'Chain is finish. I cannot help you.'

'Can you not fit a new chain?' I called, chasing after Azziz as he shuffled back into the garage.

'You need new chain and sprockets. I no have. You order online. Three weeks to come.'

This was bad news. The imminent onset of winter aside, my Tajik visa would expire in one month, and seven days was not enough time to cross the Pamirs. Despondent, I walked back into the darkness and asked Azziz again if he was sure he had no spare chains.

'I'm sorry. I cannot help,' he said, offering me a sad smile.

I wandered back out into the sunlight feeling defeated. It was warm in Dushanbe, but a month later the Pamir Highway might already be cloaked in snow. It slowly dawned on me that Dushanbe might be the place where I was forced to part with my motorcycle.

'You see, that is the beauty of the Vespa: no chain!' chimed Maxime unhelpfully.

Looking over at the Frenchman's tattered machine, lying in bits all over the floor of the garage, I was incredulous that my motorcycle had failed whereas Maxime's looked set to survive. I decided to ask Azziz one final time if there was anything he could do. Quite frustrated by now, the mechanic explained that all motorcycle chains are different and that he needed a specific kind with a specific set of matching sprockets for my cycle. It was not a case of simply being able to throw any random chain onto the machine and make it work.

This news was the final blow. After shaking hands with Maxime and thanking Azziz, I decided to go and find a quiet corner of the city in which to come to terms with the prospect of leaving my motorcycle behind in Dushanbe. I had just stepped outside and was putting on my jacket and gloves when Azziz reappeared at the doorway.

'Wait,' he said.

Walking deep into his garage, Azziz woke the sleeping drunkard, removed the cushions from his sofa, and started to throw objects out from a cavity beneath the seats. Various tools, empty whisky bottles, faded magazines, and cigarette cartons were hurled across the room to land in a pile by my feet. Books, helmets, tins of dog food, and pairs of motorcycle boots all came flying out until, from the very bottom, Azziz delicately pulled out a packet wrapped in plastic. Slitting it open with a knife, from within the packet he unravelled a long, gleaming silver chain and grunted in surprise. Stalking outside, he held the chain and two sprockets up to my bike.

'You are very lucky man,' he said, breaking into a vast smile.

The chain and sprockets had been ordered several years earlier by a woman who had left Tajikistan before Azziz had been able to fit them to her bike, and they happened to be the perfect size for my motorcycle. Twenty minutes later, thanks to a disorderly Tajik mechanic and a heavy dose of good fortune, my motorcycle was fixed.

Just before I rode away, Azziz stopped me and pointed to my license plate.

'Anglia? he asked.

I nodded, and he gave a low whistle before poising a second question:

'Anglia - Dushanbe - Osh?'

I nodded again.

'You crazy,' he chortled, clapping his greasy hand on my shoulder. In his ten years as a mechanic, Azziz had never met anyone stupid enough to try and cross the Pamirs on a cheap Chinese motorcycle.

'Me crazy? How about him?' I said, pointing at Maxime, who grinned back at me.

'Yes, he crazy too,' muttered Azziz, shaking his head and walking back into his dark garage. 'All you foreigners crazy...'

***

The Pamir Highway is the chief reason why the few tourists who travel to Tajikistan each year choose to visit the country. As the second-highest navigable highway on earth, the road runs for over six hundred miles, climbing at its highest point to four and a half thousand metres above sea level. Used as a route through the Pamir mountains for centuries, M41, as it was known to the Soviets, remains the only route for supplies in and out of Tajikistan's Gorno-Badakhshan Autonomous Region. In more recent years, it has become colloquially known as 'Heroin Highway' due to the ninety tonnes of opium that are smuggled out of Afghanistan along the road each year. Azziz had told me that most of the road was paved, but parts of it were rubble, and many sections were regularly damaged by earthquakes, landslides, floods, frosts, and snowfall. I knew without a doubt that it would be the most difficult stretch of my entire journey.

The day after my motorcycle was repaired, Jan and I left Dushanbe and headed south into Katlon province, on the beginnings of the highway. At midday, we passed Nurek dam and its bright blue reservoir, and then the road flattened into barren country, flanked by dry yellow hills. Late in the afternoon, we passed Danghara, a small, inconspicuous settlement that I might not have given a second thought if it were not for the white stone memorial and wreath of flowers which I spotted standing at the edge of the town.

If I had passed Danghara a month earlier, the memorial and the flowers would not have been there. They marked the spot where seven American and European cyclists had been run down by a car and then attacked with knives by militants claiming to represent Islamic State. Four of the tourists had died at the scene, and several weeks later, as I passed Danghara, another two were still recovering from critical injuries. A bicycle, decked in ribbons, stood beside the stone monument with the date of the attack inscribed upon it: 29.07.2018.

In recent years, sharing a border with Afghanistan had left Tajikistan vulnerable to the influence of Islamist militants, and the country had a history of defectors crossing the Pamirs to join radical groups. The power of the militants was reportedly growing, and just weeks before I passed through Tajikistan, Islamic State had made an announcement encouraging all Central Asians to attack and kill any unbelievers travelling in the region, by any means possible.

Despite the threat, on our way to Danghara, Jan and I had seen banners spread above the road declaring 2018 to be Tajikistan's 'Year of Tourism'. The government, worried about the detrimental effects the attack would have on the trade they were trying desperately to build, had delivered swift retribution to the perpetrators. Four suspects had been shot on site, and another three were 'rendered harmless', which was doublespeak for whatever flavour of torture, unlawful imprisonment, or mode of execution the local police deemed appropriate. But despite these efforts, a wave of travel cancellations had followed, destroying Tajik hopes for a bumper year of tourism.

The attacks had taken place whilst I was in Baku on the same day my visa to Tajikistan was granted. After weeks contemplating the danger, I expected to be more nervous than I was as I passed the site of the murders. In that part of the world, tourists on motorcycles are rare, which meant that Jan and I were more than conspicuous. Everywhere, people stared at us from the rear windows of their cars, but they wore looks of curiosity, not of malice. Every few miles, a car would slow beside us, and people would stretch out their arms to offer us fruit and bottles of water, pleading with us to take the gifts. There was not a shred of hostility in any of those faces. I felt deeply for the Tajiks, and I hoped that the reputation of their country would not be permanently marred by the violent acts of a radical few.

Shortly after Danghara, the highway began to climb up towards the first high pass of the Pamirs, and the smooth tarmac we had been following disintegrated into loose stones and gravel. I heeded Jan's advice, kept my arms loose, opened the throttle, and let the cycle find its own way up the mountain. At the top was the border with the Gorno-Badakhshan Autonomous Region, an area which encompasses half of Tajikistan's landmass, but which is home to only three per cent of its population. Two guards checked my passport, inspected the crude paper visa that I had been carrying since Azerbaijan, and after scribbling our names in an old paper ledger, waved Jan and I through.

Waiting for us on the other side of the checkpoint was an immaculate road that fell down from the mountain pass to the banks of the River Panj, which marked the border with Afghanistan. The road was the most exquisite I had ever seen in my life, running before us like a ribbon of glass, so natural in its curves that it seemed like it had been melted, poured, and cast in a single sitting. As we flew down it, small summits to our left marked the nursery slopes of the Pamirs, and to our right, on the other side of the torrid river, lay Afghanistan, bound by the steepest mountains I had ever seen.

As I was growing up in England, all I knew of Afghanistan came from news reports detailing horrors of war. According to Western media, it was a broken nation, beset with conflict, enmeshed in ceaseless violence. But as I rode along the banks of the Panj, the Afghanistan in my mind was suddenly transformed into a real country, its borders within touching distance just across the water, and it was more beautiful than I ever could have imagined.

Between the feet of the towering mountains, tilled fields, apricot groves, and wild orchards clung to the river-bank, sprouting in bursts of lush greenery. Above the shaded glades, nestled between tall poplars, earthen villages hung off the mountains, built high above the flood-line of the Panj. Dirt tracks connected the villages, running parallel to the Tajik road, and as I rode my motorcycle one way, I waved to lone farmers driving their mules in the other direction on the opposite side of the river, whilst far below, Afghan children threw themselves into cool shallow pools and chased each other around the trunks of mulberry trees. It was idyllic in a very ancient, biblical way. Only later would I learn that the Amu Darya, into which the Panj flows, was known in Medieval Islamic sources as Jayhoun, a name derived from Gihon – one of the four rivers that watered the garden of Eden.

Threading a thin line between two nations, Jan and I followed the road further up the valley, dwarfed on both sides by rock-walls that grew taller and taller. At Nzini Panj, we passed a bridge spanning a set of vicious rapids, linking the Tajik and Afghan banks of the river. Beyond it, a roughshod road disappeared over the tops of the mountains, leading onwards into the Hindu Kush and Afghanistan's eastern provinces.

The bridge was a vital link between the two nations, but in recent years it had gained a notorious reputation. In Dushanbe, a local guide had told me that the bridge was known to play a major role in the drug trade, and whilst heroin flowed one way across the bridge, it was not uncommon for Tajik traffickers to send slaves as payment in the opposite direction. Young boys, in particular, were coveted by Afghan elders who required dancers for Bacha Bazi ceremonies - rituals, popular across much of Afghanistan, in which boys are forced to dress as girls and dance before older men, which often lead to the young boys being sexually abused. The ancient custom of Bacha Bazi is so widely practised by Afghan elders that the government claim it is impossible to eradicate, and when U.S. troops were sent to fight in Afghanistan, they were ordered to overlook instances of abuse, as Bacha Bazi ceremonies were deemed to be too culturally important to Afghan allied forces to prohibit.

Jan and I might have slept somewhere alongside the highway that night, but Tajik soliders were patrolling the road and preventing travellers from camping as Afghan militants had been known to take pot-shots from across the river. This meant continuing until we reached Kalaikhum, a small town with a single guesthouse for the few travellers who passed that way. Though the road had been perfect asphalt all afternoon, the last ten miles to Kalaikhum were a wreck. By the time we arrived in the dust-caked streets, darkness had fallen, and we had seen enough broken Tajik tarmac to leave us fearful of the rest of the highway.

The next morning, it was not just the surface of the road which changed, but also its nature. As the mountains continued to grow in size and viciousness, their sides became so steep that the river-bank disappeared altogether. All that remained was a vertical wall of stone, running down to the water, with a crude road hewn into its side. With the sky reduced to a slither of light far above us, Jan and I crawled along the highway, bordered on one side by several thousand metres of crumbling mountain, and on the other by a vertical drop to the Panj which ran white and ferocious one hundred metres below.

Progress was slow, and despite our engines, riding became physically exhausting when it involved a constant battle to remain upright. By midday, tired and desperate for lunch, we came to a stop in a little village tucked into a cleft in the mountains. In between the small earthen houses of the village, patches of vegetables grew in fragments of sunlight, watered by an irrigation channel which ran down to the river. Aside from the sound of birdsong and the gurgle of running water, it was perfectly quiet, and the heavy, golden midday air was warm and sweet, laced with the smell of damp earth and freshly fallen fruit.

Jan and I walked around, looking for a patch of shade in which to sit and nibble some biscuits, or perhaps somewhere to buy bread, but the village seemed empty. Giving up the search, I was about to sit down at the foot of a tree when something rustled nearby. Looking up, I saw a young woman rising from a patch of vegetables, wearing a wide smile and beckoning for us to follow her. She was dressed in pale cream and gold, with dark hair plaited to her waist, and eyes as green as the grass she had been kneeling on. Smiling in silence, she turned on her heels and walked deeper into the village, glancing every few moments to make sure that we were following.

The young woman led us past more gardens and through thickly shaded bowers, never speaking, but turning often to show her smile. As she walked, a thick knot of hair swayed to the rhythm of her strides, falling in and out of shafts of sunlight. Her long plait, which had seemed dark at first, revealed itself to be coloured deep red, and as it swung between the towers of light cast down over the mountains, it glimmered like a belt of rubies.

At the far end of the village, we arrived in front of a small lawn where a group of seated women giggled as our guide led us to a table outside a modest home. The women were as pretty as they were bashful, with sharp brows, golden skin flecked with freckles, and long copper hair that pooled over their crossed legs. In Kazakhstan and Uzbekistan, the people we met had mostly been of Uzbek and Mongol blood, with round faces and monolid eyes. But the Tajiks are of Persian descent, and in the lower Pamirs, where they mix with Afghans from the Hindu Kush (who in turn can trace their lineage back to Alexander the Great), many people look distinctly Caucasian. Alongside the women, a group of men emerged from the house a moment after our arrival, all of them rugged and tough, with strong, straight jaws, tight frames of muscle, and piercing green eyes.

For Pamiris, welcoming, nourishing, and protecting strangers are innate instincts inherited at birth. So after shaking our hands, the men insisted that Jan and I join them for lunch. The owner of the house we were sat outside introduced himself as Sadam, and though we communicated almost entirely through gestures, he did know a few English phrases from his studies in Khorugh - the 'capital' of the Pamirs, a small town one hundred miles to the east. He told us that the village we were in was named Shipad and that the woman who had brought us to his table was his sister. The men joining us for lunch were a mix of Sadam's brothers and cousins, all of them farmers from the surrounding villages.

To begin the meal, Sadam's doting sister poured out cups of pale green tea which were laid upon the table beside a clutch of cucumbers and the bread (known as 'gurtha' in Pamiri) which always features at Tajik mealtimes. Circular in shape, with a thin centre and thick edges, the bread was studded with intricate patterns that spiralled towards its centre. It was sustenance, nourishment, and art, all rolled into a wheel, brushed with a bright glaze, and baked over cow dung. To accompany the bread, there was also a vast plate of plov, another Central Asian staple, consisting of a tall mound of steaming rice which cradled a handful of roasted mutton at its summit.

Whilst eating, Sadam told us how he had once fought for Tajikistan as a wrestler, travelling to Kazakhstan and Kyrgyzstan to compete. But now, aged twenty-five, he considered himself an old man and had decided to settle down. He lived in Shipad all year round, and he was eager for us to understand that Pamiri people, on both the Afghan and Tajik sides of the Panj, had their own language and culture, distinct from their respective nations. Though he recognised that he was legally a citizen of Tajikistan, Sadam identified as Pamiri. Nevertheless, he still had great respect for the two countries that bordered the Pamirs and their respective peoples. According to Sadam, Afghans were good horsemen, but bad wrestlers. Fighting, he said, was a Tajik art.

As a plate of sweet peaches appeared, alongside a dish of ripe mulberries and more tea, I pointed to the tall peaks surrounding us and tried to ask Sadam if people ever climbed them. He explained that whilst hunting, men would often go high into the mountains. The area surrounding Shipad was home to foxes, wolves, snow leopards, and the largest species of sheep on earth, named after Marco Polo, who first encountered the enormous creatures during his travels in the thirteenth century. With the mention of snow leopards, Jan and I asked if we should be worried, to which Sadam laughed. His gestures seemed to suggest that if we were to be attacked by one, we should consider ourselves lucky just to have seen one of the rare creatures in the wild.

I could have sat all afternoon at that table, laughing with Sadam and his family. Looking back, the lunch I had in that little valley was one of the most precious moments of my entire journey. To be invited into a home to break bread with its family, and to be let into their life, even if only for an hour, is to be granted the greatest of gifts. Sustenance and shelter, accompanied by generosity and kindness - those are the only things that a traveller ever really needs, and we found them in abundance at Sadam's table, seated beneath the shade of the mulberry trees, deep in the golden valley of Shipad.

***

In Wakhi (the language spoken by inhabitants of the Wakhan valley in the far south of Tajikistan), the Pamirs are known as *Bam-i-Duniah,* which translates literally to 'Roof of the World'. For four hundred miles, since leaving Dushanbe, Jan and I had been riding in darkness, following a road that wriggled along the bottom of steep valleys. But on the morning that we left the town of Khorugh, on our fourth day in the Pamirs, everything changed, and in the space of a few hours, we rose from the feet of the mountains to their summits, emerging on a high, cold plateau where I came to understand how the mountains had earned their Wakhi name.

Peeling northwards away from the Panj, the highway ascended rapidly, breaking out above the tree line, and then above the snowline, before finally emerging into a flat, lifeless landscape, bordered on all sides by ice. Gone were the green villages with their vegetable patches and meadows, gone were the fruit trees and the orchards lit with warm sunlight. The little idylls of the lower Pamirs had been replaced by a frozen, inhospitable territory which was completely empty apart from the sparse clutches of flat-roofed houses that appeared beside the road next to heaped piles of cow dung - the only fuel local people could burn in a land devoid of timber.

I had read that it was unwise to ascend more than five hundred metres each day in the mountains, but possessed by the same compulsion that had us step off the ship in Kazakhstan and immediately set off across the desert, Jan and I could not help but ride on. As the air grew cold and thin, the Pamirs became increasingly bleak, and it was not long until white yurts began to appear upon the horizon, sprouting in lone clusters on either side of the highway.

The Pamiri people, though they consider themselves distinct from Tajiks, fall into two further folds. South-west of Khorugh, in the lower Pamirs, they are closer in nature to the Afghans, but north-east of Khorugh, on the high plateau, they are more similar to the Kyrgyz. Over the next few days, yurts would become an increasingly common feature in the landscape, as the appearance, language, and culture of the people began to shift. Alongside the movable homes of these semi-nomadic peoples, the other most prominent indicator of cultural change was the sudden popularity of the kalpak - a tall, white felt hat, beloved by the Kyrgyz, which adorned the head of every man we met on the road from Khorugh onwards.

Burnt by the strong sun, blasted by the wind, and still gripped by the frosts of the previous winter, the village where we stopped for lunch looked like one of the most difficult places on earth to survive. As Jan and I brought our motorcycles to a stop, a woman with a Kyrgyz face appeared in a doorway and made a sad limp towards a dilapidated building, inviting us to follow her. The shelves inside her shop were stocked with three things: stale bread, vodka, and old chocolate bars, all covered in a thick layer of dust. The woman looked old beyond her years, withered and weakened by her harsh environment. The difference between her life and that of Sadam's in the warm, fertile village of Shipad, only a few hundred miles away, could not have been more extreme. Holding up her stale bread, she apologised for not having anything fresh, and when we asked for water, she simply led us outside and pointed to a nearby stream.

We camped that night on the shore of Lake Yashilkul, reportedly the coldest place in Tajikistan at three thousand seven hundred metres above sea level. The moment that the sun set, the temperature began to sink towards freezing, and we sat down to make a hurried dinner on our gas stoves. Starved of oxygen, the little flames could not burn strongly enough to boil water, so we settled for half-cooked rice and hunks of bread washed down with vodka. As the first stars began to appear, Jan looked over our little camp with an expression which was a mix of pride and contentedness.

'I could never persuade my friends at home to do this,' he said. 'They just wouldn't understand.'

I realised then that it would not have taken much to persuade Jan to stay up there in the mountains forever.

As the starlight grew, we tried to stay awake until it was dark enough to see the full night sky, but the cold soon became unbearable. Climbing into my tent, I wrapped myself up in my sleeping bag and every item of clothing that I owned, and then I lay there shivering in the darkness, listening to the pulse sounding in my head, unsure if it was the altitude, the cold, or the vodka which made it so loud, or perhaps all three in concert.

Our route the next day took us from Yashilkul to Murghab (once the highest town in the USSR), along a stretch of the highway that rose and fell in regular undulations, famous for inducing motion sickness. That afternoon, whilst stopping on the side of the road to take a photograph, my rear wheel slid out beneath me, and a moment later I was flat on my back with the motorcycle pinning me to the ground. I arrived in Murghab with a sickening headache, clutching a bleeding knee, and it was once again up to Jan to straighten my twisted handlebars. Luckily, he had found us a room at a home-stay, and after a supper of bread and tea, I retreated to the top of a pile of sheepskins, where I lay down to sulk over my injuries.

We thought about staying in Murghab for another day, but the faded village, hunkered against the side of a mountain, was too bleak a place to rest. Since leaving Khorugh, the Pamir Highway had taken on new qualities, remaining just as awe-inspiring, but growing increasingly provocative, testing our endurance and patience. Our machines and bodies were slowly wearing, yet there was still a long way to go. Despite the fact that my swollen knee made riding agony, I told Jan that we should press on, and we left Murghab the next day with our sights set on the Kyrgyz border.

Late that morning, we were making good progress when I spotted what looked like an abandoned motorcycle standing to one side of the road. As we came closer, the machine materialised into a tattered old Vespa, and lying flat on his back, with his brogued feet propped up on the seat, was Maxime, casually taking a nap at four thousand metres above sea level. Upon my arrival, without even looking up in surprise, the Frenchman let out a little sigh and let me know:

'Le Vespa. C'est mort,' before closing his eyes and returning to his slumber, as if he had just accepted that he would be stuck in the wilderness forever.

Gradually, we managed to convince Maxime that all was not lost, and as Jan helped him to change his air filter and clear his carburettor jets, the Frenchman told me how Azziz had succeeded in fixing his clutch, after which he had set off across the Pamirs, taking a different route to us, down a road which was in even worse condition than the M41. Along the way, Maxime had suffered two punctures, but his wheels were so small he had three spares hidden amongst his luggage. Otherwise, his plucky Vespa had performed admirably. He was only facing problems now because there was simply not enough oxygen in the air for his engine to run as it should. And the air was only getting thinner.

Making a convoy of three, we left as soon as Maxime's engine was running again, with the Vespa leading the way. It was pleasant to no longer be the slowest rider, and being able to lazily follow Maxime's wheels around potholes and craters meant that I was free to admire the landscape surrounding me without having to concentrate so much on the road. As the morning went on, that landscape became increasingly impressive, and by midday, the Pamirs had grown into slumbering giants, covered completely in snow, with the tallest peaks rising well above seven thousand metres.

In tandem with the mountains, the road was also climbing, and by mid-afternoon, we reached the Ak-Baital Pass, the highest stretch of the highway, at four thousand six hundred and sixty-five metres. I was the first of our group to reach its summit, and breathless from the ride, I stepped off my cycle to admire the view stretching in both directions. Below their white peaks, the mountains were made of red stone, and they sloped away from the pass in bands of russet and bronze. The air, though thin, was infinitely clear, and far below, at the bottom of the valley, I could just see Maxime on his Vespa, making his way up the pass, inch by beleaguered inch.

By the time Jan joined me at the top, it was obvious that Maxime was having real troubles with the altitude. My motorcycle had barely managed the climb, and it was thirty years younger than the Vespa. When Jan went back down the mountain to help, even his engine was unable to tow the struggling scooter. In the end, Jan loaded Maxime's luggage onto his bike, and the Frenchman had no choice but to push his machine to the top. Twenty minutes later, he collapsed in an exhausted heap at my feet with a faint smile on his lips. His resolve was enough for me to be sure that he would make it to Mongolia, even if he had to walk the rest of the way.

Twenty miles after the pass, as the landscape levelled out, a fence appeared, running north to south parallel to the road. This, I realised, was the border with China, and hidden on the other side of the mountains behind it was Kashgar, the Taklamakan desert, and the Chinese province of Xinjiang. For the first time since I left my home five months earlier, I allowed myself, for a brief moment, to dwell on just how far I had come on my fragile motorcycle, which against all expectations, had just crested one of the highest roads in the world.

That evening, we arrived at the shore of Lake Karakul, where it became clear we would not make the border before nightfall. Not far from the lake, we camped in the wind-shadow of a dry river-bed, close to an abandoned military post. The same guide who had told me of the active trade in young Tajik slaves across the Afghan border had also described the abandoned barracks of Karakul to me. The area had gained notoriety several years before when two tourists, camping alone, were attacked and eaten by wolves there. As the snows had not yet fallen, we hoped any roaming predators would not be hungry enough to be tempted to attack us. Even so, I slept with a knife beneath my pillow that night.

We cooked another dinner on our sputtering stoves, waiting an age to boil water for tea which was cold a minute later anyway. The wind was fiercer than it had been all day, but I was glad that we had not encountered any storms in the mountains. As we went to our beds, the sun was just setting, casting a sombre light onto the world. To our left, the lake lay like a plate of cold quicksilver, nearly three miles above the ocean. To our right, the road climbed to meet the ring of mountains that enclosed us, their frosted tips set on fire by the sunset. After we retreated to our tents, the wind continued to strengthen into the night, and I remember lying in the dark, somewhere between wakefulness and sleep, thankful that I had tied my guylines to boulders. Then, an hour before dawn, everything became quiet and still, and when I looked out from my tent, there were so many stars in the sky that it was filled with more light than darkness.

Chapter Twelve

The woods are lovely, dark and deep,
But I have promises to keep,
And miles to go before I sleep,
And miles to go before I sleep.

- Robert Frost, 'Stopping by Woods on a Snowy Evening'

Coming down from the Pamirs, the road had improved, but the mountains did not let us leave without claiming a casualty. Just past the town of Sary-Tash, Maxime's Vespa gave out, for good this time. After waving to the Frenchman as he disappeared in the back of a truck, Jan and I rode on alone, heading northwards parallel to the Chinese border. With a larger budget, I could have purchased a permit allowing me to enter China and travel through the Karakoram's of Pakistan, down into India. But as the cost of a single permit exceeded several thousand dollars, the paperwork was far beyond my means.

As there was no other way to enter China with a foreign license, from the moment I entered Kyrgyzstan, parting with my motorcycle looked increasingly inevitable. By the time I reached Osh, the second-largest city in Kyrgyzstan and the official end of the Pamir Highway, I had covered eight thousand miles on the bike - a distance just greater than the diameter of the earth. If I had been riding a straight line through the centre of the world rather than across its surface, I would have already reached the Antipodes by that point, a fact which made me happy. That it was not mechanical failure or catastrophic destruction that would bring my time with the machine to an end, but bureaucracy, was maddening. Nevertheless, when Jan and I were reunited with Maxime at a guesthouse later that day, the Frenchman handed me the business card of a motorcycle dealer he had met, and I knew I had no other option but to seek a price for my machine.

The motorcycle dealer was a German man named Dave Fucher who ran his business in Osh half like a private enterprise and half like a Christian mission. He had come to Central Asia to make money and save souls along the way, as the quote from Galatians scrawled along one wall of his garage testified. He explained that if I wanted to avoid the heavy import taxes, which were far greater than the value of the motorcycle, I would have to sell my bike on the black market. The sale was something he could arrange, but he said it would depend upon two things:

'First, the lord above must will it. Second, I must find you a buyer.'

The German's God must have been listening to that conversation because a day later, Dave offered me fifty thousand som to buy the motorcycle immediately. Before I handed over the keys, I asked if he could wait whilst I took the machine for one last ride out of the city. With a look of deep understanding, the German solemnly nodded, before helping lift my luggage off the bike.

Threading through the traffic of Osh, without any weight, I had never felt so comfortable on the motorcycle. It was one of those special days where riding felt utterly intuitive; I had only to think where I wanted to go and a moment later the bike would be there. Soon, I had left the bland streets of the city behind, and finally free from the traffic, I followed the Ak-Buura river into the countryside, where each of the previous one hundred and fifty days of my journey came flooding back to me. As I raced across empty fields and crossed over low hills, I relived every one of the thirteen thousand miles that I had ridden since leaving my home, and it was not long before the Kyrgyz road began to blur in front of my eyes, disfigured by the unexpected presence of tears.

My emotion did not stem from feelings of attachment for the cycle. The last few weeks crossing the desert and the mountains had been grievous, and I relished the thought of being able to look out of the window of a train or a bus and study the world, without worrying about my chain, or my tyres, or my ruinous knees. But selling the motorcycle did mark the end of a portion of my life, and I could not fathom that time having been any richer.

On that final ride out of Osh, I lived again through all the labours and all the fears of the preceding five months. I saw flashes of lightning in Croatia, heard the crack of rocks tumbling onto the wet road in Greece, and blinked away dust blown up into my eyes from the plains of Turkey. I swerved around reckless Georgian drivers, fell again at the mud volcano in Azerbaijan, and cursed every inch of the wrecked Kazakh road leading to the Uzbek border. Every hot day in the Kyzylkum and every frozen night in the Pamirs returned to me all at once in a single ceaseless torrent.

But the golden days returned too, starting with the afternoons in France near Esterel, where the curving mountain roads first taught me what a tonic the machine could be. Then came the pleasant shapes of Albania's coastline, the mad clamour of Istanbul, and the long ride over the Pontic Alps. After that came memories of the road near Sheki, where the lower Caucasus of Azerbaijan had seemed so like home. And finally, my mind returned to the unutterable beauty of the road south of Kalaikhum, where the Pamir Highway met the Afghan border and ran for two hundred miles alongside the white waters of the Panj.

I could not believe that such a short stretch of time could contain so much life, and I was grateful to my motorcycle for having been the agent of it all. It was a cheap, wretched, feeble machine, but it had carried me a quarter of the way around the world, through some of the harshest terrain imaginable, with barely a complaint. Though often impractical and regularly terrifying, motorcycles possess a unique ability to make travel feel very real. Riding along at fifty miles an hour with your feet only inches above the ground, separated from the world by nothing more than a leather jacket and the thin plastic visor of a helmet, inspires a much closer relationship with the landscape than can be achieved by staring through the glass window of a car. On a motorcycle, you notice the true character of a place, learn its smells as well as its sights, come to know every rut and bump in the road, and pay attention to even the slightest changes in the weather. Everything in the world around you becomes more significant and more memorable. To ride a motorcycle is to feel your way, mile by mile, across the surface of the earth, navigating a precarious line between ecstasy and disaster. There are many modes of travel which are safer, more efficient, and more sensible, but few feel so consistently glorious. And I can think of no other vehicle which would have provided me with the same calibre of freedom as my humble little machine, which carried me all the way from the Blackdown Hills of Somerset to the green pastures of Kyrgyzstan, without even a change of tyres, dribbling engine oil all the way.

***

Two days after selling my motorcycle, I was sat in a car on the road to Bishkek, feeling both relief and terror. Whilst the metal shell of the tattered Mercedes offered a sense of security that had been unknown to me on my bike, the owner of the car, a man named Samat, insisted on driving everywhere at one hundred miles per hour. The only time we slowed down was if Samat spotted what he thought might be a police patrol hidden amongst the trees, or if the engine started to smoke and steam, which it did routinely every twenty minutes.

After nine hours of driving, I reached Bishkek at nightfall, where Samat dropped me outside a hostel. On the other side of the hostel door, a long garden led to a tapchan which was full of people talking above the noise of a guitar. Walking towards a dormitory, I made a quick survey of all the faces and stopped in my tracks. Sat on one edge of the tapchan, engaged in ardent conversation with another young man, and surrounded by a small pyramid of beer bottles, was Bertie.

I laughed at finding him again, just as he noticed me and stood up to offer an embrace and bring me a beer. Dressed the same as he always was, in beige trousers and a crumpled shirt, he looked like a jaded prep school teacher who had lost himself one afternoon amongst the country lanes of Somerset, and who after years of wandering had inadvertently emerged in Central Asia.

'Fancy seeing you here,' I grinned. 'How did you manage it?'

'Aktau - Bukhara - Tashkent - Almaty. I was given free rides all the way. I never knew people could be so kind before I stepped foot in Central Asia,' he said, making the journey sound so effortless.

'And Afghanistan?' I asked.

'Oh, Afghanistan is old news. I'm heading to the Chinese Embassy tomorrow to see about a visa. You should hear what Rick has to say about Xinjiang,' he said, gesturing towards the man sat beside him.

'Nice to meet you, buddy,' said Rick, in a lazy Australian drawl.

A Tasmanian filmmaker on a hitchhiking journey of his own, Rick had spent the last few weeks living with the Uighur, a Muslim Chinese minority, known to be heavily persecuted by the Chinese state because they are considered a terrorist threat by the Beijing government.

'I've never seen such oppression before,' he said. 'You can't imagine the number of cameras on the streets of Kashgar. The state watch the Uighur's every move.'

Finished with China, Rick was now hitchhiking west, taking pictures as he went. I liked him instantly, and I quickly came to respect him, sensing that he cared deeply about the subjects he photographed. Along with Bertie, over the coming weeks, we would have many conversations about the struggles we faced in trying to do justice to the land surrounding us through photographs and words. Moved by the beauty of Central Asia, and amazed by the kindness of its people, we all felt that we had stumbled upon a remarkable portion of the world, and the fact that the countries of Central Asia were so unknown beyond their own boundaries meant that how we practised our art mattered more to us than it ever had before.

A short while later, Jan also arrived, having spent the last two days riding alone over the mountains. He brought with him two new friends named Athalia and Eddy - a kind young couple from Germany who were slowly making their way around Central Asia by bus, train, and any other means possible. Then there was another unexpected appearance in the form of Marine, the French girl from Baku, whose broken foot had gradually mended over the last month as she hitchhiked across Kazakhstan and Uzbekistan, following the same trail as Bertie.

In the space of a few hours, our little tribe had expanded rapidly, and the mood in Bishkek was jubilant. We planned to spend the night on the tapchan, drinking beer and swapping stories of everything that had happened since our goodbyes at the ferry port in Kazakhstan. But after half an hour of conversation, the owner of the hostel appeared. Shouting above the murmur of voices, she asked:

'Why are you not at the party?'

We shot each other puzzled looks.

'The party?' asked Bertie.

'Yes, today is Kyrgyz Independence Day!' she shouted, just as a firework streaked across the sky over her shoulder. 'Quick, quick. You must go to Ala-Too square right now!'

Scrambling into action, a minute later we had crammed into the back of a Marshrutka and were barrelling across the city. With few buildings greater than several stories in height, Bishkek felt like a provincial Soviet town that seemed to keep expanding forever. But as we reached the heart of the capital, the low skyline opened into a vast square, filled with thousands of people who were all staring up at a sky filled with flaming rockets.

As we stepped through the crowd, every man and boy we passed was proudly wearing a kalpak, the black and white felt caps beloved by the Kyrgyz. Not known for its tourism, Bishkek receives few foreign visitors, and we seemed to be the only tourists in Ala-Too square that night. But Caucasian countenances did fleetingly appear amongst the crush of Kyrgyz faces, typically belonging to old Russian men and women who had been relocated to Bishkek during the days of the Soviet Republic, never to return home. Their pale blue eyes and light hair stood in stark contrast to the rest of the crowd, but they chatted with their neighbours and sang the Kyrgyz anthem as loud as anyone else, looking both completely at odds and utterly at ease amid the Kyrgyz profiles surrounding them.

Once the fireworks had died down, a full orchestra appeared atop a stage on one side of the square and began a rendition of Strauss. Unimpressed with the music, the crowd turned to talk amongst themselves whilst passing around bottles of kumis - the mildly alcoholic fermented mare's milk that is adored by Kyrgyz people. As the classical orchestra played on, the muted audience remained indifferent to the Western music, which seemed a strange addition to their celebrations. But when the conductor shuffled offstage to make way for a troupe of komuz players, the mood shifted, and suddenly the air was electric.

Twelve men and women walked out and greeted the crowd, each holding a fretless three-stringed komuz, an instrument, shaped like a narrow guitar, which is so popular amongst the Kyrgyz that it has become a national symbol. Beginning slowly at first, the band began to play faster and faster, plucking strings even as they whirled their komuz over their shoulders, around their backs, and through their legs, their act as much a dance as it was a musical performance. As the tempo raced, the audience beamed and clapped and stamped their feet to old, familiar rhythms, and in a matter of minutes, Ala-Too square had transformed from a picture of indifference to the image of national pride.

At first, I had been surprised at the size of the crowd. Earlier in the day, my driver Samat had told me that some of his compatriots, particularly the older generations, were apathetic in regards to their independence. For many of those who had lived through it, Soviet rule was thought to have been a positive thing for the Kyrgyz. Samat himself had spent much of our nine-hour car journey recalling the days of the USSR with great fondness.

But the Kyrgyz are proud people, and whether the USSR was remembered longingly or not, the crowd in Ala-Too square that night was eager to celebrate Kyrgyz history. Officially, that history stretched back twenty-seven years, to when Kyrgyzstan was founded in 1991 after the dissolution of the Soviet republics, but an enormous flag flying to one side of the stage in Ala-Too bore a symbol which alluded to much older national origins.

Set against a red background, the flag featured a golden emblem at its centre, representing the roof of a yurt, surrounded by forty rays of the sun. Each ray symbolised one of the forty tribes who were united under the leadership of the folk hero Manas to fight against the Mongols, as set down in the national epic of the Kyrgyz. Below the flag, a statue of Manas himself, cast in bronze, towered above the stage. The gaze of the warrior looked down that night on the people of a nation that was only decades-old in name, but centuries-old in tradition. Though the Kyrgyz gathered in Ala-Too square were there to celebrate the twenty-seventh year of their independence, the ranks of kalpaks, komuz players, and kumis-swigging citizens all spoke of more ancient origins and unions, surviving from a time when war-like tribes still roamed the steppe, led by great men like Manas whose lives, hundreds of years later, are still remembered, enshrined in myth and immortalised in monuments of bronze.

***

When I left England, I had a vague notion of the distance that I would have to cover to reach the Antipodes, but I had no clue as to how long it might take me. I was moving at no particular pace, with no schedule or agenda, which meant that whenever my arrival somewhere coincided with a meaningful event, it felt like a happy coincidence.

Arriving in Bishkek for Kyrgyz Independence Day had been a pleasant surprise, but there was another event due to take place shortly after my arrival which was of even greater significance. I had heard of the World Nomad Games less than two weeks before, from a cyclist I met in Dushanbe. Held every two years, the games are a celebration of the ethnic sports indigenous to Central Asia, as played by the people of Kazakhstan, Uzbekistan, Tajikistan, Afghanistan, Kyrgyzstan, Turkmenistan, and Russia. For someone seeking to become better acquainted with the cultures of Central Asia, the World Nomad Games were a young writer's dream, and by sheer coincidence, I had arrived in Kyrgyzstan just as they were about to commence.

From Bishkek, it was half a day's drive to Cholpon-Ata, a town on the north shore of Lake Issy Kul where the games were being held. Now lacking my own means of transport, I joined Bertie on the main road leading out of the capital, thumb outstretched, anticipating a long wait. But true to Bertie's word, the people of Central Asia really are some of the kindest in the world, and after just five minutes of waiting, we were climbing into the back of a car full of Kyrgyz university students making their way to the tournament.

Finding a seat next to a young woman, I mumbled a few words of Russian and suddenly felt very ashamed of my lack of languages. Thankfully, she took one look at me, smiled, and then in perfect English replied:

'My name is Aisha. I'm very pleased to meet you.'

Comforted by the knowledge that we would not have to spend the next six hours in awkward silence, I fell into conversation with Aisha, eager to make the most of the opportunity to speak with a young Kyrgyz person.

'Do you work alongside your studies?' I asked, after Aisha explained that she was studying creative arts in Bishkek.

'I'm a photographer, mostly weddings,' she said, showing me a gallery of bridal portraits on her phone.

At the mention of weddings, I recalled hearing about the Kyrgyz tradition of bride-knapping or 'ala kachuu' - meaning to 'take and flee' - in which Kyrgyz grooms forcibly abduct young girls from their families and keep them captive until they consent to marry. When Jan had told me that as many as one in five brides are still kidnapped in Kyrgyzstan, I had found the fact difficult to believe. Though I realised ala kachuu might be a sensitive topic, I was desperate to hear a Kyrgyz perspective and decided to ask Aisha about the custom.

'Yes, this practice is still common in Kyrgyzstan, especially in the southern countryside. But it's something we all disagree with,' she said, gesturing to her fellow students in the car. 'Sometimes villages just act out the ritual, as if it were a performance. But other villages do take girls violently.'

'And what happens after a girl is taken?' I asked.

'She will live with the women of the groom's family whilst they try and persuade her to marry. If she refuses, she might be raped and cast out into society, but if that happens, her own family will reject her. Often the woman has no choice but to submit.'

'Are there no laws against it?' I asked.

'Yes, but they are not enforced. It is too large a part of Kyrgyz culture. The number of cases of ala kachuu are actually on the rise. But people in the cities are trying to change this. Only last week we held a big protest on the streets of Bishkek.'

It was strange to think that the same city which only days before had featured an enormous show of national pride had also recently been used as a platform for students who were ashamed of parts of their culture. Aisha explained that there was a growing divide between the young, cosmopolitan Kyrgyz living in Bishkek and the rural communities in the rest of the country who still clung to dated, sometimes violent traditions. Nevertheless, modern ideas about gender equality were not going to stop Aisha and her friends from enjoying some ancient Kyrgyz traditions that weekend. They were even more excited about the games than we were.

Cholpon-Ata, Aisha told me, was made famous during the days of the USSR as a popular site for sanatoriums, many of which were built on the shore of Lake Issy Kul facing the distant Tian Shan mountains. When Bertie and I left the students and stepped out of their car, we had high hopes for the town, and our expectations were not disappointed. The gridded streets of Cholpon-Ata themselves were unimpressive, but down by the lake, curtained by snowy mountains, the landscape was serenely beautiful. All along the shoreline, a thin fringe of forest rose between the water's edge and the town, and there, in a quiet copse of trees, beside a small sandy beach, Bertie and I met the rest of our friends from Bishkek and set about building a camp.

After raising our tents and clearing a fire-place, we all swam far out into Issy Kul and looked back towards the shore. From where we lay floating in the warm water, Cholpon-Ata seemed a small town, dwarfed by the mountains behind it. But set amongst the hotels and sanatoria, one massive structure rose above the streets - a stadium, large enough to seat several thousand people, which had been built for the games. And as we looked towards the stadium, though we were nearly a mile away, the silence of the lake was suddenly broken by the distant sound of thousands of cheers. The games, it seemed, had begun.

The next day, desperate to see some sport, we went early to the stadium, where a humble piece of paper taped to the outside wall announced the programme. We were fortunate - the first event was just about to begin, and it was set to be a dramatic match of kok boru between the host nation and their rivals from the north, Kazakhstan.

I had been hoping to watch a match of kok boru (or buzkashi as it is known in Persian) since the day I set foot in Central Asia. For the Kyrgyz, who live their lives on horseback, it is the national sport and a corner-stone of their culture. I understood the significance of the game and knew that it involved sixteen men, sixteen horses, and one dead goat, but of everything else I was uncertain. So with the rest of the group in tow, I led the way up into the stands to find us a place amongst the bristling crowd, curious as to what was about to unfold.

Finding some seats, I turned towards the field, just as two teams of horsemen galloped into view. The riders looked fierce and muscle-bound, with hunched backs and swollen shoulders, whilst the horses they rode were elegant, tense, and fizzing with nervous energy. Four players from each team rode into the centre of the pitch, where twenty metres in front of them, the decapitated carcass of a goat (known as the ulak) was lying in the dust. Beside the heap of bloodied fur, an umpire, also on horseback, stood facing the opponents, waiting for them to fall in line. A second later, the crowd fell quiet, the umpire let out a sharp whistle, and the game of kok boru commenced.

The eight riders on the pitch immediately entered a furious race, galloping towards the ulak. Each man wielded a whip, striking furiously at his horse as well as at the other riders around him. As the charge neared the dead goat, the Kyrgyz captain placed his whip between his teeth, lent down from the saddle, and reached for the carcass, grabbing a bloody limb with one hand and a fistful of fur with the other. With incredible strength, he hauled the ulak up onto his lap, just as the Kazakh riders closed ranks around him and began to rain a barrage of blows upon his head, doing everything they could to wrestle the carcass from his grasp.

Within a matter of seconds, a vicious melee had formed, cloaking the eight players on the pitch in a cloud of blood, dust, and spittle. Occasionally, the goat would appear for a moment, thrown high into the air above the envelope of dirt, before vanishing again amongst a forest of grasping hands. Huge screens standing on the side of the pitch displayed close-up shots of the action, showing the faces of the riders, twisted in pain as they fought with one another, vying for the goat's bloody limbs. Whips, fists, feet, and heads were all being used as weapons - even the horses seemed to have been trained to bite at one another's necks.

Then, suddenly, one of the Kyrgyz players managed to break from the scrum, beating Kazakhs away as they attempted to chase after him. He made off across the pitch, riding at full gallop, with his reigns hanging limply around his horse's neck as he clutched the ulak in both hands. At the end of the pitch, a large stone bowl called a kazan awaited, and as the Kyrgyz player approached, he made no attempt to slow down. His horse kept riding at full speed, until its front legs crashed against the concrete, sending both rider and goat flying through the air into the kazan. A second later, the Kyrgyz rider stood and showed his bloodied face, holding the goat carcass aloft, and the crowd let out a mighty roar in praise of his valiant effort.

The ulak was returned to the centre, eight new riders took their positions, and within a minute the game was live again, filling the stadium with the crack of bone striking bone and the sharp snap of gnashing horse teeth. The violence was intimate and extreme, and whilst the horses swung their necks and kicked and bit one another, players pulled at each other's reigns, attempting to drag their opponents to the ground.

Every time a horse or man went down, or some other act of brutality was spotted, huge cheers would erupt around me, the crowd never so spirited as when the action was at its bloodiest. Later in the game, I met an English-speaking nurse who was at the tournament to provide first aid to injured players. Only the day before, she had treated a Kazakh horseman for a triple skull fracture, an injury he had received whilst diving headfirst from his horse into the kazan with the ulak clutched in his arms. She told me how the player had simply seen the injury as a necessary sacrifice. These were hard men playing a hard game, and broken bones meant little in the face of national victory.

As the game drew on, Kyrgyzstan began to establish a comfortable lead, which they held for the remainder of the match. Throughout the whole sixty minutes, the horses had been running everywhere at full gallop, showing astonishing stamina and intelligence. They knew instinctively where their riders wanted to go, and it would take only a single stroke of the whip for them to turn around, to halt, to feign a change in direction, or to break into a gallop and not stop until their shin-blades met with concrete. But such prowess was to be expected from animals of their stock, descended from the horses that the Mongols once used to conquer a quarter of the world.

When the game finally ended, the victorious Kyrgyz captain galloped around the pitch with the flag of his nation streaming behind him like a cavalry general celebrating a military victory. With the win secured, the Kyrgyz crowd jumped to their feet, cheering, embracing, and calling out to the players as they paraded before the stands. Meanwhile, on the far side of the pitch, taking advantage of the break between games, two boys on small black colts galloped after each other, whipping their horses with branches plucked from nearby trees, and leaning out of their saddles to brush the ground with their hands, clutching at invisible ulaks: the next generation of kok boru stars, already impatient to take to the field.

***

The following day, our camp decided to leave for Kyrchyn, a valley in the mountains to the north of Issy Kul where more events relating to the games were being held. The steep-sided gorge, green from valley-floor to mountain-top, was littered with white yurts and had a river running down its seam. Drinking from the river and chewing on the grass in the meadows, animals roamed in abandon, whilst young Kyrgyz horsemen galloped from one side of the valley to the other, weaving through crowds of people wearing the traditional dress of dozens of different nomadic groups from across Central Asia and beyond.

Alongside horses, the nomads had brought with them a wide variety of other beasts that were considered integral to their ways of life. There were yaks, camels, bison, eagles, and elegant Taigan hounds. There were goats, sheep, hawks, hares, and wolf pelts for sale at the price of twenty thousand som. As well as livestock, whole lambs were roasting over open fires, and huge pots were full of mutton simmering in fat, waiting to be added to vast cauldrons of plov. On our way to the valley, we had even seen some Kyrgyz men using a chainsaw to slice up the carcass of a horse, piling the meat into their cars to be taken to Kyrchyn to be eaten. To these nomads, every inch of every animal was precious: nothing was ever wasted.

In the centre of the valley, a large market had been established where goods from across the region were being bought and sold. There were Tajik steel-smiths selling large hunting knives, Kazakh tanners selling leather saddles and whips, and Kyrgyz farmers offering jars of honey and hundreds of bottles of kumis. By this stage, I had been surrounded by kumis for weeks and felt guilty for still not having tasted any. Sensing my guilt, a Kyrgyz lady at the market offered me a bowl. Sour, chalky, and acidic, it had a slight effervescence and tasted of rotten cheese. Luckily, Bertie was on hand to pass me a plate of beshbarmak - a mix of potatoes, onions, and horse meat - which was just enough to distract from the taste of old mare's milk, and to save me from embarrassing myself in front of the Kyrgyz lady.

As we ate our beshbarmak, Bertie and I watched the final round of the mounted archery competition. One at a time, women wearing the national dress of their country came thundering down the valley, shooting arrows at a line of goat-shaped targets. As each horse passed, I could feel the thud of their hooves through the earth, and I shuddered as the riders effortlessly sank their arrows into the goat-like silhouettes. First prize was awarded to a young Mongolian woman who celebrated by galloping around the valley standing on her head in the saddle, flashing an inverted grin as she passed us in the crowd.

There were countless other competitions taking place, from spear-throwing and horse-racing to falconry and hunting. In the evening, there was also a series of boxing and wrestling matches held just before sundown. Some of the opponents fought on foot, and some wrestled on horseback, the crowd cheering loudly as competitors tried to drag one another to the ground. The feats of athleticism taking place all around were staggering, as was the sheer diversity of life on display. Only months before, I had not even known that the country of Kyrgyzstan existed, and yet at the World Nomad Games, the small nation seemed like the cradle of the earth, temporarily home to hundreds of different ways of life, each of them rare and precious.

But the World Nomad Games, as well as a celebration of nomadic life, was still a tournament, which meant that one nation had to be crowned the winner. Fortunately for the hosts, Kyrgyzstan had outperformed their rivals in almost every single event, and on that final evening in Kyrchyn, the Kyrgyz were declared overall victors. With the announcement, a deafening cheer ripped through the valley, and the mountain pastures changed their skin from green to red as thousands of national flags were unfurled in a riotous display of Kyrgyz pride, with people emerging from their yurts to dance, embrace, and raise toasts with bottles of kumis, their golden smiles beaming out at neighbours all across the valley.

The atmosphere was infectious, and at nightfall, our group from Bishkek built a great fire at the edge of the forest. Piling the wood high, we burnt it all at once, dancing around the flames in a frenzy. Across the orange glow, ash-flecked faces stared at one another, gleeful in the light of the fire, each of us feeling blessed to be surrounded by friends who not long ago had been total strangers. I think by that stage, after weeks of wandering around Kyrgyzstan, building a community for ourselves each night in a new portion of the wilderness, we felt a little nomadic ourselves, like a waylaid tribe, who, having travelled far, had finally found a home in the wooded foothills of the Tian Shan mountains.

As the fire sputtered out, the night grew cold, and Bertie confessed that he had only a light summer sleeping bag. Everyone laughed as we made donations of blankets and jackets to the man who was probably the bravest and most ill-prepared of us all. Over the previous few months, Bertie had slept not only in the wilderness but in parks, graveyards, and petrol stations, anywhere he could find space for the tiny one-man tent that collapsed on him every night. Though fearless, he had grown accustomed to a warm desert climate, and Kyrchyn was his first real taste of the cold. So as well as borrowing our blankets, he lifted hot stones from out of the fire and piled them in his tent, where he lay down beneath a mountain of jackets, atop a bed of boiling rocks, and dreamt of being back in the desert, just as a soft rain began to fall outside, trickling down from the surrounding mountains.

***

When we returned to Bishkek, we found that the city had grown cold in our absence. Summer was gone, the snows were on their way, and overnight our little tribe began to crumble.

Eddy and Athalia left first, bound for Kathmandu. Then Marine left for Indonesia, Rick went east to Uzbekistan, and Bertie turned south, making for Osh, still unsure if his Chinese visa would be granted. Last to leave was Jan, who had his sights set on Mongolia. Before he went, the Dutchman turned to me one last time and said:

'Are you sure you don't want to try and find another motorcycle and keep riding for a little longer?'

For the last seven weeks, I had spent almost every waking moment with this man. Beyond family, to spend so many successive days with a single person is rare. With some people, it might have been intolerable, but to spend those days with Jan was a privilege. I would have liked nothing more than to follow him all the way to Ulaanbaatar, but like the eye of a reader, which begins in the top corner of a page and ends at its opposite, I had been tracing a path south-eastwards across the world, making for the Antipodes. Though my motorcycle was gone, and the means of my travel had changed, the guiding line that I followed still remained the same. For me, India called, and after that, the green claw of Southeast Asia, before Indonesia, Australia, and New Zealand.

'I'm sorry, Jan, but Mongolia just isn't on the way,' I said, clapping him on the shoulder. He nodded his understanding, then left at dawn the next day on his motorcycle.

I was alone once again.

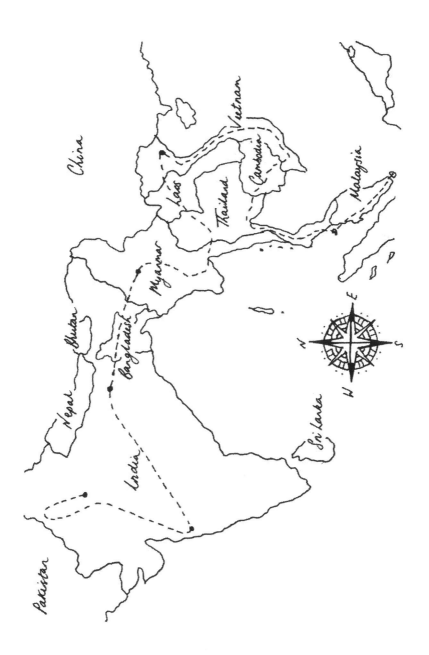

Chapter Thirteen

The way to make people trust-worthy is to trust them.

– Ernest Hemmingway, Letter to Dorothy Connable

Home to a throng of thirty million people, Delhi is made of several cities, clumsily piled atop one another over the course of many centuries, each sporting its own ailments and infirmities. The congestion there is the worst in the world, the air is famously toxic, and every day, Delhi's rickshaw drivers must crash their way down narrow old roads, attempting to navigate through an unpickable knot of traffic which never comes undone.

The first rickshaw I hailed in India dropped me in Old Delhi, the heart of that unpickable knot, where the streets are at their narrowest, the buildings at their blackest, and where the sun is permanently eclipsed beneath a steady drench of smog. Only hours before, I had been standing in the crisp Kyrgyz air, waiting to board a flight at dawn. After so many months watching the world roll by six inches beneath the soles of my boots - each culture, place, and people bleeding into the next – in the space of just a few hours, it had suddenly undergone an unfathomable change.

164

My flight that morning had left me suffering from an acute bout of melancholy, local to thirty thousand feet. Shut inside the aeroplane cabin, it had felt as if the whole world was imploding under a barrage of pressure. Even the gentle blue arc of the earth, just visible through the windows, could be seen bending under the weight. As I flew over Tajikistan, the Pamirs, which only weeks before had been such visceral, formidable things, appeared miles below - nothing more than a flat image, smudged with light and shadow - the mountains crushed to dark ink scuffs on a crumpled, throwaway page. After the freedom of my motorcycle, stuck in that aeroplane, I had felt barren and shrunken, dried out and grey, as if there was a drought in my soul.

But hot, clamorous, unruly Delhi, with all its cluttered life, was the perfect antidote to that melancholy. From the seat of my first rickshaw, everywhere I looked, the city was teeming with creatures: cows ambling down the road, dogs sleeping in doorways, and monkeys scrambling along telephone wires. Immense noise, incredible heat, and the ceaseless racket of motor engines commingled with smog and dust and dirt to form a choking, sticky brew that seeped through my pores and clung to the insides of my lungs. Filthy, vigorous, and vital, the whole city was wrapped in a seductive sense of chaos, and I sensed that I would like Delhi immediately.

I decided to stay in an area named Chandni Chowk, in a hostel opposite the russet steps and marble domes of Jama Masjid, the largest mosque in India. Built by Shah Jahan, the Mughal Emperor who commissioned the Taj Mahal, Jama Masjid sits at the centre of Delhi's old Muslim district, from where the Mughals once ruled their Hindu subjects. Under Shah Jahan, Mughal imperialism reached its zenith, but the empire would have been nothing were it not for Babur – the great-great-grandson of Timur - who in the early sixteenth century left his native Central Asia, swept down through Punjab with his army, and then overthrew the Lodi dynasty, establishing what would go on to become one of the richest kingdoms in the history of Asia.

But this area of Delhi was not only famous for its Mughal heritage. I had been told that some of the best food in India could be found on the streets of Chandni Chowk, and as I had not eaten since my final bowl of plov in Bishkek the night before, as soon as I left my hostel, I set out in search of lunch, promising myself that I would stop and eat at every street stall I encountered.

It was not that I disliked Central Asian food, but I had been looking forward to my first meal in India for some time. For the past month, I had survived on a diet of plov, lag'mon, and bread - nourishing but sober foods, which had left me craving something more vigorous. Luckily, the first vendor I spotted in Chandni Chowk, a kachori seller, provided just that. Taking a little silver plate, the kachori-wallah placed a hot brown pocket upon it, then pierced the fried lentil cake with his thumb and drizzled tamarind sauce into the crater. I took one bite and was staggered. It was like crunching on a dark cloud, shot through with spices, which hid at its heart a vial of sweet heat.

Next was the panipuri stall, home to more crispy envelopes, pumped full of a pale yellow liquid that tickled and shimmered on its way down my throat. Clean, delicate, and subtle, these were not the brash, clumsy tastes of any Indian food I had tried before, but elegant flavours, wonderfully complex, veiled with spices from the far reaches of the subcontinent. A samosa followed the panipuri, accompanied by a glass of mausabi, a sweet drink made from lime juice and rock salt, which was the perfect remedy for the humid afternoon.

With my appetite only growing, I started looking for one of the small roadside restaurants, known as dhabas, that are common all over India. By chance, my search led me down a narrow lane at the heart of Chandni Chowk, and halfway along the shadowed alley, I looked up to see a huge Sikh man smiling at me from outside a dhaba where he sat stirring an orchestra of pots. Lifting an arm of thickly corded muscle, he took his silver ladle and motioned for me to step inside, where a crowd of diners, their cheeks ballooned with food, sat chattering and feasting side by side.

A minute after I sat down, the Sikh brought me a silver tray which was split into several compartments. In the first was a stack of slightly charred chapatis that steamed as I tore them apart. Turning to the second section of the tray, I took a scrap of chapati and heaped a pile of dal onto the bread. Stained yellow with turmeric, heavily salted, and laced with chilli, the humble lentils tasted honest and earthy, and over the coming weeks, I would recognise their flavour in almost every Indian meal that I ate.

Beside the dal lay some curried vegetables, accompanied by a well of minted yoghurt and a heap of raw red onions, sprinkled with salt and lime juice, which no thali plate is ever without. Two further compartments held a pair of chutneys, one sweet and thick, the other dark and bitter. And after all that, there was still one portion of the tray un-tasted. Clawing off another piece of chapati, I finally turned my attention to the centrepiece of the meal: the paneer butter masala.

Coloured bright orange from Kashmir chillies, with green splinters of coriander and white pearls of cream dribbled across its surface, the butter masala was a marriage of the three colours of India in a single, exquisite dish. Currents of cumin, cardamom, and clove powder ran through the silken sauce, married with turmeric, ginger, garlic, bay leaves, and waves of garam masala. It was too complex, too sophisticated a mouthful to register all the flavours in a single bite, and then there was the paneer – soft as a whisper, spiced on the outside, but bright white and snow-fresh within.

But lunch did not end there. Finishing my last tatter of chapati, I looked up to see the turbaned owner smiling down at me from his pots, chuckling at the mess I had made eating with my ungainly hands. He told me that if I was looking for something sweet after my thali, I had only to walk two streets and I would arrive at the oldest jalebi shop in Delhi. Not one to ignore recommendations, I soon found myself standing in a queue, watching a jalebi-wallah squeezing spirals of white batter into a vat of boiling oil. After the syrup mix had been deep-fried, the orange curls were fished out with a large steel net and set aside to cool, temptingly close by.

Reaching the front of the queue and handing across some rupees, I finally received a small paper parcel dripping in grease. The jalebis inside were crunchy and hot, and as I bit into the first of the crispy orange coils, I punctured its outer shell, unleashing a molten core of liquid syrup which was thick and deliciously sweet. Having spent barely any money at all, I walked back to my hostel, munching greedily, thinking to myself that there are few simpler routes to happiness than feasting upon a labyrinth of deep-fried sugar, plucked from between the sheets of an old Indian newspaper.

***

On its way out of Delhi, my train to Amritsar crawled past vast heaps of litter which rose like mountains at the fringes of the city. Squatting in the trash, women sifted through the rubbish, whilst their children stood nearby, burning piles of plastic. Crude homes, built from tin and wood, came right down to the tracks where railway workers stood and dropped their picks into pools of black mud, staring up at the train with gaunt, thin faces.

The city went on like this for some time, but Delhi did eventually dwindle, and the train passed out of the capital into green fields compressed by a white haze of heat. Before long I fell asleep, and several hours later, I woke to find that we were gliding across the brown plains of Punjab. My first waking thought was of my motorcycle, and of how it might have felt to ride across such wide, empty countryside.

The morning after my arrival in Amritsar, I went in search of the Golden Temple (Harmandir Sahib) – the holiest site in Sikhism. Arriving at the temple's gates, I was instructed to leave my shoes upon a shelf, wash my feet, and to tie a cloth over my head. A moment later I was inside, walking around the edge of a large white marble quadrangle, filled in the middle with a green pool, at the centre of which stood a large and ornate inner sanctum, covered from top to bottom in bright, shining gold.

Though Sikhs have been worshipping at the Harmandir Sahib for four centuries, the temple had not always been golden. It was not until 1830, when Ranjit Singh, leader of the short-lived Sikh empire, donated a small fortune to the temple that it acquired its precious plating. And Singh was not a man to do things by half measures. From where I was stood, every possible surface both in and outside the temple looked to be gilded. An electric fan, which blew cool air out onto the crowd of thousands waiting to gain entry, had even been spray-painted gold, in keeping with the temple's extravagant skin.

As well as the vast crowd queuing to enter the sanctum, thousands of other pilgrims were walking around the edges of the temple, many of them stopping to wash in the green water of the pool. Committed male devotees were undressing to their kaccheras (the cotton underwear Sikh's must wear), and tying their kirpans (the daggers Sikh's must carry) to their turbans, before submerging themselves in the stagnant, filthy, sacred water. Nearby, an enclosed jetty led down to the pool, beside a post which read: 'Holy Dip for Women', scrawled in the colourful, childish font which adorns every sign in India, marrying the puerile with the divine.

One hundred thousand people visit the Golden Temple every day, and the longer I stayed, the thicker the crowds became. But after an hour of pushing past long lines of pilgrims, a warm shower suddenly broke, sending everyone fleeing for shelter. Unperturbed by the rain, I kept walking around the quadrangle, almost entirely alone. When the clouds cleared as fast as they came, there was a brief moment when the empty temple was filled with nothing but the shimmer of the inner sanctum, which gleamed like a colossal ingot under the newfound sun. Even the dark green pool, which only a moment before had been lightless and curdled with rain, was suddenly lambent, and the empty walkways surrounding it, reflecting every beam of light, changed into paths of gold.

As I strolled around the quadrangle, I noticed that many memorials were etched into the damp stone walls of the temple, carved to commemorate martyrs who had given their lives for their religion. Early Sikhs were known for their warrior culture, hence the dagger that all Sikh men wear, and as I stood gazing at one memorial, I heard a tourist nearby ask a Sikh to show her his kirpan.

'I'm afraid I cannot show you,' he said, 'for I only draw my kirpan in times of peace.'

'In times of peace?' the woman asked, questioning the paradox.

'When an enemy presents himself to a Sikh, the Skih will vanquish the threat before it even has time to develop. A Sikh quells conflict so quickly, the moment he draws his kirpan is the moment peace is restored. Though we are warriors, peace is the heart of our religion,' said the man, before graciously bowing his head and continuing his walk around the temple.

Alongside peace, the second sacred tenet at the heart of the Sikh religion is charity, which is why at the centre of the Golden Temple, as can be found in all Gurdwaras, there stands a Langar hall - a place where visitors and pilgrims, Sikh and non-Sikh alike, can sit down beside one another to receive food and take shelter.

Although Langar halls can be found across India, few feed as many as the one at the Golden Temple, where nearly half a million meals are prepared each week. As I walked up a flight of stairs on my way to the vast brick building, I caught a glimpse of the work necessary to fill so many stomachs. In front of vast copper pots, dozens of cooks stood stirring small oceans of dal with ladles as tall as themselves, whilst porters poured five-kilogram tins of masala mix into the cauldrons two at a time. Long trains of women sat shaping thousands of chapatis and throwing them onto hot plates, whilst their neighbours peeled, sliced, and diced small mountains of chilli, garlic, and ginger. It was an immense operation, military in its scale and efficiency, but conducted entirely in the name of charity, and it runs all day and all night, every day of the year.

Finding a space in the Langar hall, I sat down beside businessmen wearing white starched shirts and gold watches, and beside men dressed in tattered rags with no earthly possessions other than the cloth wrapped around their frail bodies. Cross-legged on the warm stone floor of the hall, everyone was equal, and when volunteers began to walk down the lines of people, throwing chapatis into outstretched hands, every pilgrim sat with their arms held high and their head bent in humility. Each man, woman, and child accepted their common status as beggars, elevating the toss of every chapati to a scared act of charity.

The meal was simple, unassuming, and nourishing, featuring a metal tray piled with dal and vegetables, which was replenished again and again until each guest was full. It was not a social event - people mostly ate in silence - but the quiet only added a sense of reverence to the meal. It was food reduced to its most pure and innocent form: a gift of sustenance from the community to the community. Here was the real treasure at the heart of all Gurdwaras and the Harmandir Sahib - not great gold shrines or stores of riches, but the promise that as long as Langar halls stand, no pilgrim, whatever their creed or religion, need starve in sight of a Sikh temple.

***

The next day in Amritsar, I woke to the sound of dripping. Outside my dormitory window, fangs of rain were falling faster than the streets could drain and shopkeepers sat in front of their stores ankle-deep in water. I watched as a cycle rickshaw made its way down the street, pieces of litter surfing on the bow wave that ran before it. The rain was the spawn of a cyclone that had spent the last few days ravaging northern India, and the owner of my hostel proclaimed it the worst deluge Amritsar had ever seen. In the space of a few hours, the entire city had turned to soup, with red rivers running through its streets. All the power had gone out, and in front of every home, old men stared out of their windows clutching little clay cups of chai, which when finished were cast out onto the water to go floating about the city like tiny terracotta boats, perfuming the streets with the smell of steamed cinnamon and cloves.

After a damp rickshaw journey, I arrived at Amritsar station and boarded the first of a succession of trains that would take me to Jaipur.

Buying rail tickets in India had proven more difficult than I had expected, the task not made any easier by India's complicated class system - 2AC, 3AC, CC, FC, SLEEPER, GENERAL, SS, being but some of the options. For the first two trains, I managed to book myself an air-conditioned carriage, with comfortable seats and a breakfast service. But on the final four-hour leg of my journey, I found myself in general class, in a hot, cramped metal chamber, sat on a hard wooden seat, with the weight of several hundred passengers pressing heavily against me.

After finally reaching Jaipur, I fled the train station and was waiting at the edge of a busy road, looking for a break in the traffic, when a short man appeared at my side and levelled a brilliant white smile at me.

'In India, you have to learn how to wait,' he said, clapping me on the shoulder.

'But you also must know when to go!' he then shouted, grabbing me by the arm and pulling me across the road through the narrowest of gaps between two speeding cars.

'My name is Ismail Khan, but you can call me Smile. I drive Indian helicopter,' he said joyfully, gesturing towards a nearby rickshaw. 'You are new to Jaipur? Come, let's get some chai.'

In his late forties, with deep black curls and sparkling brown eyes, Ismail had a vivacious charm about him. True to his name, he also had the finest set of teeth I saw in India, and once he started talking, nothing in the world would quiet him.

'There is a single law for Indian roads,' he said, as we sat down at a chai stall surrounded by rickshaw drivers. 'The small makes way for the big. The weak make way for the strong. The walking man makes way for the cycle rickshaw, the cycle rickshaw for the auto-rickshaw, the auto-rickshaw for the car, the car for the bus, the bus for the truck, and everything makes way for the cow.'

'You have been a rickshaw driver for long?' I asked.

'It seems like a lifetime, but I am from Nepal originally. I had a jewellery shop in Kathmandu before I came to Jaipur. Let me ask you, what do you know about stones?'

'Stones?' I said.

'Yes, stones – emeralds, rubies, diamonds…' he purred.

'Absolutely nothing,' I admitted.

'Baba!' he shouted, beckoning a driver sat nearby. 'Show this man your sapphire. A beautiful stone,' Smile said, turning to me.

Baba - a hairless, wizened old man - hobbled over and held out his hand. On one finger sat a silver ring which cradled a deep blue gem at its centre.

'The beauty of stones is that they are a universal currency. Baba here knows that wherever he is in the world, this stone is enough to pay for a respectable funeral. We hope Baba will not die in a foreign land, *inshallah,* but if he does, this stone will ensure his body is treated with respect,' said Smile, patting the old man's hand whilst looking longingly at the gem.

When he was not dealing in precious stones or driving his rickshaw, Smile had a wife and five children to care for, and he also played a small role in his family's textiles business. For half an hour, we sat, drank chai, and talked. Smile was happy to practise his English, and I was glad for a glimpse into the life of a Jaipuri rickshaw driver, which seemed to mostly entail sitting around and drinking tea with old friends. But there were parts of the city I wanted to see, so eventually, I stood up to leave, just as Smile asked:

'Sam, what are you doing tonight? I want to show you my favourite bar.'

'Your favourite bar?' I asked in surprise, knowing that Smile was a Muslim and lived in a Muslim part of the city.

'Yes, my favourite bar. It is a secret bar,' he said. 'Meet me here at eight, ok my friend?'

That evening, Smile was waiting for me at the chai stall with his rickshaw. It was a short drive to his cousin's textile shop, where a crescent of three rickshaws had been parked around the entrance to hide a set of stone steps. On top of the steps, four men sat huddled close together, and beside them, hidden in brown paper bags, were two crates of Kingfisher beer.

'Welcome to bar Ismail,' gleamed Smile.

Vikram, Mohammed, Ajay, and Ahmed were all related to Smile and in some way connected to the textile business. In the glow of the Jaipuri twilight, they gave me a warm welcome, made space on the stone step for me to sit, and handed me a hot Kingfisher, grinning at the strange sight of a foreigner come to join them for their evening beer.

'They are all brothers,' Smile explained. 'They grew up together in Jaipur. And though I did not spend my childhood with them, they have only ever treated me like a brother too.'

Everyone spoke a little English, but whenever something was

misunderstood, Smile stepped in to translate. We passed an hour in usual bar-side chatter, with Vikram asking me about English cricket, Mohammed complaining about his wife, and Ajay, clearly the family salesman, doing his best to persuade me that I was in need of a new suit.

Somewhere between our third and fourth beer, Smile must have been struck by a pang of hunger because he suddenly decided that as his guest, I must be fed. After a quick discussion amongst the men, and a draw of matchsticks to determine who had to go and fetch a batch of chapatis from the bakers, a small iron fire pit was dragged out from the shop, lit on the street, and within moments the evening air was thick with the smell of frying spices.

After a meal of mutton curry, several more beers followed, and the conversation continued more slowly as each man reclined on the steps, revelling in the satisfying lull of Indian lager and a belly full of meat. Mohammed, a more conservative Muslim than the rest, had refrained from drinking, but after eating he pulled a ball of Nepalese hash the size of a fist out from under the canopy of his rickshaw and rolled himself a long joint, which he sat smoking contentedly, blowing out thick clouds of perfumed smoke as the rest of us sipped our beers.

An hour later, Smile had his arm wrapped around me in a show of fraternal affection when he said:

'Why is it you trusted me, Sam? I'm no fool – I know the reputation that Indians sometimes have. Not all tourists would have willingly got into a rickshaw and spent a night eating and drinking with strangers.'

'I wanted to trust you, so I did,' I replied.

'This is a good way to be,' nodded Smile in return.

As he was driving me back to my hostel that night, swerving across the empty road, I asked Smile what might happen if the police caught him driving whilst drunk, even if the rickshaw was moving no faster than a donkey's trot.

'Let's just say I have several friends amongst the Jaipuri police force,' he said, turning around and flashing me a wicked grin.

Once we reached my hostel, I shook Ismail's hand, thanked him for everything, and had begun to walk away when he called out to let me know that he would come and collect me at eight the following morning.

'Why?' I asked.

'To show you India! I am your guru now!' he giggled, steering his rickshaw out into the moonlight.

***

True to his word, Smile was waiting for me in his rickshaw the next morning. Together, we spent a day exploring all the sights of Jaipur: Galtaji temple, Man Sagar Lake, Hawa Mahal Palace, and Amer Fort – the rich remnants of a lost Rajput kingdom. Throughout it all, Smile was a diligent guide, but by lunchtime, he had grown bored of the crowds of tourists, and as we were walking down the steps of Amer fort, he caught me by the arm and said:

'You know, Sam, Jaipur is just a museum. None of this old stuff means anything in the real India.'

'But history is surely important to Indians?' I asked.

'Pah, you think the average Indian believes that? Tell me what the poor man in the village knows about Indian history? No, if you want to see the real India, we must go to visit my family in Shekhawati.'

'Well that's a nice idea Smile, but - '

'You are right,' he interrupted. 'It is a nice idea. We shall leave tomorrow.'

Indians have a great talent for affectionate abduction, and though their motives are usually innocent, the method can sometimes seem sinister. During my time in India, there were many occasions when a friendly face took me by the arm or invited me onto the back of a motorcycle and led me away to an unknown location. Often my guides just wanted to share a cup of tea at a chai stall or introduce me to a family member. It is a difficult thing to accept at first, this benevolent kidnapping, but India is all the richer for it, and no man was quite so talented in the art of abduction as Ismail Khan.

In a single afternoon, by unclear means, Smile acquired a car, and after bundling me into the back, with Vikram behind the wheel, we were soon tearing along an Indian highway. All I knew was that we were heading north-east, to a region of Rajasthan named Shekhawati, where Smile's cousin Hassan reportedly lived.

'Trust me, Sam,' said Smile. 'I will show you the true side of India.'

Once we passed out of the city, the landscape shifted to brown, arid scrubland and never changed back. Smile insisted that this was farming country, but to me, the plains seemed barren and empty. I knew that in the distance, three hundred miles ahead, the land would eventually crumble into the sands of the Thar desert. For all I knew, we were heading straight to the heart of that hot crucible, or perhaps we would drive even further, out to the far reaches of Rajasthan.

Fortunately, after four hours of driving, we had not yet reached the desert when Vikram pulled off the road into the fringes of a small village. Surrounded by fields of thin grass, a collection of single storey homes, built from faded bricks, were set amongst gardens of brown fruit trees where goats dozed lazily in the shade. In the middle of the village, outside a small square home, Vikram brought the car to a stop, just as a colossal figure appeared in the dark doorway.

Emerging from the house, a towering chieftain with wide shoulders and a dark thrust of a beard walked forward to stare quizzically at our car, obviously suspicious of outsiders. Behind him, a woman clutched a newborn baby, whilst two older girls lingered at her side. Coming closer, the man peered at me through the window, defensive and distrustful. But when Smile emerged from the other side of the car, the man's solemn expression cracked into a wide grin, and after salaaming Ismail, he walked around and lifted up his cousin in a warm, familial embrace.

'Sam, meet Hassan, and welcome to Rolsabsar,' said Smile.

'As-salāmu ʿalaykum,' said the mighty Hassan, taking my hand.

'Wa ʿalaykumu s-salam,' I replied, relieved that the giant had turned out to be friendly.

Hassan spoke no English, but words are not required to convey hospitality when it is genuine and instant. Leading us to a shaded part of his garden, our host seated us amongst his goats and began brewing four cups of chai over a small fire that smoked in the centre of the paddock. After a long drive, Vikram was glad to relax, whilst Smile was clearly content to be back in the countryside, and I was busy taking in my surroundings, stunned at how quiet the village was. I had never thought such peace would be possible in India.

Hassan's small herd of goats provided the main source of sustenance for his family, but as I would later learn, he also earned an income as a labourer. As Smile translated and told his cousin about my travels, Hassan revealed a passport full of dozens of stamps for Saudi Arabia, each denoting a trip to the Middle East. Alongside millions of other Indians, valued for their cheap labour, Hassan went west as often as possible, sending almost all the money he earned back home. Riyadh and Rolsabsar, those were the two poles of Hassan's existence; it was difficult to imagine two places more different.

Hassan was as generous and kind-hearted as Smile, but he also shared his cousin's propensity for sudden and unexplained misadventures. I had not even had the chance to finish my cup of tea when he ushered us all into the car and sped off towards a neighbouring village, desperate to make the most of the rare opportunity of having access to a vehicle. Swerving wildly along dirt tracks, giddy with excitement, Hassan leaned around from the driver's seat, and rubbing my rough cheeks, made it known that if I was to stay for dinner, then I was in need of a shave.

Five minutes later, before I could protest, I was lying back in a chair watching a barber sharpen his straight razor on a leather strop, with six pairs of eyes staring down at my foam-flecked face, in what might have been the most remote barbershop in India. As the barber removed my beard (but not the moustache), Smile spouted from one corner of the room. One at a time, the six other men waiting for a shave, who had come from neighbouring villages, were firing questions at him which I could tell from their persistent stares were all related to me. Ismail paced up and down, waving his hands, shaking his head, and telling them his version of my life. At one point, I even heard Smile mention my time at Oxford, which was met by a general head bobbing, and after another few seconds of speech, a loud chorus of laughter.

Once I was done, Smile slapped my smooth cheeks and lay down himself in the chair. Soon, he also emerged gleaming from beneath a hot towel, his impish grin brighter than ever. Outside the barbers, I asked what the men had been laughing at inside after he mentioned my time at university.

'They wanted to know how educated you were,' he said with a wink. 'I told them that you studied at Oxford, and some of them knew the name. Then someone asked how we are related. I explained that I am teaching you about India, which I realised makes me the tutor of an Oxford man. Ha! You will call me Professor Smile from now on.'

After a tour of the village, involving countless cups of chai with Hassan's many neighbours, it was already dark by the time we returned to his home. In the courtyard outside the house, Mirha, Hassan's wife, squatted beside a vast copper pot, cooking mutton curry. But before we sat down to the meal, Vikram called me over to the still smouldering fire where he was toasting something on the end of a stick.

'Here, Sam, for you. A kind of nut,' he said, dropping a hot grey oval into my palm and motioning for me to eat. Dubious, I bit down on the steaming orb, which was smooth and soft and overpoweringly salty, whilst the three men broke into giggles around me.

'Good man,' boomed Hassan, slapping me on the back.

I looked across to Smile, and in between fits of laughter, he let me know that I had just eaten a roasted goat's testicle, the previous owner of which was currently stewing inside Mirha's pot.

Soon after, the meal itself was ready, and the men sat down together in a chamber of the house, separate to the women who dined outside. In a ritual as old as time, brothers broke bread with brothers, and as Hassan, Vikram, Ismail, and a collection of other men from across the village shared food, I was invited into their little fold. Mirha, it transpired, was a fabulous cook, and in her hands, the slaughtered goat had been transformed into a masterpiece. As each man ate, scarcely a word was spoken. We were all too involved in our own contentment to risk breaking the spell with the unnecessary addition of speech.

After dinner, we sat around the fire outside whilst Hassan's two eldest daughters ran around in the dark. Some of the men passed a thick roll of charas between them, taking no pains to hide it from the children. Smile, meanwhile, went skulking to the car to drink the two beers he had smuggled into the village, which had to be kept out of sight in case the Muslim elders took offence. That was the essential formula of Ismail's character: equal parts mischief and respect.

'Sam, do you think you will write about this place?' he asked, as we stared contemplatively into the fire.

'Almost certainly, Smile.'

'It is important to tell the truth when you write.'

'I try to when I can.'

'And will you write about me?'

'It would be wrong to not give my guru a mention,' I said, watching his grin gleam in the firelight.

'Well then, there are some more things you should know about my life if you are going to tell the truth. I have told you already about my arranged marriage at sixteen, and about my jewellery shop in Kathmandu, but I haven't told you why I moved to Jaipur.'

'I thought it was because you wanted a change?' I asked.

'I loved Kathmandu,' he said, a look of heavy remembrance in his eyes. 'I would have stayed there forever, but my gem store attracted the wrong sort of attention. The truth is, Sam, that whilst in Kathmandu, my business wasn't completely legal. What started as a few favours to friends soon grew into something more serious, and before I really knew what had happened, I was involved with a gang. I would sell stolen gems for them, and in return they protected my shop.

'I wasn't happy about the situation. I didn't want to live that way, but it can be hard to get out of a mess like that. Things were fine for a long time, but then some men from a rival gang visited my shop one day. My protectors sent some people to help, and a man was beaten nearly to death. I was sent to prison for two years, just for being a witness.

'A Nepalese prison isn't such a bad place, especially if you have friends like I did. I worked in the kitchens as a butcher because I was one of the only prisoners trusted to be around knives. Two years and I never once fought in prison. The only weapon I have ever used in my life is my tongue. Few people realise its power.

'But parts of prison were hard. The guards were very cruel. Every day I changed the bonds of an old man who had to be tied up because he had tried to kill himself. He used to plead with me to beat him. I never did, but the guards always got to him. He would beg and beg for more as they kicked him again and again, never stopping until he passed out, which was exactly what he wanted. It was the only time the old man ever felt any peace.

'Even after two years, it was too dangerous for me and my family to stay in Kathmandu after I left prison. We had no choice but to pack up our home and move to be with our distant family in Jaipur. You can't imagine how different my life is now, driving a rickshaw every day in India.'

'Do you think you will ever go back to Nepal?' I asked.

'To Kathmandu? No. If I move from Jaipur, the only place I will go is here,' he said, casting his arm about the darkness. 'I'd like to buy a plot of land next to Hassan's. I can see myself as an old man out here, growing peanuts on a farm. Can't you?'

Whatever Smile said, I knew he would never leave the city. Prison had led to a reformation of kinds for Ismail, but not a pacification. He had too much spirit and energy, and too habitual a taste for mischief, for him to ever leave the bustle of Jaipur. I could see that Hassan loved him dearly, but the differences between the cousins were profound. Hassan was at peace by the fire with his goats, whereas Smile favoured the mad throng of the city.

'I only told you that because I want you to trust me, and there are no secrets between friends,' he said, placing his hand on my shoulder.

'I trust you, Smile,' I said.

Away from electricity, air conditioning, and running water, my body returned to the old rhythms it had known in the wildernesses of Central Asia. Darkness brought with it tiredness, and after Ismail's story, I soon found myself falling asleep before the dying fire. Smile, Vikram, and Hassan began to struggle too, and before long, Hassan stood, passed his baby to me, and said he would lay down some mats on the roof for us all to sleep upon.

As Vikram went to fetch water from the car, Smile went hunting for some blankets, and I was left alone with the sleeping child. Black paint lined the baby's eyes, and a single vermillion streak stained his little forehead. He slept soundly, gurgling now and again, as the fire crackled and the goats tussled between the trees. The night was black and clear, with no moon at all in sight, and though their existence hadn't seemed possible in the midst of Delhi, Jaipur, or Amritsar, for the first time since my arrival in India, I looked up and could see stars in the darkness, glittering above me like hot gems flung across the wide Rajasthani sky.

Chapter Fourteen

Within you there is a stillness and sanctuary to which you can retreat at any time and be yourself.

- Hermann Hesse, *Siddhartha*

After leaving Ismail in Shekhawati, I made a furious tour of Rajasthan, beginning in Bikaner where huge black camels paced past the gates of grand havelis, built by gem-merchants who grew rich trading with the West. From Bikaner, I took a train to Jaisalmer, the gold-stone fortress-city in the heart of the Thar desert, where Indian Air Force jets danced ceaselessly along the horizon, patrolling the Pakistan border. Jaisalmer led to Jodhpur, home to Mehrangarh Fort, which cast its vast shadow across a city painted blue in honour of Lord Shiva. Last came Udaipur, aristocratic and elegant, with its ornate palaces and chain of ancient lakes. From there, a bus had taken me out of Rajasthan in the night and crossed through Gujarat, to deliver me to Mumbai, where the state of Maharashtra dips one toe tentatively in the ocean.

But peeling back the curtain of my sleeping cabin, as I looked out at the gathering traffic, Mumbai did not seem like a city by the sea. Dozens of motorcycles followed our bus, like pilot fish mobbing a whale, and the black lacquer tops of the rickshaws reminded me of turtle backs from above, but otherwise, as I looked out at the city, any sense of the ocean was absent.

This was because since its origins as a bustling port, Mumbai has gradually been expanding inland, growing year on year. In the 1970s, construction started on a new planned city - Navi Mumbai - designed for a population of two million inhabitants, built fifteen miles from its progenitor. But in the last five decades, Mumbai has swollen to such a size that Navi Mumbai will soon be swallowed by its original, as the once small port city continues to balloon by over ten thousand people each week.

The humidity in Maharashtra was the worst I had ever known, and after a restless night of travelling, I had no energy to do anything but sit and read. Spread across the front page of that day's edition of the *Times of India* was the picture of a huge garbage flow (known as a nullah) found in the slum of Dharavi, reported to be decades old. These garbage flows were contributing to rising rates of malaria and dengue fever in the slums, and on page three, a storyboard described the life-cycle of a blood-thirsty mosquito named Rita, listing all the best ways to kill her.

Other headlines included news of a butcher's shop in Byculla which had narrowly escaped disaster after posting an advert for buffalo meat incorrectly labelled as beef. Locals, believing the butcher to be slaughtering holy cows, had started a minor riot and tried to burn the shop to the ground. Elsewhere, an eighty-six-year-old holy man and activist, Swami Sanand, had starved himself to death campaigning against pollution in the Ganges. News that the Diwali holidays would be shortened from twenty-one to fifteen days had sparked national outrage. And most chilling of all was a report that revealed some parts of Maharashtra were already suffering water shortages, despite the monsoon rains finishing only several months earlier, threatening the lives of millions.

After such a sobering read, I felt the need to take a walk, and late in the afternoon, I eventually ventured out for a stroll along the Colaba, Mumbai's main boulevard. Filled with cafés, restaurants, and street vendors, selling all manner of trinkets and fake treasures, this touristic part of the city was infamous for its criminal links, and my mood was not helped by the fact that I could not walk five steps without a man rising from the shadows to offer me dollars, drugs, women, or stolen gold.

I soon came to Leopold's, the city's most famous café, where bullet holes could still be seen in the walls - remnants of the 2008 terrorist attack, left as memorials to the one hundred and seventy-six people killed across Mumbai by an extremist Islamist terrorist organisation hailing from Pakistan. Leopold's café was specifically targeted during the attacks, as was another Mumbai icon standing just around the corner: The Taj Mahal Palace Hotel, one of the grandest hotels in all of India.

Rising opposite the Arabian sea, grandiloquent and impressive, the Taj Mahal Palace Hotel was once a worldwide emblem of colonial opulence. When it opened for business in 1903, the hotel housed Mumbai's first bar, and years later it launched the city's first discotheque, which in a cruel stroke of irony was named 'Blow Up'. Though the attacks in 2008 left the Taj badly damaged, it has since been fully restored, and the hotel has once again regained its glittering status as a honey-trap for Mumbai's international elite.

As a symbol of India, the Taj Palace is known around the world, but leaving the hotel, I found a monument of even greater fame before me. Like all the major temples and memorials of the subcontinent, as I approached the Gateway of India, it was hidden beneath a cloak of grubby pigeons. But on my walk towards the monument, the noise of a nearby engine startled the birds, and their sudden departure was like an unveiling. As the gateway shed its grey feathers, three pale stone archways were revealed, standing like massive portals to the rest of the world.

A threshold to another era, the gateway was built in 1911 to commemorate George V's coronation as Emperor. But as I stood beneath its middle, I noticed an inconspicuous little plaque which told of the monument's other, more significant role in history. It was there, under the archway, that the last British troops left India on the 28th of February 1948 in the final days of the Empire. Those troops, as written on the plaque, were from the Somerset Light Infantry, garrisoned at Jellalabad barracks in Taunton, Somerset, not half a mile from where I grew up.

Every day as a boy, I remember waking and looking out of my bedroom window to see the red-brick keep of Jellalabad glowing in the sun. By the time I was born, the barracks had been empty for decades, but I knew that soldiers had once lived there, and I spent many mornings wondering what adventures the regiment might have had around the world. I had never once seen them mentioned in books or histories until

I was stood in Mumbai and read the plaque, just as dusk was falling. With its thick pillars and looming turrets glowing red in the sunset, the Gateway of India even looked a little like the keep of Taunton's Jellalabad barracks - a passage not just to another world, not just to a distant decade, but also to a fragment of home.

***

Unlike the crushed heart of Old Delhi, Mumbai's streets are wide enough to walk along, and on my second morning in the city, after a breakfast of fresh coconuts, I set off on foot despite the heat. From Wellington Fountain, I followed a road past the National Gallery, around to the law courts, where be-robed barristers paced between the creepers of Banyan trees, wigs in hand, rehearsing their closing arguments. Rushing past them, stepping onto the orange lawns of the Oval Maidan, crowds of schoolboys were dragging cricket bags, eager to join one of the many games already underway in the vast park.

At the far end of the Oval Maidan, I encountered Churchgate station, a chaotic tumble of trains and locomotives, running out across the city in all directions. Though it was pleasant to walk, the trains in Mumbai have no doors, and I knew that there would be no better way to see the city than hanging outside a moving carriage, with the ground rushing by underfoot, whilst watching the lives of thirty million people hasten past.

A minute after arriving at the station, I was riding in a carriage heading north, dangling outside the train, watching the city slip through my fingers. Large towers rose up all around, swaddled in fumes, and I was so engrossed with the view that I failed to notice another train coming in the opposite direction. With a second to spare, a thoughtful passenger pulled me back inside, just as a dozen carriages flew past, inches from my nose. The passing train disappeared in a heartbeat, but behind it, imprinted in the smog of the city, a thousand faces lingered in the air - a catalogue of souls, paraded past at fifty miles an hour, then lost on the hot Mumbai breeze.

I was not riding the train aimlessly; I had a destination in mind. Though I had been in Mumbai only a day, I had been approached countless times by touts offering tours of Dharavi, one of the city's poorest districts and one of India's most famous slums. At first, I had been shocked. Slum tours seemed like a sinister form of poverty tourism, patronised by wealthy voyeurs who wanted to be reminded of the comfort of their own lives. But the truth is that nearly half of Mumbai's population live in areas designated as slums. To not visit those places would have been to ignore how fifteen million Mumbaikars live. So at Churchgate station, I had asked a ticket officer how to reach Dharavi. His response had been emphatic:

'Take a train to Mahim junction, sir, and then simply follow the smell.'

I got off at Mahim, a nondescript station, and soon found myself crossing a walkway which rose above a thick current of litter. It took a moment for me to realise that I was actually stood upon a bridge and that the flurry of rubbish below me was a river. Either side of its banks, lines of small shanties made from concrete blocks, corrugated iron, and sheets of tarpaulin were perched precariously atop one another, marking the walls of the slum. The whole thing looked like it had sprung up in an instant, each home piled haphazardly above the next, so fragile that it seemed the slightest touch might have been enough to send whole streets tumbling into the rotten waters below.

In front of me, a single road cut through the solid mass of scrap metal and plastic. Joining a crowd of people rushing down it, I walked towards the slum, and just as the ticket officer had promised, I soon became aware of a smell, but it was not the stench of sewage, of putrid life, or poverty. It was all the smells of India – the sweet spices of chai, the choking scent of chilli, the smell of frying pakoras, of fresh paneer, and of cut coriander heaped atop mutton, just richer and in greater concentration than I had ever known them before.

Without realising it, I had already entered Dharavi, with its restaurants and chai shops, its jewellers and tailors, its chemists, mills, schools, mosques, factories, temples, and even its white good shops offering finance. It was a city entirely of itself, just like other Indian cities I had visited, except built to a smaller scale - a place where an inch was ample space between neighbours and a hand's breadth felt like a mile. I had expected filth and sadness and destitution, but Dharavi was simply India in miniature, the same joyous, vibrant, maddening world, packaged tight in a single square mile.

Steering past children running out of school gates and shepherds herding goats down the road, I turned into a tight alley, heading towards the heart of the slum, where the world disappeared in darkness. In the narrow passageways, beneath the shade of the plastic sheets that stretched across the rooftops, no sunlight reached the ground. Here, the slum was a city of shadows, of indiscernible shapes creeping through the dark. But my eyes soon adjusted, and all sense of the sinister quickly disappeared as the indecipherable shapes changed into old men and women, sat smiling on the doorsteps of their homes, waving to me as I went by.

People have been living in Dharavi for over one hundred years, ever since a community of tanners first moved to the district from central Mumbai. The cost of one month's rent there is one thousand rupees - the same as the price of a beer in the Taj Palace Hotel's harbour bar. But as well as homes, Dharavi is also crowded with businesses, from potteries to textile shops, and even recycling plants which process waste from the rest of the city. Glimpses of these factories and workshops appeared as I walked: lines of workers hunched behind machines, diligently labouring in the hot twilight of the slum. To me, Dharavi looked like a centre of industry, a place where people worked hard, lived happily, and strove to build a better society, and yet, despite all of this, the slum remains one of the most misunderstood places on earth.

After walking for half an hour through an endless procession of illegible streets, I eventually emerged into an open space which had the remnants of a collapsed building piled at its edges. In the middle of a small square of dust, a group of skull-capped boys were playing cricket, using sticks as wickets and a piece of piping for a bat. Before I had even stepped out into the light, a crowd of hands had me by the wrist and were pulling me over to the pitch, desperate to see the foreigner play.

The boys were a range of ages, from fifteen through to six, and every one of them insisted on introducing himself. Shehzad, Salman, Rizwan, Sched, Asif, Shariq, and Ayaran all lived nearby in the slum and were all one day destined to play cricket for India. Pleasantries complete, a serious game soon got underway, and I quickly realised that I was out of my depth. The boys laughed at my amateurishness, coached and goaded me, but in the end, they threw up their hands in despair. They had never met a man so bad at cricket before.

Between them, the boys had a favourite chant, which they shouted over and again: 'Dharavi Lala Bolte' - 'we are the Dharavi Lala' - a gang name that this impish little crew had assigned themselves. During a break in the game, we sat down to rest in the dust, and as I let them scribble in my notebook, somebody muttered the name of a rival band of boys from another part of the slum. Instantly, the eldest cricketer pulled a dull black blade from his pocket and did his best to conjure a look of menace.

But these were not rough slumdogs destined for a life of crime. I had seen sharper blades at my sleepy Somerset comprehensive. The boys of Dharavi were young and unruly, but innocent, and after a few seconds of trying to look dangerous, the boy collapsed in giggles and gave me his knife to inspect. It was a crude, blunt tool, no more dangerous than a spoon, but he was clearly proud of it. After pretending to study its merits, I handed the knife back to him but suggested that he and his friends would be better to solve their rivalries through games of cricket rather than scuffles in the street.

When I stood up to leave, the boys sensed that I was lost and pointed me in the direction of Mahim station. For a while, I retraced my steps down narrow alleys, but before long, I found myself at a flight of stairs leading up to a raised walkway twenty metres above the ground. Muttering a silent thanks to the Dharavi Lala, I climbed up onto the pathway which stretched out above the roof of the slum, running for half a mile towards the station in the distance. On all sides of me, the plains of Dharavi unfurled in a single street-less sheet of corrugated iron, stitched together with plastic - a tattered, improbable skin, stretched tight across the city, with one million people living under its shadow.

But not every denizen of Dharavi was contained beneath that billowing ceiling. As I walked towards the station, I began to notice that people had climbed up onto the rooftops and were sat alone on rafts of sheet metal, adrift atop the slum. Some were muttering into telephones, others were reading books, and some just lay still, sheltering from the bustle below. In a country of over one billion people, where privacy is so rare, these little sanctuaries seemed unimaginably precious, each one of them an island of solitude, hidden from the teeming chaos underneath.

***

Many say that trains are the best way to travel across India, but a train is no use without a ticket. Unfortunately, I had arrived in the country ahead of the Hindu holidays, and most of the trains I wanted to catch were fully booked. So after a brief sojourn in Goa - where I spent a week cooking fish on the beach and riding a Royal Enfield through the jungle - I took a bus back to Mumbai, and from there I had no other choice but to book a flight onwards to Varanasi, landing in the holy city just in time for Diwali.

Sat in my plane seat, I was wondering if Indian passengers would be as loquacious in the air as I had found them to be on railway lines when the man next to me offered his hand. He then delivered a well-practised and overblown introduction in perfect Queen's English:

'My name is Rabuil. I am the Assistant Income Tax Commissioner for West Bengal. A pleasure to make your acquaintance, sir.'

In his mid-thirties, Rabuil had been in the Indian civil service for a little over a year. Business had taken him to Mumbai, but he was making his way back to Kolkata, via Varanasi, where he planned to spend Diwali with his family. All this he explained in his peculiar, exaggerated accent, pronouncing every syllable with care, treating each word as if it was a thing liable to betray him.

'For a long time, I worked for British Telecommunications. I used to have daily elocution lessons there, so as to sound more British on the telephone. Though, as you can imagine, this caused a bit of a stir when I moved to United Healthcare - an American company. Who knew that so many Americans would object to speaking with a British man, even if he was really an Indian?'

Noticing a newspaper in my bag, as the plane ascended, Rabuil nodded towards it and asked:

'Are you aware that the world's tallest statue has been unveiled today? A one hundred and eighty-two metre tribute to the independence leader Sardar Patel, built in the state of Gujarat?'

'I was just reading about it this morning. What do you think about the project?' I asked, knowing that the four hundred and thirty-million-dollar statue had caused local outrage in Gujarat, one of India's poorest states.

'With this statue, Modi's government are not doing anything less than the Mughals did in building the Taj Mahal,' said Rabuil with conviction. 'They are trying to cultivate a heritage purely for their own interests. They will let Gujarati farmers starve so long as they have their bright shining symbol to win votes from the rest of the nation.'

'But will the statue not improve business and attract tourists, being the tallest in the world?' I ventured.

'Pah! The moment it was unveiled, the state of Maharashtra announced that they are already halfway to completing a two hundred and twelve metre statue of Shivaji which will be finished within the year. Nobody will go out of their way to visit the second tallest statue in the world, will they? I'm afraid even our governments are that petty.'

'But if you dislike government so much, why do you work in the civil service?' I probed.

'Because we are in India, young man. I disagree with so much that Modi's government do - such as their irresponsible civic projects and their attempts to turn this country into a Hindu state - but you see, an Indian will do anything for prestige. We are walking, talking paradoxes. The most hypocritical men in the world. Yes, I used to work for British Telecoms where I learnt to speak English with a fine accent and earned a good salary, but now I am the *Assistant Income Tax Commissioner for West Bengal*, and I would not trade that title for the world.'

I nodded in understanding as Rabuil reclined in his chair, proudly muttering his title again to himself.

'But enough about me. You must be excited to see Varanasi? It is a very special place,' he said.

'I am indeed.'

'The Ganga is the most important river in India: it brings life to our nation. You will see many sadhus bathing in its holy waters, but do not be tempted to join them. Bathing in the Ganges requires an Indian constitution. Only last month, a German tourist swam between two of Varanasi's bridges. A short time later, he died of an indecipherable infection - a mystery for the doctors who treated him. Though Varanasi is one of our most cherished cities, the pollution there is, unfortunately, some of the worst in the world. You will see for yourself later...'

That afternoon, stood on Dashashwamedh ghat, Rabuil's words took on new meaning. Varanasi was cocooned in such a deep haze of motorcycle fumes and crop-smoke that from where I was stood on one side of the Ganges, I could not see the opposite riverbank. Though the pollution was made worse at that time of year because farmers were burning their crops in the surrounding fields, Rabuil had explained that Varanasi's smog was always thick, and deep enough even on the best of days to block out the sun.

'At least it means you can save on the sunscreen,' he had joked, 'even if the cost is emphysema.'

At the bottom of the ghat, the stone steps I stood upon seemed to lead down to the edge of the world, and as I gazed across the Ganges, I felt like I was looking upon an image of the earth's primordial oceans, the last remaining portion of the filthy, fizzing soup from which we were born. But what I could see was also an image of the future, a picture of how the world would come to look if we continued to burn things, and bury things, and pour poisons into our streams. Floating out on the oily water, alongside the waste of one million people, I could see the carcasses of dead dogs, slick chemical spills, and rafts of plastic spinning in the current. To me, the Ganges seemed to harbour not life but death – a photographic negative of the fecund seas from which we came, pregnant with venom.

From Dashashwamedh, I walked for miles down the ghats, past palaces, havelis, temples, and all the crumbling antiquities of India's oldest city. In the water, willow-thin men dressed in loincloths were submerging themselves, whilst young buffalo keepers stood oiling the curved horns of their beasts. On the stone steps and muddy banks, squealing boys ran in packs, catching pilgrims in the tangle of their kite-lines. It was ordinary Indian city life, strung along a river, not especially spiritual or profound. But then I arrived at Manikarnika ghat, and looking down towards the water, I saw a dozen dead bodies lying atop funeral pyres, slowly crumbling to ash along the edge of the Ganges.

Hindus believe that cremation on the banks of the Ganges can break the cycle of death and rebirth, resulting in ascension to heaven, an event known as *moksha*. Demand for cremations in Varanasi is so high that bodies burn on the riverbank day and night, every day of the year. At Manikarnika, a huge industrial cremator standing at the top of the ghat receives most of the dead, but on the steps before it, men stand beside weighing scales and huge piles of timber, waiting to sell wood to the most wealthy families - the rich few who can afford to have their loved ones cremated in the open air and have their ashes cast into the hallowed river.

As I looked out across Manikarnika, blinking away the smoke, a group of men emerged at one side of the ghat carrying a body between them that was wrapped in white cloth and covered in fresh garlands of flowers. I watched as they silently carried the thin bundle to a stack of dry logs waiting beside the Ganges. As the corpse was set down, the cloth covering it slipped, and a moment later it fell away completely, revealing the face of the dead man beneath, with its shock of white hair, gaunt yellow cheeks, and purpling mouth crowded with black teeth.

After placing smoking sticks of incense around the pyre, the men took turns kissing their hands and touching the body's feet, before stepping back and forming a solemn crescent, heads down in reverent contemplation. The atmosphere was peaceful, sombre, and in keeping with the occasion. At least, it was for a few short minutes, until a boisterous goat appeared amongst the mourners, walked up to the pyre, and then began nibbling at the flowers placed upon the corpse, quickly inspiring mayhem.

Immediately, the men nearest the body launched forward to beat away the goat, hurling stones at the animal as they ran. In their haste, one of them slipped, and as he fell forward, his flailing arms knocked the corpse and set the pyre wobbling. The crowd let out a gasp of horror, and for a moment, it looked as if the whole thing - logs, cadaver, and goat - would go tumbling into the river. But then a waif-like Brahmin appeared through the smoke, shimmering like a spectre, and holding out a thin brown hand, he steadied the teetering pyre.

In his other hand, the Brahmin carried a clutch of burning grass, and with jeopardy averted, he walked five times around the pyre, chanting as he went, before kneeling to blow a fistful of sparks into the timber. As the fire took hold, the attendant men returned to the crowd, wearing expressions of relief, whilst the Brahmin remained to ensure the body ignited. Once satisfied, he stepped away and disappeared back amongst the fires, the white folds of his shroud trembling in the hot mirages spilling from the bodies slowly turning to embers all around him.

Looking at the men gathered on the ghat, I could see little sadness. Bodies burn every day at Varanasi, and in a crowded country of over one billion people, few Indians are unacquainted with death. Drinking tea and chewing paan, it was impossible to tell which men sat on the stone steps of Manikarnika had come to honour their dead, and which had simply come to socialise. But one detail did stand out. Of all the figures in the crowd, not one of them was a woman. In Varanasi, women are explicitly barred from the funeral ghats, a measure tragically made necessary by a history of grieving widows throwing themselves onto the burning pyres of their dead husbands in acts of self-immolation.

Alongside the burning of the bodies, hundreds of other ceremonies take place up and down the ghats of Varanasi every day - the necessary rituals of a four-thousand-year-old religion that boasts thirty-three million deities, every one of which requires worship and devotion. Alongside these daily rites and traditions, Varanasi is also the epicentre of many religious festivals, and celebrations there outstrip those held in any other Indian city. Which was fortunate, because the day that I arrived marked the beginning of the most famous Hindu festival of all: Diwali.

Dedicated to Lakshmi and Ganesh, the gods of auspiciousness and patron deities of artists and writers, the Hindu festival of light celebrates the victory of good over evil and of knowledge over ignorance. In India, it is a time for Hindus, Sikhs, and Muslims alike to cleanse themselves, cleanse their homes, and celebrate new beginnings. And in Varanasi, it is also a time for young children to take to the streets, with armfuls of rockets, firecrackers, and cherry bombs, to spend their evening lighting fires and doing their very best to burn India's holiest city to the ground.

As I walked back towards Dashashwamedh in the evening, the first sign of the celebrations was a thread of camphor lamps that I spotted floating down the Ganges, their elegant flames forming a pretty ribbon of fire stretching from one end of the city to the other. Above the river, cordite clouds had begun to gather, as children and men appeared firing missiles, lighting fireworks, and shooting cannons into the sky. Every few seconds, after the ignition of a monstrous rocket, a false star would arc over the river and hang suspended for a moment above Varanasi, before burying itself between the city's streets and bursting into a bright explosion amidst a chorus of panicked screams. I had been told that every year there are many fires and that every year there are deaths. Irrespective of the danger, sadhus and pilgrims still lay outstretched on the ghats, their saffron robes pulled over their faces, as motionless in their slumber as the bodies that were still burning on the pyres only a short walk away.

I soon learnt that a crowd of sprinting children, coupled with the sound of a menacing hiss, usually heralded the imminent blast of a banger. Whenever a gang of them began to run, anybody standing nearby would look for cover, diving over walls or hiding behind the hulls of upturned coracles, waiting for the explosion to boom along the riverbank. When thought safe, one by one, people would emerge from their hiding places, and following the trail of flames dripping onto the street, they would crane their necks to see if any buildings were burning, some of them looking up with eager eyes, urging the flames to take hold.

Amongst the camphor lamps floating on the water, there were men launching rockets from boats, nearly sinking themselves in the process. I watched as one vessel, half aflame, had to beat a rapid retreat to shore, and the giddy crew were so happy to survive that they gifted me a cherry bomb to light in their honour. After igniting the sputtering fuse, I was three steps away when the whole thing blew up, leaving a bright white hole in my vision and draining the world of sound. Turning around, I could see the men cheering, but their congratulations were lost beneath the screech of my eardrums which from that point onwards kept up a gentle ringing for the rest of the night.

Wandering the city for half an hour felt like traversing a warzone, and as the night progressed, the explosions only became more violent. Some celebrants preferred more gentle devices, launching peaceful paper lanterns that rose slowly into the sky. But the lanterns would only climb so high before being shot down by a rocket and then falling to earth in a heap of burning debris, becoming steady street-fires around which Varanasi's cows gathered to warm their skinny hides.

Eventually, I turned back towards my hostel, and I was only a few streets away from the relative safety of my dormitory when a group of men appeared, howling with excitement, one of them clutching a fizzing orb the size of a coconut. As the fuse burnt lower, the man began to panic, and in the end, he decided to drop the bomb in the middle of the road. As people fled in fear, the ball exploded in a violent theatre of flame, sending bits of wood and plastic flying past my face, riding on a wave of menacing heat. A moment later, a motorcyclist appeared and rode through the burning remnants of the firework. Five seconds earlier and he would have been ripped to pieces.

The city was hell-bent on carnage, as if in the grip of a riot, but everyone ran around wearing smiles of glee. People were tying bangers in bunches, trying to make the biggest explosions possible, their loud shouts ringing out above a backdrop of shattering glass. Holy is not the word to describe it, but it was epic and otherworldly, especially when I went up to the roof of my hostel and found that half city was ablaze. And though I had been told that the rockets would stop at midnight, when I finally fell asleep in the early hours of the morning, white flashes were still lightning up the streets, and bright bruises of colour were still blooming high above the darkened banks of the Ganges.

Chapter Fifteen

But from himself the Phoenix only springs:
Self-born, begotten by the parent flame
In which he burn'd, another, and the same.

- John Dryden, *Metamorphoses*

As my flight descended into Mandalay, I could see the outline of the city from the window of the aeroplane. A small hill, spiked with shining stupas, rose beside a square palace which set the pattern for Mandalay's streets. One box eclipsed the next, square encompassing square, until the edges of the city met a wall of hot, sullen country, pimpled with gold pagodas. Outwards from there, the land was empty, save for a few solitary temples that stood gleaming in the jungle or shining on the banks of the Irrawaddy.

I had hoped to cross into Myanmar from the Indian state of Manipur, but the border between the two countries had been closed for travellers unable to afford the extortionate price of a private guide. This left me with no choice but to take a flight from Kolkata, and as I walked out of Mandalay airport, I braced myself for the inevitable barrage of bus conductors and rickshaw drivers that I had grown accustomed to in India. But I was met, instead, by silence. No-one accosted me, nobody begged, there were no entreaties or pleas. A placid ticket officer simply sold me a seat on a bus, and within minutes, the airport was behind me, and I was on the road to Mandalay.

The bus dropped me by the moat of the square palace that only an hour before I had admired from the air, and immediately I set off walking through the city, eager to get a sense of a new country after so long spent in India. There were echoes of the subcontinent here: red paan stains on the roads, Hindu temples, and lithe, pregnant mongrels with tortured dugs hanging halfway to the ground. But the sometimes subtle, sometimes drastic differences that mark one country from the next were present too. Instead of short bidi cigarettes, the men smoked thick green cheroots that let out clouds of herbaceous smoke. Instead of pale brown uniforms, the police were dressed in black and rode two-up on motorcycles, the pillions clutching pump-action shotguns. And instead of bare-skinned sadhus with banks of matted hair, claret-clad monks ambled down the streets, their shaven heads glinting in the sunlight.

Despite his famous poem, Kipling never set foot in Mandalay. If he had, he would have known that it is not a city by the sea but one which lies at the centre of a vast plain, the only feature for miles around being Mandalay hill, the landmark which gives the city its name. From the foot of the hill, I followed a snaking path to its summit, pagodas and monasteries appearing at every turn, occasionally framed by a parade of young boys, dressed in pink robes, on their way to study. Alongside the boys, women with yellow circles painted on their cheeks cycled past, their make-up made from a tincture containing thanaka wood, worn by ladies across Myanmar to protect against the Burmese sun. By the time I reached the top of the hill, that same powerful sun had risen high in the sky, and as I emerged into its blinding glare, I found myself on the terrace of Su Taung Pyae Pagoda, looking down at the city of Mandalay far below.

Though the golden tiles of the pagoda were incandescent in the morning light, a few merciful patches of shade remained, and a cool marble slab provided me with first a bench, and then a bed, as I lay down to rest for a while and quickly fell into a light sleep.

Often whilst travelling, I found myself sitting up in a park, a church, a mosque, or a pagoda after a short nap, and for the first few minutes of syrupy wakefulness, I would have no recollection of where I was. Rubbing my eyes, the world would return to me as it comes to a child, entirely novel, entirely strange, and brimming with curiosities. Only by slowly studying the details and stitching fragments back together would I come to remember which country I had woken up in. For five minutes after each of these sleeps, the world was a depthless inventory of wonders, and I was a boy again, free to discover them all.

That day in Mandalay, when I woke on my stone bed in Su Taung Pyae Pagoda, I found three giggling women wrapped in light dresses staring at me. One of them came forward, and without speaking, she pointed to her camera. Still blinking away sleep, I obliged their requests for photographs, as each of the women came and perched on my knee, posing for a picture. Flattered by this attention, I started to wonder if this was reality or reverie, just as the final woman grasped my hand.

'Thank you,' she said, in a voice two octaves deeper than my own. It was only then that I noticed the masculine jawbone, the black hairs on the back of the hand, and the raised lump of an Adam's apple. As the three figures strode off, waving at me coquettishly, I quickly looked away in embarrassment. In one corner of the temple, a grave-looking monk stood watching the scene unfold. I locked eyes with him for a moment and half-smiled an apology, to which the holy man burst into a fit of uncontrollable giggles, his plump belly rocking with laughter beneath the thick folds of his robes.

Coming down from the hill, I walked past Kuthodaw pagoda, which like many of its neighbouring temples consisted of a gilded stupa surrounded by hundreds of rows of smaller shrines. Kuthodaw, however, is unique amongst the pagodas of Mandalay because housed within the small white shrines of the temple are seven hundred and thirty stone tablets, inscribed with one thousand four hundred and sixty pages of the Buddhist Tripitaka, making Kuthodaw the largest book in the world. Never having stood inside a book before, I went and strolled amongst its pages, each stone tablet as big as myself and filled with tightly curling characters, wondering at the effort that would be required to read, let alone build such a tome.

Standing inside Kuthodaw made me realise that I was in want of some reading material, so I was glad when I stumbled across a street-side bookseller in the centre of Mandalay. His table was littered with poorly printed copies of Orwell's *Burmese Days* and Kipling's *Collected Poems,* but there were more contemporary titles amongst his collection too. After leafing through his library for a while, I finally settled on a book which I had hardly expected to find in Mandalay:

Azeem Ibrahim's *The Rohingyas: Inside Myanmar's Hidden Genocide.* I had first learnt of the Rohingya crisis several years before when Western media began to document the struggle of the world's largest stateless population - an Islamic ethnic group living in Myanmar's Rakhine state, named the Rohingyas (meaning 'from the Rakhine'). Though the Burmese constitution officially recognises one hundred and thirty-five ethnicities as comprising the population of Myanmar, the Rohingyas are not included in that list, and for decades they have been denied citizenship and forced to live under the oppressive watch of the Burmese military.

The crisis began to demand global attention in 2016 when fighting broke out between the Rohingyas, the police, and local Buddhists. As the violence continued to escalate, within the space of a year, over seven-hundred thousand Rohingyas had fled to Bangladesh as refugees. In his book, first published in 2015, Azeem Ibrahim warned that Myanmar was on the brink of genocide. In an afterword written two years later, defining genocide as the massacring of a people or the systematic destruction of their culture, Ibrahim argues that genocide has undoubtedly occurred in the Rakhine, accusing the Burmese government of systematically destroying the Rohingyan way of life.

At the time of my visit, in November of 2018, the crisis was still developing. The same morning that I bought Ibrahim's book, Amnesty International stripped the Burmese leader, Aung San Suu Kyi, of her Ambassador of Conscience Award for her failure to condemn the violence. Once celebrated for rescuing her country from military dictatorship and setting Myanmar on the path to democracy, in the eyes of the international community, Suu Kyi had fallen far from grace, with many accusing the leader of being complicit to genocide.

The situation, however, was complicated. Although Myanmar celebrates its diverse population, it is an overwhelmingly Buddhist state, and the majority of its citizens are ethnically Burmese. Included amongst the Buddhist demographic is a small group of radical extremists who are fervently anti-Muslim, and in Myanmar, where all Buddhist boys are expected to spend some time in a monastery, the monks hold great political power. Added to that, although the military junta officially ended in 2011, the army still holds a quarter of the seats in parliament and exercises enormous influence. For Aung San Suu Kyi, it was a choice between reprimanding the military and risking another coup or staying silent when Burmese soldiers started killing in the

Rakhine.

The intricate situation has deep historical roots. Many Burmese are critical of the Rohingyas, claiming that the Rohingyan people have no claim to the land in the Rakhine and that they migrated there from Bangladesh when Britain relinquished control of Myanmar in 1948. But a small number of others are more sympathetic, recognising that the Rohingyas have lived in the area known as the Rakhine for hundreds of years, and some Burmese argue that the Rohingyas should be welcomed as citizens of Myanmar along with the one hundred and thirty-five other officially recognised ethnicities.

Because of the ongoing struggle of the Rohingyas, I questioned if I should even visit Myanmar, and I contemplated boycotting the country, as many other tourists had, fearing that any money I spent might find its way into the pockets of a government guilty of crimes against humanity. In the end, I decided that I could justify travelling through Myanmar as long as I educated myself on the issue of the Rohingyas and shed light upon it in my own writing. Reading Ibrahim's book on my first afternoon in Mandalay was the beginning of that education, but it would not be its end.

***

On my flight into Mandalay, the Irrawaddy river had shone like a scar from the air - a smooth, brown rift, cleaving Myanmar in two. When I left the city on an old boat furnished with chairs torn from a Russian airliner, the river had changed into a stretch of pale water, slow and languorous, that leeched past damp slopes of silt. Higher up its banks, the sides of the Irrawaddy were clotted with green foliage, intermittently broken by the wooden stilts of a house or the gleam of a golden pagoda. Otherwise, for over one hundred miles, the riverbank passed by unchanged, lifeless aside from the groups of women who came down from their villages to wash clothes in the water, spending their days throwing armfuls of wet lungis against the hot rocks of Asia.

After an eight-hour journey on the old boat, I arrived at Bagan, the ancient capital of the Pagan Kingdom, which at its height eight centuries earlier had stretched as wide as the borders of modern Myanmar. Sleepy from a full day of Burmese sun, I soon found a hostel, and having heard that Bagan was at its best at dawn, I went straight to bed, preparing myself for an early morning.

I woke before the sun was up, and borrowing a bicycle, I pedalled out into the night, following a road that left the town to turn towards the jungle. Critters shook the bushes all around, and beside the sandy trail I followed, huge forms began to rise in the darkness. Pyramids of shadow, growing taller and taller, continued to loom over me as I wobbled onwards, unable to properly discern their shapes. Then a drop of light flared in one corner of the sky, sending a breath of wind blowing through the scrub, signalling the imminent arrival of dawn.

Finding a small hillock, I climbed to its top, just as the sun began to show above a ridge of distant hills. The feint wind that I had felt stirred the morning mists, and standing up above the writhing cloud, like rocks rising in a drying tide, hundreds of stone pagodas began to appear. These were not gold, or white, or silver pagodas, but old stone temples, wrought of red bricks, crooked and cankered with age, that rested amidst the jungle like a herd of sleeping creatures dreaming in the dawn. As day broke, more and more continued to appear, pushing up the sun with their bronze spikes, until thousands pierced the sky, slowly fading in colour beneath the bright light of day.

Taking to my bicycle again before the unbearable heat arrived, I rode deeper into the ruins. In the morning light, I could now see that the trail I followed branched into many others, peeling away past bushes sheeted with spider's webs and through fields that I had been warned were full of cobras. The trails, some of them no wider than a man, ran to every stupa, pagoda, and monastery of ancient Bagan, built by kings, nobles, and wealthy men to atone for their sins and to secure a favourable reincarnation. There were once twice as many monuments as those that stand today, but in the last fifty years, earthquakes had levelled thousands. I took their number as a sign that Bagan had been home to a lot of guilty men over the centuries, many of whom had clearly suffered a crisis of conscience in their later lives.

Of all the characters from the history of Bagan, one man is remembered as particularly evil: the notorious King Narathu, who ruled from 1167-1171. Aggressive, obsessive, and vainglorious, Narathu murdered both his father and brother to take the throne, and upon his ascension, he ordered the construction of a grand temple named Dhammayangyi. To be sure of its strength, the king insisted that no space be left between the bricks of his temple, and he was known to use a needle to test the workmanship of his masons for even the slightest gap. Those of inadequate craft were killed, whilst the best labourers were allowed to continue until their section of the temple was complete, after which Narathu would cut off their hands to ensure that they would never build anything so great again.

In the end, Narathu murdered his wife and was killed in retribution by her father. He died before Dhammayangyi was finished, and the temple can still be recognised today by its unfinished roof, which no stonemason since the evil king has ever dared to complete. Amongst a plain of one thousand spiked stupas, Dhammayangyi stands alone as the only temple with a flat top. Inside, instead of the typical Buddha found within most of Bagan's pagodas, three statues commemorate the father, brother, and wife who were the victims of Narathu's familicide. Behind them, like almost all the pagodas of Bagan, an inaccessible chamber is enclosed by four walls of brick - the pregnant heart of the temple, hiding nine centuries of secrets in its impenetrable bosom.

I spent my day in Bagan cycling amongst the ruins, stopping to read in the shade of the temples and passing through villages made of bamboo. At the edges of the villages, men shepherded cattle through the scrub and tended fragrant fires, whilst outside their wooden homes, women cradled children and sifted pans of rice. Hazy with wood-smoke and profoundly quiet, the villages looked as if they had survived unchanged since the days of Narathu. Shielded from the rest of the world by fields of tall grass and collapsing pagodas, they had lingered for eight hundred years, the last living remnants of a once-mighty kingdom.

As I pedalled back to my hostel in the evening, an old man driving a horse trap came to a halt at my side. With a flick of his whip, he motioned for me to load my bicycle into his cart, and a moment later, I was bouncing through the sunset, being pulled along by a Burmese pony. Pausing to chat with other drivers, we toured a handful of villages as the old man went about his errands, smoking cheroot after cheroot. Finally, we turned towards the new town of Bagan, but before we left the ruins, the driver pulled his cart alongside a break in the trees so that I could take one last look at the throng of pagodas cast across the jungle, each of them fading to enormous shadows, like a herd of giants settling down for the night amongst the bush, resting in precisely the same pattern as they had risen at dawn.

***

Leaving the Irrawaddy, a night bus carried me from Bagan to

Nyaung Shwe, a town on the northern shore of Inle Lake, where I arrived on the eve of the Tazaungdaing festival. Held every year to celebrate the end of the rainy season and the conclusion of Kathina (the period in which monks are given new alms and robes), Tazaungdaing is celebrated across Myanmar. But the best place to see it, at least according to the Mandalay shopkeeper who first told me of the festival, was Taunggyi, the capital of Shan state, which was just one hour's drive from Nyaung Shwe.

The shopkeeper in Mandalay had told me that the festival was at its most interesting at night, so after idling all day alongside the lake, I climbed into the back of an open truck destined for the hills of Taunggyi, carrying with me an unshakeable sense of nervousness. Only the day before, Taunggyi city centre had been evacuated after armed police discovered three bombs planted outside a marketplace. The military had swept the festival ground, finding no other explosives, but like many parts of Myanmar, Shan state was affected by intermittent clashes between the local Shan ethnic minority and the national military, a tense situation which drew foreboding parallels with developments in the Rakhine.

Civil unrest aside, there was another reason for my nervousness. The shopkeeper in Mandalay had warned me that the festivities at Taunggyi were so dangerous that deaths occurred there every year. He did not explain the precise nature of the danger, but he had repeated one piece of advice over and over again:

'Don't get too close to the balloons.'

Arriving at the edge of the festival, I followed a crowd into a maze of food stalls, bars, and old fairground rides, affronted by light and sound. There were stalls selling clothes, spices, medicine, and thanaka, alongside little restaurants offering shrimp pancakes, skewered pig tails, and mountains of moon cake. Tall towers of whisky bottles and pyramids of beer rose beside decrepit old Ferris wheels that juddered and shuddered as they span. Despite so many distractions, the crowd kept moving slowly forward, eventually spilling out into the bowl of a wide valley, where the spectacle which made Tazaungdaing festival so famous was about to begin: the launching of the Taunggyi fire balloons.

Stood on a small ridge, I looked over an audience of thousands of people, packed worryingly close together, all of them singing, dancing, and trembling with anticipation. At the centre of the crowd, a group of men had started to unfold a vast sheet of fabric, just as three flaming torches appeared at the edge of the valley. Slowly, the men who carried these torches made their way through the press, until they reached the unfolding balloon, where they stopped to light a fire. As the fire began to inflate the balloon with boiling air, people came forward and fixed hundreds of lighted candles to the floating fabric. Ten minutes later, the monstrous lantern had swollen to the size of a hot air balloon, bulging above the crowd. Covering its thin skin, painted in a tapestry of flames five metres high, was the image of a Buddhist monk knelt in solemn prayer.

People began to cheer once the final candle was fixed in place and the balloon's full illumined form was rotated for everyone to see. Then a vast candelabra, several metres across, was hung below the canopy – a tail of flickering light to mark its path skyward. For a while, it hung motionless in the valley, a taught, shimmering inferno, straining at its anchor-ropes. Then, at last, the balloon was released and allowed to begin its gentle blaze skywards, amidst the roars of a crowd erupting in ecstasy.

I watched as half a dozen of these huge lanterns were inflated, paraded, and then released, each one designed and created by a team competing for the prize of most impressive display. But after the sixth balloon, a truck drove into the centre of the crowd, and suddenly the atmosphere shifted. From the back of the truck, a white pallet was unloaded and placed on the ground beside another balloon which had just begun to rise, but this balloon was not clad in candles, for it would be carrying far more volatile cargo.

As the excitement increased, so did the nervousness of the crowd. Several men came up to me, clapping me on the shoulders, grinning wide whisky smiles that were crossed with a mixture of fear and delight. Once the balloon was filled, all attention turned towards the pale crate strapped beneath it and two long threads that had been lain across the ground. As the lantern strained against its ropes, the crate was lifted off the earth, and a moment before it was released, two men stepped forwards and held a pair of flaming torches to the threads, causing the fuses to fizz into life, just as the canopy began its climb.

For a few seconds, nothing happened. The balloon rose peacefully above the silent crowd, lifting higher and higher. When it was still less than one hundred metres above the ground, a single scouting rocket shot out from the pallet, arced over the valley, and then detonated with a pop that was watched from below by ten thousand restless eyes. Another intake of breath. A multitude of nervous heartbeats. And then suddenly the whole sky burst into flame.

Flying out in all directions, streaming across the hills and shooting straight down to earth, plumes of fireworks burning white, red, green, and blue erupted from beneath the balloon and sent the crowd screaming and squealing in all directions. The temptation was to turn away and seek protection from the rockets, but as the balloon climbed higher and the threat of being burnt subsided, people began to turn their unbelieving eyes towards the helix of flickering fire that was gradually being strung above the valley.

Burning away the clouds, its flight unfaltering, the balloon continued upwards, unleashing an endless stream of fire as it went. Then, just as it began to fade out of sight, one enormous volley sounded, and a single rocket in the shape of a glowing bird began spiralling down to the crowd, vanishing in flames only twenty metres above us like a phoenix dissolved in fire. And still the balloon kept climbing, firing rockets and sprouting tails of light, roaring its way up towards unknown heights, vicious and graceful and beautiful beyond measure.

I was stunned into silence. At first, I thought the balloon must have been a special creation, launched to mark the pinnacle of the Tazaungdaing celebrations. Then, five minutes later, another truck appeared, another pallet of gunpowder was unloaded, and another balloon began to rise, this time less than fifty metres from where I stood. As the torchbearers passed me in the crowd, I felt the heat of their flames, and suddenly the danger was real. Caught amidst the impassable scrum, I had no choice but to turn and watch as the balloon was filled, the fuses were lit, and another floating bomb was released into the night. But it was only a matter of seconds until I realised that the flight of this balloon was doomed.

Initially, it rose steadily and looked marked for success. Then, suddenly, a flame from one of the fuses set the canopy alight, and a ribbon of red tore up one side of the fabric, ripping the balloon in two. As the whole bright bulb collapsed in on itself, the crate of loaded explosives dropped down to earth, streaming flames as it fell, and the crowd below drew breath and contracted, bracing themselves for a tragedy.

The moment the fireworks hit the ground, a cavernous ball of fire engulfed the nearest spectators, as ten thousand others screamed and ran in wild, animal panic. Turning my back to the explosion, I began to flee like everyone else, just as a rocket struck my left shoulder, sending a volley of pain along my arm. The crowd managed several panicked steps until someone ahead of me fell, and then before I knew what had happened, I was lying in the dust and bodies were falling all around me.

Struggling to my knees, I emerged at the surface of the fallen crowd only to see that rockets were still streaming everywhere. In front of me, a man running with a baby in his arms was violently pushed, sending the child flying through the air. The father rose from the ground and punched the man who had pushed him, splintering his jaw with a crack that was loud enough to be heard even above the nose of the unceasing explosions. It was sheer, unmitigated panic, brutal in its terror, and by the time it was done, one man lay dead in the smouldering crater that the fire balloon had left behind.

Deaths, however, were commonplace at Taunggyi, and after firemen had doused the burning debris and the injured had been carried away, another balloon was unpacked and sent upwards to light its own path across the valley. It was still firing as I sat in a truck and rolled back down the hills to Nyuang Shwe - a slow, silent, lethal blossom, rising higher and higher, burning all the way, like a sputtering star being blasted back up into oblivion, the very picture of loneliness.

***

I ate mohinga every day that I was in Myanmar. A cloudy, peppery, rich fish broth, filled with slender rice noodles, chilli flakes, vegetable fritters, and chunks of lime, it made for the perfect breakfast. But no bowl of mohinga tasted as good as the one I ate by the side of the road in Yangon, at six o'clock in the morning, on my first day in Myanmar's capital.

I had taken a night bus to reach Yangon, which dropped me outside the National Museum. The museum's doors opened at eight, which meant that I had time after my mohinga for several cups of earthy black coffee, made with beans grown in the mountains of Shan State. When finally inside, I found the first four floors of the archives to be predictably filled with artefacts from the Pagan era and displays centred on the Burmese and Buddhist elements of Myanmar's past. The fifth floor, however, housed a much more interesting exhibition, dedicated to the ethnic minorities of Myanmar - those one hundred and thirty-five peoples officially recognised in the national constitution.

Amongst the exhibits, there were weapons, tools, crafts, and traditional dress from the most remote tribes, collected from the far corners of Myanmar's seven states. Photographs of Padang women with their long necks stretched by golden hoops hung next to images of Naga warriors wearing hats made from the tusks of wild boar. Portraits of Archa girls from the Chinese border stood beside stills of Chin ladies, their faces covered in elaborate tattoos. There was even a video of Inle Lake fishermen at work, famous for propelling their narrow boats by rowing with oars clutched in their feet.

Though it was meant to be a celebration of the ethnic diversity of Myanmar, the exhibition felt more like a memorial predicated upon the extinction of the very culture it sought to preserve. To have the exhibition bracketed off from the rest of the museum made it seem as if Myanmar's history did not quite belong to the ethnic minorities, as if they were just an afterthought. And it came as little shock to learn that nowhere in the museum was any mention made of the Rohingyas.

Outside the museum, I read an article in a Burmese newspaper providing an update on the situation in the Rakhine. Rohingyan refugees in Bangladesh had rejected the first attempts at repatriation, refusing to return to Myanmar despite Bangladesh's efforts to eject them. As long as the Burmese government denied them citizenship rights, many Rohingya feared that returning home would only lead to further violence. It was a bitter stalemate, with no resolution in sight, unless the Burmese government was willing to grant the Rohingyas national identity.

Over the past week, I had tried to broach the topic with the few Burmese people I encountered who could speak English, but I had met with little success. The shopkeeper in Mandalay who had eagerly encouraged me to visit Taunggyi refused to discuss the topic and was reluctant to even call the Rohingyas by name, referring instead to the 'supposed victims living in the Rakhine'. He maintained that the Rohingya had arrived in Myanmar as refugees from Bangladesh when the British Empire fell, and as far as he was concerned, the best thing they could do was give up their citizenship claims and vanish altogether.

Elsewhere, when I asked a café owner in Nyuang Shwe about violence in the Rakhine, he had quoted an old Burmese proverb:

'If there is one person alone in Myanmar, everything is well. If there are two people together, they will start a fight. If there are three, there will be a rampage.'

For him, the massacres and violence were nobody's fault. In a turbulent and crowded country of so many different ethnicities, some tension was inevitable. The real problem, he said, originated with the British and their decision to lump together so many disparate tribes, regions, states, and peoples in a single nation before abandoning it. Matters were little helped by the fact that the Rakhine is the poorest state in an already poor country, and in poverty, people cling to their religion, which is why the café owner thought the Muslim Rohingyas clashed so frequently with the local Buddhist majority.

It was clear that the issue of the Rohingyas was a complex one, and I was grateful for every conversation I had that provided a new perspective. As well as talking to shopkeepers and café owners, I had asked friends from home if anyone had contacts in Myanmar. For a long time, my requests went unanswered, but when a university friend told me that he knew someone studying history in Yangon, I sensed an opportunity and immediately asked for an introduction.

I met the student, who asked to be called Charlotte, in a café close to Sule pagoda, in the centre of the capital. Like most of the people I had spoken to, she was Buddhist and ethnically Burmese, but she was also young, liberal, and cosmopolitan. Fortunately, she was very eager to talk, despite coming straight to the café from a long shift at a nearby school where she was working as a language teacher alongside her studies at Dagon University.

'The problem,' said Charlotte, 'is that the people of Myanmar are so closely tied to their land. Unlike many Burmese, I do believe that the Rohingyas have lived in the Rakhine for a long time, definitely since before the end of the British Empire. But recognising the Rohingyas as citizens would mean giving them land, and in Myanmar, all the land is accounted for. No Buddhist in the Rakhine will give up his fields for a Muslim.'

'How bad do you think the situation is? Are people right to use the word genocide?' I asked.

'To tell the truth, I think the situation with the Rohingyas is beyond hope. A few years ago, I used to teach a Rohingyan boy in one of my classes. He was bullied by the other children because of his different religion, his darker skin, and the strange language his parents spoke to him. After a few months, he left the school. I don't know where he is now. Harmful attitudes towards the Rohingyas are so deeply rooted in our society, but I also worry about the fate of other ethnic minorities, like the Shan and the Kachin. They're increasingly coming into conflict with the military too.'

When I told Charlotte about my recent trip to Shan state, and of my surprise at the relaxed safety measures at Taunggyi, she laughed and replied:

'The Burmese look for cures, not preventatives. A mother doesn't smooth the edges of her table to stop her young son from hitting his head, but she'll always have plasters ready for when he does. I guess what has happened with the Rohingyas is something quite similar. Right now, we're trying to struggle through the mess that we've made, but more should have been done to prevent it in the first place. That's what worries me about the other ethnic groups - that something like this might happen again to them because we haven't learnt from events in the Rakhine.'

'Do you think the Burmese government care about international criticism? Or are worried about the tourist boycott?' I asked.

'You need to understand that it's only Western tourists who have stopped coming. This year Myanmar has seen more Chinese visitors than ever before. That's mostly because of the way the situation has been portrayed in Western media. European and American journalists are quick to criticise, but the complexities of a country like mine can't be explained in a single news article. The only way to get a grasp of this situation is to read as much as possible, and to speak to as many people as you can.'

With this in mind, before we parted, Charlotte scribbled the address of another coffee shop on a napkin and handed it to me. Years before, following the unexpected death of her father, she had attended poetry readings at the café to help her deal with her grief. She remembered that the owner at the time had been a Rohingya, and she thought that if he was still there, then I should try and speak with him.

After thanking Charlotte for her time, I set off walking across the city, pushing through the creepers of the banyan trees that hang over every pavement in Yangon. The Burmese have the best smiles of any people on earth, and every face I passed on the street beamed back expressions of kindness. Those smiles made the violence occurring on the nation's fringes seem all the more harrowing. I could not fathom how a country of such gentle, welcoming people could also be a breeding ground for genocide.

After half an hour's walk, I arrived at the address of the café written upon the napkin. Inside, a middle-aged Burmese lady greeted me with a grin that stretched from ear to ear. She invited me to sit, poured some green tea, and asked what I would like to order. When I asked if the café was still owned by a Rohingya man, her face suddenly fell, and her voice became grave and inflected with anger.

'No,' she said emphatically. 'There is nobody here from the Rakhine. You are very much mistaken.'

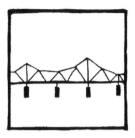

Chapter Sixteen

One does not reproach a child in the east.

- Graham Greene, *The Quiet American*

The world has not yet shrunk enough for an average lifetime to be ample time to see it all, and after eight months of journeying, I became more discriminate in the way I spent my days. From Myanmar, my route lay east, through Thailand and Laos, two countries I had visited five years before. Aged eighteen, those nations had been a marvel to me, but as I stepped across the border into Thailand for a second time, I knew that it would not be the place that it had once seemed half a decade earlier.

The transition at the border was profound, and it was mostly a matter of money: Myanmar was poor, Thailand was rich. This was in part due to the success of the Thai tourist trade, but it was also because Thailand's fortunate geography had sheltered it from the designs of colonial powers when the rest of Southeast Asia was being ravaged in the late nineteenth century. Whilst the English and French were busy colonising Myanmar and Laos, Siam was left as a convenient buffer between the two territories, surviving largely unspoilt, and the implications of this are still felt today. Beyond the border at Myawaddy, the Thai road was immaculate, the cars that lined it were modern and expensive, and just visible in the distance, glinting in the sun, was the first of a thousand shopping malls.

Seven hours later, I was in Chiang Mai in the north of the country, fighting my way through the nocturnal melee that is the city's famous night market. Caught amongst a crush of damp, bilious tourists, it was half an hour before I found a seat at a restaurant and sat down to a bowl of Tom Yam soup. Looking out at the crowd, the only Thai face I could see was a poster of King Maha Vajiralongkorn, plastered across one side of a building, looking gormless and bewildered above a sea of khaki-clad Americans.

I had grown too accustomed to the privilege of travelling through places that barely received any visitors. The crowds in Chiang Mai threatened the vanity in my heart, the same vanity that can be found in the heart of most travellers: the desire for unique and rare experiences. Instead of pushing past the crowds and searching for something meaningful in a country saturated with millions of tourists, as a better writer might have done, I ran from them, horrified, and after just a single night in Thailand, I was alone again in the back of a night bus, rushing through the unlit jungle.

A day later, I arrived in Luang Prabang, another place already known to me. In the dawn light, processions of monks were making their slow way to the temples, whilst shop owners gulped bowls of steaming broth on the roadside. It was a flicker of Asia, surviving against the odds, exactly as I remembered it. But by lunchtime, just as with Chiang Mai, Luang Prabang was teeming with tourists, and as I walked amongst the artisanal bakeries, the cafés, bistros, and wine bars, I felt like I was wandering through a Parisian arrondissement, rather than an ancient Laotian city.

That night, I stayed in a dank dormitory on the banks of the river Mekong where I was reminded that I was not in Paris after all. The only other person in the dormitory was an Irish chef who spent the evening sat in one corner of the mosquito-riddled room, shaping a waxy ball of opium into thin black noodles and smoking them one by one. Resting around the chef's feet was a crescent of glass whisky bottles with dark creatures coiled inside – half-rotten snakes, scorpions, and millipedes – the beasts favoured by Luang Prabang's famous distillers who sell their spirits in the local market, infused with all the critters of the jungle. The Irishman had come to Luang Prabang to buy a stock of bottles which he hoped to sell to tourists in Bangkok. I was inspecting them one by one when he pulled a vast jar out from under his bunk. Looking down, I saw a black paw pickling in liquor and realised that surrounding it, drowned in drink, was the butchered body of a moon bear.

By the time I boarded another night bus the following day, my journeys eastwards from Yangon had melded together into a single hellish mural, one hundred nightmares long. Hungry and exhausted, I had spent three days being thrown from side to side on winding mountain roads, unable to sleep, unable to write, barely able to read in the moonlight. Only two splinters of memory remain from the sleep-starved fog of those days. The first is the image of an overturned truck, a disaster of steel and glass, wrecked just beyond the Vietnamese border. The second is the sound of the passengers on my own bus screaming as we went sliding down the mountain in an uncontrollable skid, rescued at the last minute by the driver, just as we were about to plummet over the edge of the cloud-wrapped mountains.

By the end of it all, nothing in the world could have persuaded me to step onto another bus. And thankfully, I did not have to, because waiting for me in Hanoi was an old friend and accomplice, sat astride a shiny new motorcycle, with a space on the back for me.

***

I first met Steven aged fourteen in a park near my house. Searching for a lost rugby ball, I had parted the leaves of a bush and found him crouching inside, hiding from a group of boys intent on giving him a beating because he had sold them a bag of tea leaves disguised as tobacco. He promised me five pounds if I pointed them in the wrong direction, which seemed a fair price, and I have been trying to keep up with the ceaseless string of melodramas which constitute his life ever since.

On a whim, Steven had left England a year earlier with a forged teaching certificate, and after surfacing in Hanoi, he had won himself a job at one of the best schools in Vietnam. Prone to all manner of calamities and disasters, I was amazed that he had lasted so long in Southeast Asia without crashing a motorcycle or contracting an exotic disease. But when I saw him at Hanoi bus station, sat atop a thundering Suzuki and chatting to a policeman in Vietnamese, he looked the image of a well-adjusted expat, and I knew right away that Hanoi had become his home.

'Xin chào!' he shouted, upon seeing me step off the bus. 'You took your time getting here. It's only been eight months.'

'Isn't that bike a little big for you?' I jested, nodding to the Suzuki, knowing that Steven had no licence.

'Sam, it's Hanoi. Nobody has a licence. Come on, let's go get a beer.'

After hundreds of miles confined to buses, it was a pleasure to sit on the back of a motorcycle and look about me for once, guided by a driver who knew his territory intuitively. Though I had arrived in the dark underbelly of Hanoi, amidst a clot of highways and flyovers, Steven knew every inch of the city by heart. Racing through streams of traffic, he rode with a sixth sense, slotting the bike through invisible gaps and roaring past lines of blackened high-rises, on through the ugly, cluttered body of Vietnam's capital.

After twenty minutes of riding, we emerged on the northern edge of West Lake, the blank heart of Hanoi, just as a lilac dusk was falling. Like Paris with its empty tower, Hanoi is a city centred on nothingness, the whole metropolis being wrapped around a liquid paw-print which spreads for a mile from one edge of the city to the other. Dark and lifeless, the lake was as still as a puddle of oil and totally empty except for two fishermen paddling a frail boat out to its middle, pulling up strings of little silver fish as they went.

Steven, a keen photographer, had always had an artistic eye, and he timed our arrival at the lake to perfection. As we raced around its fringes, the lights of the city flickered into life, and bright skyscrapers began dripping streams of neon onto the vast black mirror beside us. Out over the water, thousands of birds and bats had left their roosts and were dancing in a frenzy, feasting on clouds of plump bugs that flocked to the false lights in the lake. The air was so thick with flying creatures that they brushed our faces as we passed, Hanoi's bulbs shining through their thin skins, lighting their wings with glowing veins.

Before long, we turned off the lake towards a part of the city named Tây Hồ, where Steven lived in a shared house with several other foreign teachers. As we stepped off the bike, we could hear loud music coming from inside his house, and Steven issued a brief warning:

'Just so you know, the people I live with aren't your typical teachers. Hanoi attracts a certain type of expat, drawn to the city for the abundance of jobs and high wages for foreigners, but they don't necessarily make good role models for their students.'

Intrigued, I stepped inside and was met by cheap wine fumes, drunken song, and a ball of half-naked humans writhing around on the floor. Casting my wide eyes at Steven, he simply shrugged, then did his best to introduce me to the few individuals who were still sober enough to mumble greetings from the ground. Shortly after, realising that they had run out of wine, one of the group suggested heading to a bar. One by one, they clambered onto the back of a small fleet of motorcycles resting outside the house and went wobbling off into the night. I noticed that one of them, the most drunk and the last to mount his moped, walked with a heavy limp.

'Ah yeah, that's Joe,' said Steven, when I asked why the man limped. 'He lost his leg about a year ago.'

'How?' I asked.

'He was drunk and fell off his motorcycle,' said Steven with a wince. 'Welcome to Hanoi.'

***

Despite the blatant danger of Hanoi's roads, with the price of motorcycles so cheap, and with a long, thin country ahead of me, I could not resist getting another bike. The machine I bought in many ways resembled my first - a Vietnamese cousin to its Chinese predecessor. It was made chiefly of plastic, howled whenever the brakes were applied, and it left a sticky trail of black smoke wherever it went. The headlights were smashed, the chain was rusty, and the clutch cable had broken and been tied back together. It was a pathetic specimen, doomed for the scrap-yard, and I loved it from the very beginning.

I had been in Hanoi only a few days and had just collected the motorcycle when Steven called and explained that his old boss was in need of a cover teacher, before asking if I would be willing to ride to the school and teach for a day. Having taught English abroad before, and with no plans, I agreed, and then immediately set off in search of the school, which stood five miles away on the other side of the city.

My journey took me out of Tây Hồ and into the centre of Hanoi, towards the old quarter and the colonial heart of the capital. There, the thick ring roads and congested roundabouts of the outer city gave way to wide avenues lined with honeyberry and dragon-plum trees, which framed colonial mansions painted in cream and gold. Beneath the shaded bowers, hung with an air of fading elegance, Hanoi's old imperial relics stood proud and inviolable, resisting the burgeoning city that crowded all around. But the string of grand, stately homes was as brief as it was handsome, and soon the road broke out into a large square, where the city changed nature once again.

Standing in the centre of the square, looking austere and imposing, was the mausoleum of Ho Chi Minh. Cast in concrete and adorned with armed guards, it stood in stark contrast to the colonial palaces surrounding it. I would later learn that deep within the inner tomb lay Uncle Ho's embalmed body, still immaculately preserved fifty years after his death, tended by the same team of scientists responsible for Lenin's corpse in Moscow. It was a bold, brutal monument, and always had a crowd of pilgrims stood outside, come from across the country to pay homage to Vietnam's founding father.

Leaving the mausoleum and the historic centre, I edged my way back out onto Âu Cơ, the six-lane highway running around the capital, stuffed with the five million motorcycles that collectively make Hanoi one of the most polluted cities on earth. On that road, everywhere I looked, human forms sat atop mopeds, wrapped in silicon raincoats and hidden beneath facemasks - mere silhouettes of humanity. Rather than a road, it was as if I had ridden into a giant, wretched machine, one that carried commuters along on a vast belt before ejecting them at whim. The only thing that disrupted the flow were accidents, though I only ever saw their remnants, from smashed flower pots, to twisted bicycles, to crushed helmets, ominously abandoned at the side of the road, resting beside sinister crimson stains.

Fortunately, it was not long before I left the highway for Cầu Long Biên, an old, rusting bridge that stretches across the Red River like a buckled copper snakeskin. Wrapped in mist and quaking with the weight of thousands of motorcycles, the mile-long bridge seemed to hover in the air, floating above the wooden sampans and the sand barges pushing through the reeds below. Built under French rule, the bridge was repeatedly bombed by American planes, but each time Long Biên was damaged it was rebuilt by the citizens of Hanoi until it became a symbol of Vietnamese defiance. Riding beneath its tall russet ribs, I felt as if I was passing through a portal that led to the past, and in a city which had much of its history obliterated in the war, the old bridge stands apart as one of Hanoi's most cherished relics.

Eventually, I found Đoàn Thị Điểm school in the grounds of Hanoi's eco-park, an expensive part of the city where the rich elite send their children to be educated amongst green ponds and palm trees that stand in discord with the rest of the capital's concrete sprawl. Waiting for me in reception was the mercurial Miss Quyen, a tiny, agitated woman who threw a textbook into my arms, told me that I had five minutes to prepare for my lesson, and wished me luck, before promptly disappearing.

Although I had only a small amount of teaching experience, I had spent enough time in schools to know that as a teacher, if you walk into the room and find two pupils stood on their desks jousting with broken badminton rackets, and another trying to hang his nemesis by his shoelaces in the corner of the classroom, things are going to go badly. Added to that, Miss Quyen had given me the wrong textbook, the children spoke no English at all, and the Vietnamese co-teacher who was meant to be my aid seemed happy to sit in the corner and watch me crumble. From the outset, I knew that I was doomed, and even worse, every eight-year-old in the class knew it too.

At first, I stood at the front of the room for five minutes, waiting for silence, but all I received was a volley of missiles trained at my nose. Tired of waiting, I eventually bellowed at the children as loud as I could, hoping that by proving my lungs were bigger than theirs, I might submit them into silence. These children, however, had never been shouted at before. Not understanding what a shout was, they were totally impervious to its power. In response, they simply stared at me with their big insensible eyes, quiet and oblivious, until one of them bounced another eraser off my forehead causing the whole class to erupt in laughter again.

I did my best, but the students were beyond hope. The fifty minutes of the lesson seemed interminably long, and I spent much of it breaking up fights, confiscating weapons, and foiling the efforts of escape parties. On the rare occasions that I managed to engage the students, I could only ever get them to be quiet one at a time, and as soon as I knelt down to listen to their mumbled attempts at English, the rest of the class made a game of running forward and fighting with one another to pat the top of my bald head, which was shining like a beacon under the bright electric lights of the classroom. When the lesson finally ended, lunchtime was announced by the caretaker who stood in the playground beating a vast drum, its rhythm ripping through the building like a call to war. Without waiting for my dismissal, the students stood up and ran for the door, making for the lunch hall which they descended upon like a voracious plague, leaving me to tidy the devastated classroom.

'Thank you for today,' mumbled the Vietnamese co-teacher on her way out. 'I hope you stay longer than the last three...'

As I rode back to the city across Long Biên, still recovering from the lesson, a chill wind blew down the Red River bearing storm-clouds. When the rain broke, it fell with all the intensity of an Asian downpour, but it was cold and icy, signalling the imminent onset of winter. Knowing that I had probably been caught in the deluge and that I would need to be comforted after my first experience of a Vietnamese classroom, Steven called and directed me to a quiet corner of Tây Hồ, to a roadside restaurant where, according to him, we would find the best bowl of phở in all of Hanoi.

I had read about phở before and had heard its virtues extolled by many travellers, though I was sceptical that the noodle broth - typically a Vietnamese breakfast dish - would be enough to lift me out of my damp mood. Nevertheless, trusting Steven, I took my place opposite him at a small table, just as an old woman, wrapped in enough layers to lead an arctic expedition, placed two wide bowls before us.

Peering into the dish in front of me, at first I lost sight of my surroundings as a billow of steam rolled up and enveloped my face, banishing the cold in a cloud of aromatic heat. Inside the bowl lay a raft of white rice noodles, soaked in a pale brown broth, which supported a little pile of pink beef shin slowly melting in the perfumed waters. Following Steven's lead, I added a dash of chilli, some slices of pickled garlic, a pinch of coriander, and then taking chopsticks and spoon in hand, I had my first taste of Vietnamese phở.

The translucent noodles, like flat strips of silk, were delicate but firm. The meat, bewitchingly soft, was rich and hearty. And then there was the broth, boiled down from beef bones in the huge cauldron at the front of the shop which never stopped bubbling. That is the wonder of Vietnamese phở - each bowl is part of something greater than itself, the offspring of an original potion which is kept constantly simmering, enlivened day after day by an endless supply of animal parts and herbs. Every bowl is a remnant of all the other bowls that have gone before it, a delicious phantom, refined and powerful, but one that radiates warmth rather than cold, and which lingers long after it passes.

Steven, in between laughing at my astonishment, ordered a basket of bánh quẩy - deep-fried breadsticks used to suck up the broth and add extra bite to the dish.

'I told you it was good,' he smiled. 'You should never have doubted the culinary talents of the Vietnamese. After all, Ho Chi Minh was a chef before he was a politician. Do you know the secret ingredient in phở?'

I shook my head.

'Wintertime,' he said.

And Steven was right. If it had been summer and forty degrees outside, then the phở would not have tasted so good. But there and then, as the icy water fell in sheets just six inches from where we were sitting, I could not have imagined a more perfect meal. Great food is more than just good cooking and fine ingredients - it is timing and occasion too, and nothing in the world could have done more to raise my freezing spirits than my first bowl of steaming phở, gulped down on an open roadside, as I looked out at the soaking city of Hanoi, drenched in the first rains of the Vietnamese winter.

***

The next day, Miss Quyen called Steven and asked if I would be interested in teaching classes for the next two months until they found a permanent replacement teacher. Strangely, despite the horror of the previous day's lessons, I consented, and suddenly I found myself with a little life in Hanoi that I had neither solicited nor expected.

I was not the first fledgeling that Steven had welcomed to the city, and within a matter of days, he had introduced me to a wide network of mechanics, tailors, shopkeepers, and restaurateurs who would cater for my every need. But I cannot pretend that Hanoi was an easy place to live. The black rain that fell on my first day at school heralded the approach of a morbid winter that once settled, did not lift for weeks. The tall, thin house in Tây Hồ, which was designed to keep cool in summer, became a pillar of cold misery, and I lived at its frozen summit. But it did have a room and a bed which for a short while I could call my own, two privileges unknown to me during the previous eight months.

Outside, the city was grey, wet, and miserable, but it also became familiar, and fondness often follows familiarity. An inexplicable part of me even used to enjoy my melancholy commute, trapped amidst six lanes of congestion, rumbling my way to school. It was worth it just to cross Cầu Long Biên every day - that anxious, fragile, beautiful bridge that looked like it might fold at any moment and drop me into the sluggish waters of the Red River, a state of precariousness that made every crossing feel like a triumph.

In time, I even grew fond of my school and my class of thirty terrors, not that their behaviour ever improved. I did, however, win over my Vietnamese co-teachers - Miss Van and Miss Surong - who collectively possessed more patience than I had thought humanly possible, and who I suspected were both secretly angels. Neither were from Hanoi, both lived far from their families, and they worked harder than any teachers I have ever known. I knew they had finally accepted me when they allowed me to enter the staff room, where every lunchtime the blinds were pulled down low, and all the female teachers congregated to fall asleep upon each other, filling the corridors for an hour with the sound of their gentle snores.

Amongst my students there were the usual characters: the dreamer, the clown, the enforcer, the devotee, and the renegade always covered in ink. They were mischievous, hilarious, and had an abnormal proclivity for violence. But after a few weeks of teaching, I did believe that they had come to respect me a little. By Christmas, I even thought that I had assumed enough authority to take them outside the classroom and treat them to a placid game of duck-duck-goose. This judgement proved to be a mortal error.

The second we stepped outside, the children scattered, like debris from a detonating bomb, disappearing into every crevice of the playground. Panicking, I tried to collect them one by one, but it was not long before a boy discovered a sprinkler in the bushes and started to shower his classmates with it. In response, his archenemy took cover in the vegetable patch and began to launch a steady battery of rocks and mud, which when they missed their intended target clattered against the headteacher's window. There were yelps and screams and cries of terror as children were mown down by jets of water and flying clumps of earth. It seemed that things could not possibly get any worse, but then I watched with horror as a boy on the other side of the playground appeared with a pair of scissors smuggled from the classroom. He ran around screaming battle cries, waving the scissors like a maniac, and before I could do anything to stop him, he had amputated a little girl's pig-tails, unleashing pandemonium.

The rest of the lesson was spent trying to contain the mob of rioting eight-year-olds, whilst failing to calm down a murderous Vietnamese girl intent on battering the boy who had snipped her hair. In the end, looking up to see a minor brawl unfolding in the playground, the head-teacher emerged and managed to get the children to settle. But she disappeared as fast as she arrived, and it was impossible for me to convey the rules of duck-duck-goose without a translator. Instead, I tried a demonstration, but quite predictably, this simply led to the thirty students forming one long line and taking turns to run full tilt towards me, clattering my head as they passed. All I could do was sit on the grass and accept my fate, ruing my decision to ever let the children outside, praying for the caretaker to appear and ring the war-drum of lunchtime, which was the only distraction that might possibly bring an end to the children's violent spree.

***

On my last weekend in Hanoi, my oldest friend - a man named Deej - revealed that he was in Southeast Asia and had decided to make a spontaneous trip to Vietnam. Deej and I had first met at primary school, aged five, and we had been best friends ever since. He was there on the morning that I left my home at the beginning of my journey, and I knew that he would be there on the day that I returned, but the eight months that had elapsed between me leaving home and reaching Vietnam was the longest we had ever been apart since our first encounter in a sunny Somerset playground. The news that he was coming to Hanoi was one of the greatest gifts of my journey.

Deej had recently become engaged, and he arrived in Vietnam with his fiancé Eleyna on the weekend of his birthday, which provided double cause for celebration. After two months of living in Hanoi, I was happy to play the tour guide, dragging Deej and Eleyna back and forth across the city to each of my favourite places. Together, we ate phở in Tây Hồ, raced around West Lake, crossed Cầu Long Biên, and sipped Vietnamese coffee beside the wreckage of a B52 bomber at Huu Tiep lake. We visited museums, played cards in the old quarter, drank wine on our rooftop, and tasted every dish Vietnam is famous for. And then on the final evening, we went with Steven and everyone else from our house to Lotte Tower, Hanoi's tallest skyscraper, to toast Deej's birthday and drink whisky at the rooftop bar, sixty-five floors above the city.

After eight weeks trapped amongst the chaos of Hanoi's streets, I suddenly found myself three hundred metres above them, staring down through purple mist at the glittering halo of West Lake. The capital, at times, had been a difficult place to love, but all great cities look beautiful from above, especially when one has come to know them intimately. In the end, I felt nothing but fondness for Hanoi, and looking down through the clouds, surrounded by friends, I realised I had caught the city at a crucial moment in its lifetime.

From the top of Lotte, I could see all of the construction sites wriggling like weeds through the topsoil of the city. The Vietnamese capital was growing at such a rate that its future was clear: before long it would inevitably become just another Southeast Asian behemoth - a vast, sprawling, cosmopolitan city, with barely any room to stand in. Looking down, I had a vision of Hanoi's future. Its lakes had been drained and populated with skyscrapers, its parks had been ripped up to make way for more highways, and every empty space had been filled with concrete and steel. All its distinction and all its character had been lost beneath the mirror of a modern metropolis. It was a cypher without a face, indistinguishable from a hundred other megacities around the world.

But Hanoi had not reached that point yet. I had been lucky enough to know the city at a time when it still possessed a local charm, where its hidden parts still felt real and provincial. It was ugly, no doubt, but it was honest, with a personality entirely its own, and I will forever be grateful for my time there. Staying long enough in a place means that when it comes to parting, a portion of it goes with you, but a little of yourself also stays behind. I had laid down a life in Hanoi, a life that was soon to be committed to memory. My present, and everyone in it, was to become a past, and I would be released to seek out another life, however temporary. I had a chain of these existences, stretching all the way back to home. A hundred brief lives, lived intently, each claiming a part of myself. That is the great burden and gift of travel: you divide yourself into little parts and scatter them around the world, and each division hurts, but the reward is a type of immortality.

Chapter Seventeen

The great affair is to move.

- Robert Louis Stevenson, *Travels with a Donkey*

I left Hanoi just before Tết, the most important date in the Vietnamese calendar, which marks the beginning of the Lunar New Year. On my way out of the capital, I joined an exodus of city dwellers, all leaving to visit their families in the provinces. One of the many traditions upheld during Tết amongst the northern Vietnamese is the decoration of their homes with kumquat trees and pink peach blossoms, which bloom in allotments across Hanoi towards the end of winter. On the eve of Tết celebrations, all of these trees are uprooted and strapped to the back of motorcycles to be taken as gifts to distant family, and it was in the midst of this movable forest that I left the city, wobbling my way through a flurry of bouncing kumquats, following a trail of pink blossoms that led southwards and stretched into the distance, painting the narrow spine of Vietnam in pale petals.

The high-rise towers of Hanoi rapidly dwindled, and it was not long before I was riding amongst rice paddies and fields of grass, following narrow lanes between little towns decked in red banners and lanterns.

Stopping to eat a bowl of phở for breakfast, I used a pantomime of hand gestures to ask the owner of a roadside restaurant which animal of the Vietnamese zodiac was being celebrated that year. For a long while, the phở-seller remained silent, staring at me with impassive eyes. Then, all of sudden, the restaurant owner pointed out to the street as a man rode past on a motorcycle with a freshly butchered carcass balancing under one of his arms: evidently, it was the year of the pig.

After two months of riding through smog and grime, the damp country air smelt sweet and promising as I turned south-eastwards into Hòa Bình province. When the low morning cloud cleared, it revealed a belt of green fields, studded with tall limestone towers covered in jungle-skin. Clinging to those ethereal pillars, a thousand different species of leaf, branch, stem, root, creeper, and vine were growing so thick that at times the stone underneath was invisible. It was as if the jungle itself had grown spires and turrets, standing up in mountains built of nothing but trees and leaves that stretched up into the lingering clouds and cast their shadows over quicksilver rice paddies.

The road I followed was a gorgeous two-lane track, known as the Ho Chi Minh Highway because it roughly followed the route of the old Ho Chi Minh trail. During the war, the twelve thousand miles of jungle paths, roads, and tracks that had made up the trail played a vital role in transporting Vietnamese troops and supplies from Hanoi in the north to Saigon in the south. It took a force of two hundred and thirty thousand adolescents to build and maintain the tracks, and during the war, three million tonnes of American explosives were dropped on the Laotian section alone - more bombs than fell on France and Germany in the Second World War combined.

It was difficult to imagine such destruction as I rode through pristine jungle, happy to be free of the city and glad to have the whole of Vietnam in front of me. But I would later learn that the trail was facing a new threat, as the Vietnamese government had recently announced plans to replace the modest road with an eight-lane highway. For the large highway to be built, countless trees would have to be ripped up, and many miles of farmland spoilt, which hardly felt necessary given that a major parallel road already lay completed twenty miles to the east. For the Vietnamese, however, ruined beauty was a small price to pay to remain the fastest growing economy in Asia.

My first night on the road, I stayed in a village cloaked in smoke and cradled by limestone karsts, somewhere in Hòa Bình province. There was nothing there but a few homes, a single restaurant, and a nhà nghỉ - the Vietnamese version of a motel - where a room cost just a few thousand đồng. The bed was hard, the shower rusty, and it only took a matter of minutes for a whole host of insects to settle on my skin and begin feasting. But it was shelter and sanctuary, and I was suddenly alone again, surrounded by novelty, reacquainted with the thrill of travelling for no other purpose than to pay attention as the world changed around me.

Winter still clung to northern Vietnam, and on my second morning of riding, I found myself speeding through fields of cold fog, denied even a fleeting glimpse of the surrounding landscape. Staying on the Ho Chi Minh Highway, I followed the narrow shaft of Vietnam's crooked body ever southward, passing from the jungle into wide green plains. Then, as the fog cleared, rising up out of the fields beside little wooden villages, huge stone churches began to appear next to the road - gothic relics left behind by the French colonialists and Jesuit missionaries who, alongside Christian temples, gave the Vietnamese their Latin alphabet.

By lunchtime, I reached Phong Nha caves where I turned towards the coast, pointing my motorcycle east into clear skies and warmer weather. For miles, I rode beside a flawless beach, watching white rollers creep their way across the yellow sand, up to the feet of pine trees which ran down to the surf along gently sloping cliffs. Fresh, empty, and patterned with sunshine, Vietnam's coast was the antithesis of Hanoi, and after a day spent riding along its edge, I felt glad that there was still such a vast distance between myself and the Antipodes.

I rode till it grew dark, then I stopped at another nhà nghỉ, uncertain and unconcerned with where I was. All that my way forward required was that I keep the South China Sea to my left for the next six hundred miles. Aside from that guideline, I was free to be lost.

The fact that I did not have to be too geographically precise was fortunate because although I knew I had stopped in a village somewhere beside the sea, I could not place myself within a hundred square miles of my location on a map. Walking towards the centre of the village, I found a restaurant full of revellers clutching glasses of iced beer, swooning over plates of fried squid and boiled langoustines. Taking a chair, I ordered some noodles, and then I let myself be swallowed by obscurity. Busy enjoying the festivities, nobody in the crowd even noticed my presence. I was an inconsequential stranger, a ghost from a far-away land, and no-one in the world, myself included, knew for certain where I was.

The false belief that we are the centre of the universe is a stubborn fiction written into the heart of every man and woman, but more than any other endeavour, travel has the power to weaken that fiction. Alone, lost, and surrounded by strangers in a foreign land, I had never felt so unimportant as I did that evening in rural Vietnam. But rather than troubled, the sense of insignificance left me feeling liberated. As I watched the villagers raucously celebrating all around me, utterly indifferent to my presence, I remembered that the world would not cease to spin if I suddenly disappeared from it. Humbled and unburdened, I derived a very simple and very pure joy from being reminded of how small I was compared to the vast world around me. I came to look upon that joy as the chief privilege of travel, and I felt it many times during my journey, but it was never so strong as it was that night in the little Vietnamese fishing village, somewhere on the shore of the South China Sea.

Curiosity, however, won out in the end, and after returning to the nhà nghỉ where I was staying, I unfurled a map and asked my host to point to our location. His tobacco-yellowed finger began scanning the map, before stopping just above the Bến Hải River. Without meaning to, I had chosen to rest for the night atop the seventeenth parallel, the dividing line which once demarcated the boundary between north and south Vietnam. Exactly fifty years earlier, when the northern Vietnamese and the Viet Cong launched the Tết offensive, the surrounding area had seen some of the fiercest conflict in the entire war. Half a century later, like much of rural Vietnam and Laos, the land around Bến Hải is still littered with unexploded ordnance, which made me thankful for choosing to stay in a nhà nghỉ that night, rather than sleep wild on the beach - a prospect which only hours before had seemed tempting.

My Vietnamese motorcycle was faster than my first, and the next day I was riding at speed down a narrow coastal lane when I failed to see the sign for a small bridge. The bump in the road sent me flying a metre into the air, and the impact of my landing caused the steel rack supporting my luggage to snap clean in half, spilling my bag onto the side of the road where a handful of farm-dogs were tussling in the grass. Stopping the bike, I gingerly stepped over the dogs, hoping that I might retrieve my bag without them noticing. Five seconds later, I was gunning the motorcycle at top speed, holding my luggage under my arm, with seven angry canines snapping at my bag straps.

The reason why Vietnam is such a wonderful country to travel by motorcycle is not because of its beauty, the quality of its roads, or the kindness of its people. It is because every village, however small, is home to a mechanic who will fix anything for a small fee and a packet of cigarettes. Having lost the dogs, I stopped at the first village I passed, and within minutes found a garage. Seeing the fractured steel rack under my arm, the mechanic snatched a pair of pink plastic sunglasses from his baby daughter, and after firing up his welder, immediately set to work. After completing the repair, without my asking, he also decided to check my engine, which led to a grave diagnosis:

'SHIT-IN-FUEL-LINE!'

Taking the initiative, the mechanic blew a jet of compressed air into my tank, sending a spray of petrol up into the sky, inches from the lit cigarette dangling in his mouth. For this quick fix and near-fatal encounter, he charged me twenty thousand đồng, the equivalent of seventy English pence, before sending me on my way with a pat on the back and a broad, toothless smile.

The weld lasted no more than five miles, and it took four further attempts until it held properly. But it was the final repair that was the most important because the mechanic who performed it had his garage just before the Hải Vân Pass - Vietnam's most famous road - and a broken weld at the summit of Hải Vân would have meant disaster.

Snaking over a spur of mountains, bordered on one side by misted green peaks and on the other by a precarious drop down to the South China Sea, the Hải Vân Pass is a motorcyclist's dream. Quite predictably, it was teeming with backpackers, wobbling their way up the mountain on mopeds, a worrying number already swaddled in bandages. Normally, such crowds would have left me frustrated, but on my haggard Honda Win, held together by the dubious work of five mechanics, I realised that I was just another motorcyclist in the traffic: one of the thousands of tourists who ride the length of Vietnam every month. I passed dozens of backpackers on the road every day, engaged in precisely the same journey as me, but that afternoon, I was barely conscious of their presence. Like all great roads, the Hải Vân Pass reduced the world to a series of captivating bends, and as I raced across its surface, the road seemed to exist only for me - as if each of its twists and turns had been built for my journey and my journey alone.

Once on the other side of the green mountains, I could see the butter coloured beaches of Da Nang in the distance and the bright sea washing over them. It had been a long ride since leaving the Bến Hải river that morning, and I would have liked nothing better than to have thrown myself onto a beach and to have stayed there for the rest of the day. But I was compelled to ride past Da Nang and on towards the ancient port of Hội An, known as one of the prettiest cities in Vietnam, because that night I had a dinner date.

***

I had worked for Miss Quyen - the head of the school I taught at in Hanoi - for two months, but as with many other Vietnamese, I had found her impossible to read. Demanding, erratic, and with a great talent for confusing simple situations, she nevertheless was unfailingly kind and worked incredibly hard, managing her school duties with the challenges of being a single mother to two children. From the day I met her, I was curious about her life and how she came to be the head of a school in Hanoi, so when she told me after my last lesson in the capital that she would be in Hội An for Tết and that she wanted to take me for dinner, I had promised to join her there one week later.

We met by the waterside in Hội An, just as the first lanterns were being lit. Sliced by waterways and canals, Hội An's inner town was slowly growing brighter under the glare of thousands of flickering lights that had been cast out onto the water as part of the Tết celebrations, and visitors had flocked from across the country to watch the Thu Bồn River sprout into flame at twilight. Alongside the floating candles, lanterns hung up and down the riverfront, each shedding their light upon a portion of Hội An's patchwork past. Chinese shops, Japanese pagodas, and French colonial townhouses were all glowing side by side, their pretty pattern a testament to Hội An's past as a major trading port which once connected all the great nations of eastern Asia.

As soon as we sat down in a restaurant overlooking the river, Miss Quyen handed me a little parcel wrapped up in leaves, tied with pale brown string.

'This is Bánh chưng cake,' she said with a smile, 'a Tết tradition that for many years I used to make with my sister.'

I took the parcel and thanked her as she gazed back at me with her unwavering stare.

'You must be wondering why I am not with my family at Tết like everybody else?' she asked, casting her eyes to the table. 'The sister I used to make Bang Chung Cake with died not long ago. I cannot go home because it reminds me too much of her.'

The Vietnamese are stoic by nature, rarely showing emotion, especially when it comes to matters of grief. But that evening, Miss Quyen seemed to be feeling unusually sentimental. As we chatted, she gradually slipped into a narrative of her life, and I realised that with a busy career and two young children to care for, her uncharacteristic loquaciousness was probably inspired by the fact that for the first time in a long time, she was sat across a table from someone who was genuinely willing to listen.

'I grew up in the rural provinces, where my father was a farmer. All we ever ate was rice and potatoes. Whilst my father worked in the fields with my brother, my mother taught in a nearby school. She did not earn much money, but she inspired me to teach. When I was old enough, I went to a university for teachers, and I began to study English, always hoping I might one day have a school of my own.'

'You became a teacher as soon as you finished university?' I asked.

'No. I wanted too, but at that time, the government were recruiting English speaking Vietnamese to help in a civil project. After graduating, I agreed to work for several years as a translator because my English was good. I became part of a team who were tasked with uncovering the fate of lost American soldiers reported missing in action during the war.

'It was my job to translate the recovered diaries and letters of the soldiers, to try and piece together their final movements and discover where they might have died. It was difficult work. On one page, the Americans would write about what they had for lunch and what new songs had played on the radio. Then, on the next page, they would describe slaughtering entire families and burning villages to the ground. They were soldiers, after all.'

As she talked about these diaries, Miss Quyen pointed to my own black leather notebook lying on the table.

'They looked just like that one,' she winced.

'Do the Vietnamese still feel any hatred for the Americans?' I asked.

'Some of the younger generations don't even know that we had a war. For them, there is no hatred to hold on to. For older Vietnamese, things are harder to forget. My mother, for example, still has an American bullet buried inside her body. It's been there for nearly fifty years, but the doctors say it's too dangerous to remove. She will die with that American metal inside her.

'In the end, the project closed down. Some soldiers were just too difficult to find. Then I was able to finally start teaching, so I moved to Hanoi to increase my chances of getting a job. I married, had two children, and things were going well. But as my responsibilities at school grew, I had less time to spend at home, and my marriage began to break. I've been separated from my husband for four years now, but we haven't divorced yet. A divorce would cast a shadow over my family. This is another reason why I find it easier to not be with them during Tết. I don't like to face questions about my husband.'

After dinner, we strolled around the town, admiring the Tết decorations and listening to folk singers perform in the street. Everyone was happy and at ease, staring with astonished eyes at the rivers and canals covered in floating lanterns. As we walked, it was Miss Quyen's turn to ask about my life. She had never travelled beyond Vietnam and wanted to know everything about every country I had visited. She wanted to know about England too, how it looked and felt and smelt, and which days we held to be sacred.

'How long have you been away for, Sam?' she asked at one point.

'Ten months now,' I replied.

'But how can you be away from your family for so long? Did you not miss them at Christmas? People should be with their families at times like that.'

But as she said this, Miss Quyen realised the contradiction at the heart of her words. Stood with me in Hội An during the most important holiday in the Vietnamese calendar, far from her own relatives, she was hardly in a position to lecture on the importance of family.

As we said goodbye later that night, Miss Quyen seemed pensive, as if her earlier words had affected her.

'Where do you go next?' she asked.

'I'll keep heading southwards, along the coast, until it's time to turn inland to Ho Chi Minh City. And you? Will you go straight back to Hanoi?'

'Me?' she said, looking thoughtfully across the river. 'I have a little while before I need to go back to school. It's been a long time, but I finally feel like going back to the provinces. Tết is a time to be at home. After tonight, I've decided that I'm going to go back to my family.'

***

The deserted stretches of Vietnam's coastline were undeniably pretty, but along the populated parts, I met with much ugliness. On my ride south, I stopped at Nhơn Hải, a tiny fishing village which might have been a paradise if it was not for the tide of litter covering its shoreline. The next day I reached Nha Trang, and though the beach was pristine, it was cast into shadow by the high-rise hotels looming behind it, pressing their silver bellies up to the edge of the surf.

Sensing that the coast had changed for the worst, I turned inland at Nha Trang, climbing up into the mountains, past sections of road torn away by the rains. I stopped often to eat roadside bowls of bún riêu cua - a staple dish of southern Vietnam made from noodles topped with the meat of freshwater crabs harvested in the rice paddies. The spicy broth was welcome in the cool mists of the Central Highlands, but as I rode higher, I eventually broke through the cloud-line, emerging onto a plateau of pine forests which hid amongst their trunks miles upon miles of greenhouses and fruit vines.

I had reached Đà Lạt, Vietnam's fertile southern city, once known as the elephant hunting capital of the world. As a temperate mountain settlement, famous for its climate and its strawberries, I had heard the city praised many times. Half the nation's fruit and vegetables were sourced from the area surrounding Đà Lạt, and in my mind, I had been hoping to spend several days relaxing amongst the quiet streets of a pastoral town. In reality, due to Tết, Đà Lạt's, usual population of two hundred thousand had swollen to over four million, transforming the city into a chaotic mob.

I was glad to have been in Vietnam during Tết, but the festival did make travelling across the country difficult. Major destinations like Đà Lạt were bloated beyond recognition, whilst small towns and villages were empty, with most shops, restaurants, and hotels closing for the duration of the celebrations. This meant that I could not always stop where I wished, though riding a motorcycle again for eight hours every day had been more of a pleasure than I had expected it to be. If I could, I would have kept riding my counterfeit Chinese Honda until I ran out of road. But I had been riding the bike illegally, without the correct paperwork, and I knew that if I attempted to cross the Cambodian border then the machine would be confiscated. Two weeks after leaving Hanoi, as I entered the fringes of Ho Chi Minh City, I realised for a second time that I would soon be parting with another motorcycle.

Fortunately, there is a peculiar phenomenon in Vietnam, a migration of sorts, which sees young backpackers flying to Ho Chi Minh City and riding motorcycles north to Hanoi. This means that demand, and therefore prices, are naturally higher in the south, and I had been in Ho Chi Minh City for less than five minutes when an old lady on a moped approached me and asked to buy my motorcycle. Despite the shattered luggage rack, its countless faults, and over two thousand miles of wear and tear, I battled with the woman until we eventually agreed upon a price one hundred dollars higher than the sum I paid for the machine. Pleased at finding myself an adequate match for a wily Vietnamese businesswoman, as soon as I had sold the cycle I set off exploring the city, with four hundred fresh dollars burning a hole in my wallet.

Ho Chi Minh City, previously known as Saigon, immediately felt different to the northern capital. It was taller, wider, neater, far more cosmopolitan, and the traffic actually stopped at red lights. It still had the mad, erratic busyness of a vast Asian city, but that was tempered by a modicum of order, and it was so hot that everything, even the motorcycles, seemed sluggish. The remnants of colonialism were more apparent too. In just a short walk about the city, I passed Notre Dame Cathedral, Saigon Central Post Office, and countless grand old hotels, built in the French style, where old colonialists used to drink and dine.

With an afternoon to spare, I decided to visit the War Remnants Museum, and when I arrived, it seemed every other tourist in Ho Chi Minh City had the same idea. It is a sad truth that in this portion of Asia, particularly Vietnam and Cambodia, half the tourist trade is predicated upon places of outstanding beauty, and the other half upon the relics of wars and genocides. After the mountains and the beaches, the biggest draw for visitors in this part of the world are the battlegrounds and killing fields where some of recent history's bloodiest episodes unfolded. And though I recognised that educating people in regards to such horrors was vital, that did not change the fact that the horrors of the museum were made all the more harrowing by the crowds of backpackers in neon vests and flip-flops, about to spend two weeks getting drunk on the beaches, but stopping first to visit exhibits on genocide, war, and torture.

By the time I returned to my cheap hostel, I was in a black mood. Walking up to the rooftop, I hoped to find a quiet place to sit and write for an hour. Instead, I discovered a loud bar full of teenagers drinking shots and slurping huge pitchers of beer. I resorted to finding somewhere quieter in the city, but after leaving my hostel, I inadvertently walked onto Bùi Viện street, Ho Chi Minh City's answer to Khao San Road, which was a grave mistake.

As a young man abroad in Southeast Asia, it is nearly impossible to walk through the centres of the major cities and not at some point be accosted by a prostitute. The second I stepped onto Bùi Viện, the touristic centre of Ho Chi Minh City, several women immediately walked forward to stroke my chest, bouncing their fists together and whispering lewd promises. It is a distinctly unpleasant experience, receiving offers of false love - it makes one feel seedy just for existing, and for me, that night in Ho Chi Minh City, it ushered in a crushing loneliness.

Fleeing Bùi Viện, I bought a beer and sought solace in the darkness of a nearby park. From the bench I sat upon, I could hear music blaring from my hostel rooftop alongside the repetitive clamour of drinking chants. In Southeast Asia, tourism has stripped cities like Saigon of their identity, and in those cities, I felt stripped of my identity too. I no longer existed as a traveller or a writer. To the Vietnamese on the street, I was just another tourist come to desecrate their country, a perambulatory wallet there for women, drink, drugs, and nothing more. To most of the other tourists, I was a boring, bookish stranger, clearly just passing through. Utterly at odds with the world, in the ten months since leaving my home, I had never felt such weariness as I did that evening in Ho Chi Minh City.

I stayed in the park for a while, watching a bat skim across a black pond, the still surface flashing lilac every time the creature dipped a toe and trawled for his dinner. I was so lost in the bat's flight that I barely noticed when a man arrived and sat down on the bench next to me. He smiled, lit a cigarette, and took a long, greedy drag. When I tried to speak to him, it was clear he knew no English, and despite my best efforts, even after several months in the country, I still found tonal Vietnamese impossible.

The man sat there quite happily, taking deep, satisfied breaths, staring at me intently. After a while, I went back to my beer and paid him no attention. A few minutes later, the man motioned to my chest and smiled, then he stroked his face to imitate my beard and gave a lustful nod. Before I even knew what was happening, he had sidled over to me, put one arm around my shoulder, and then with his other hand, he reached out to grab my leg.

I pushed the man violently away, then quickly stood up to leave, as he sniggered and lit another cigarette. It seemed that wherever I went in Ho Chi Minh City that night, I would be ill-fated. All I could do was trudge back to my hostel and retreat to my dormitory where I lay awake for hours, bitter and restless, impatiently waiting for sunrise and the chance to move once again.

Chapter Eighteen

Time seems to overlap, likes the shadows of leaves pressing down on other leaves, layer upon layer.

- Tan Twan Eng, *The Garden of Evening Mists*

Ever since my time aboard the *Antares* in Croatia, I had been eager to get behind the helm of another sailboat. Leaving Vietnam, I remembered that my cousin Jennifer had learnt to sail in the waters surrounding Langkawi, an island that lies off the western coast of the Malay peninsula in the southern Andaman Sea. With no antidote for my lingering melancholy other than to keep moving, and intrigued by Langkawi (which in Malay means land of the eagles), after leaving Ho Chi Minh City, I found myself speeding across Cambodia and Thailand, travelling towards the Malaysian island as fast as the haphazard buses of Southeast Asia could carry me.

After a week of travelling, I finally boarded a ferry in Satun, one of Thailand's southern provinces, and sailed across to 'Langkawi, the Jewel of Kedah', as the island is affectionately known by Malays. At the ferry-port, a pair of relaxed customs officials welcomed me with a warm smile and a nod. They were surrounded by the same tell-tale aura, common across the globe, that surrounds all happy islanders - a quiet contentedness, coupled with a respectful lack of concern for anywhere in the world that does not lie within the thirty-mile perimeter of their little universe. I could sense that I would like Langkawi and its people immediately.

From the ferry-port, it was a short walk to the Royal Langkawi Yacht club, where I soon found *Sade 2,* the yacht on which my cousin Jennifer had learnt to sail. Coiling ropes on its deck was a deeply bronzed mariner named Keith, a stern but thorough Scotsman who had a reputation as one of the finest sailors to be found in the Straits of Malacca. Splitting his time between the tropical islands of Southeast Asia and the freezing waters of the North Sea, Keith was a seasoned instructor, and fortunately for me, he had one space amongst his crew for his next voyage: a circumnavigation of the island, setting sail at dawn the next day.

I had gone to Keith because I wanted to learn how to sail properly, and he took my request seriously. The following morning, the second we were clear of the harbour, he handed me the helm, told me that I was skipper, and bade me command the crew of three other novices as I saw fit. Uncertain of where to turn, as I edged the boat out into the lurid blue ocean, a single ladyfish stood up on its tail and ran across the surface of the water, fleeing from the prow of the yacht. Judging this to be an auspicious omen, I gave the command for the mainsail to be hoisted and turned the boat to follow the kicking tail of the creature, just as a sea eagle swooped down from above and impaled the fish on one of its long, curving talons.

Thankfully, we fared better than the ladyfish that morning, and we were soon making good progress, sailing at six knots on a western heading. On our starboard side, the main island of Langkawi bubbled up out of the Andaman Sea in a clump of low green hills, emblazoned at its edges with bright sand beaches and turquoise coves. Surrounding the large island, a halo of green splinters rose up on both sides of our yacht, and it was through this network of uninhabited islets that we would navigate for the next five days, dodging lone clumps of jungle that looked innocent from above but which stood atop menacing outcrops of rock hidden below the waterline.

As we sailed lazily on through the midday heat, Keith sat in the rear of the cockpit, gulping mug after mug of boiling tea, whilst slowly unloading his encyclopaedic knowledge of Langkawi. After several decades spent teaching people to sail in the surrounding area, he not only knew the name of every island we passed, the depth of every channel, and the height of every hill, but he knew their histories, their myths, and their secrets too.

'The Malaysians are some of the most superstitious people on earth, and Langkawi is famous for its folklore. Does anyone here know the myth of Mahsuri?' he asked, on the first afternoon of the voyage.

Each of the crew shook their heads, which was all the encouragement Keith needed to begin recounting the story.

'Mahsuri was a beautiful woman, born on Langkawi two hundred years ago. At that time, the Malays were constantly waging war against the Siamese. Mahsuri married a local warrior, but soon after their wedding, her husband was sent away to fight, leaving her alone.

'Whilst Mahsuri's husband was away, one of her rivals accused her of adultery, a crime which was punishable by death. Local villagers tied Mahsuri to a tree, and after a rigged trial, she was found guilty. Several times the villagers tried to execute her, but each attempt failed. People began to wonder if Mahsuri was immortal, but eventually, she called out to the crowd and explained that she could only be killed by the blade of her father's keris, hoping that the villagers would admire her honesty and decide to spare her.

'The dagger of Mahsuri's father was fetched, and from the wound where the blade entered her body, white blood flowed, revealing her innocence. The shocked villagers tried to save her but failed, and as Mahsuri slowly bled to death, she placed a curse upon the island, condemning the people of Langkawi to seven generations of bad luck.

'At first, the Langkawians thought little of the curse, but soon after, the island suffered a wave of attacks from the Siamese. Alongside the fighting, for decades, the island's crops failed and its people starved. Langkawi suffered for nearly two hundred years under the curse of Mahsuri. Things only changed when the tourist trade exploded towards the end of the twentieth century, exactly seven generations after Mahsuri's death. To this day, many locals still celebrate the island's recent prosperity as a sign that the curse has finally lifted.'

Keith kept up a steady stream of similar narratives from the back of the boat over the following five days, until the crew knew the history of half the rocks in the Andaman Sea. On that first afternoon of our voyage, appearing on our port side, we passed Pulau Dayang Bunting (Pregnant Lady Island), home to a lake with healing properties, believed to cure infertility in women. On the second day, we spotted two islands - Pulau

Kentut Besar and Pulau Kentut Kecil - meaning 'big wind' and 'little wind', named after an unfortunate prince who had once suffered from a legendary bout of flatulence after eating some undercooked rice. A day later, we passed Pantai Pasir Hitam, a black sand beach, supposedly formed from the crumbled bones of mariners, in front of which, at certain times of the year, a ship-devouring whirlpool was rumoured to appear. I had never encountered a place so enshrouded in myth as the ninety-nine islands of Langkawi.

In between telling stories, Keith also taught us all how to sail. From dawn until dusk, we spent every day navigating tight passages, racing around headlands, and practising manoeuvres on the warm, flat sea. In the evenings, we cast anchor in quiet coves and deserted bays, and I slept on deck beneath a ribbon of stars, woken at midnight by the green lights of squid boats drifting silently by.

Although most of the voyage was relaxing, it seems that I am unable to spend a week on a boat without some calamity unfolding, and on the final day of our passage, as we were sailing down the east coast of Langkawi, a mayday sounded on the radio. To my unaccustomed ears, all I heard was a garble of distress. Keith, however, understood the situation immediately, and he quickly began barking orders, instructing the crew to sail as fast as possible back to the marina, where a passenger ferry had reportedly burst into flames.

In the end, we were too far away to help, but later that evening, Keith and I found ourselves sat in a bar with a captain who had been one of the first at the scene. Clutching a beer and looking out at sea, he shook his head and explained:

'We could see the smoke from a mile off and I could tell straight away it was ship's fuel that was burning. By the time we arrived, there were already a lot of people in the water. After we fished them out, there were still others stood on the ferry, their backs right up to the flames.

'The Malays were afraid of the waves. Some just refused to jump, despite the fact they were all wearing life jackets and were about to be burnt alive. They shouted for me to tie up alongside, but that would have risked my boat and everyone we'd already rescued. In the end, the captain appeared and gave them a good shove, and then we hooked them out of the sea kicking and screaming. It's astonishing that no one was hurt.'

'I wouldn't be surprised if we see a bomoh down here tomorrow,' said Keith, looking out at the burnt hulk of the ferry still floating in the bay.

'What's a bomoh?' I asked.

'A bomoh,' replied the captain, 'is a Malay shaman. A witch doctor, if you like. They carry out spiritual ceremonies, brew traditional medicines, and have a habit of turning up in the aftermath of disasters.'

'Are their many bomohs?' I wondered aloud.

'More than you would expect. Some are quite well known.'

'You remember the flight that went down in 2014?' said Keith. 'MH370, a Malaysian Airlines flight from Kuala Lumpur to Beijing that disappeared and was never found? When the authorities admitted that their searches had failed, a bomoh was taken to Kuala Lumpur airport to conduct a ceremony that was meant to weaken the evil spirits that had brought down the plane. I'm sure Langkawi's shaman will have something to say to the spirits who set fire to the ferry.'

'I've been around the world more times than I can remember, but I've never known a place so full of magic as Malaysia, and not all of it good,' said the captain, draining his glass and casting his suspicious gaze along the coast.

After another beer with the two old mariners, I left alone to watch the sunset from the shoreline. The short path through the forest to the beach was teeming with creatures, mostly monkeys and monitor lizards scurrying after each other in the leaf litter. Keith had warned me of a serpent native to the island known as the 'hundred steps snake', named for the number of paces one could expect to take after being bitten before dropping down dead. Looking anxiously about for the coiled body of a sleeping reptile, I was glad when I finally stepped out of the forest onto the open beach, just in time to spot a pair of brahminy kites tumbling over the water, jousting with each other for a fish.

Once on the beach, I followed a line of jellyfish washed up by the tide to an empty cove, where I closed my eyes and lay in the final rays of the sun, mulling over the many myths and stories that I had heard told over the last few days. Close by, I could hear the noise of the lapping waves, and further off, I could hear the jungle-rustle of little creatures scampering through the treetops. They were gentle and relaxing sounds, the innocent music of day fading into night, and gradually I felt myself drifting towards sleep.

But a moment later, the peace was shattered by a loud, harsh bark that sounded from within the jungle and echoed around the gathering darkness. Turning, I listened as the angry, juddering rasp grew louder, waiting expectantly for a monster to come crashing through the tree-line. Then, just as the sun began to dip below the sea behind me, two huge black wings, fringed with white, stretched up above the green canopy. With a flurry of heavy wing-beats, a single Great Hornbill pumped itself up into the air, and after pointing its unwieldy beak straight towards the sunset, flew out over the water to its roost on a distant island. I stayed and watched the bird disappear into the dusk, and then I walked back along a beach bristling with crabs, whilst bright blue flecks of luminescent algae sparkled in the surf, and I understood why the old captain had told me that he knew few places on earth as enchanting as Langkawi.

***

When the engines of the ferry I took to Penang stopped abruptly halfway through its crossing, it was clear that the previous week's fire was on every passenger's mind. As the ship came to a halt in the middle of the sea, a chorus of sirens began to sound, just as an engineer went flying through the passenger lounge, making for the engine room. Panicking tourists began scrabbling for life-jackets and looking for the nearest exit, but after a loud quarrel between the engineer and his engine, the ship rumbled back into life. A few minutes later, we were once again steaming in the direction of Penang, an island fifty miles south of Langkawi, similar in size to its northern counterpart, but very different in nature.

Georgetown was the first English colonial outpost established in Malaysia, founded by Captain Francis Light when he leased the island of Penang from the sultan of Kedah in 1786 on behalf of the East India Trading Company. When he arrived in Penang with the company's officers, Captain Light was confronted with the challenge of building a colonial settlement on an island of impenetrable jungle. His solution was to pack cannons with coins and fire them into the forest, promising the native people that if they cleared the land, they could keep whatever treasure they found along the way. A quarter of a millennium later, the city of Georgetown is now the second largest in Malaysia and sprawls across half the island, stretching far further than the blast of an eighteenth-century gun stuffed with silver ever could have reached.

Stepping off the ship at Butterworth Ferry terminal, Georgetown's colonial heritage was plain to see. The historic centre of the city was an exhibition of white imperial buildings, green cricket squares, protestant churches, and memorials to Queen Victoria, all pristinely preserved. It was old English stuffiness, but painted bright white, and kept clean by a pure, unrelenting heat. And rising at every street corner, statues of company men and imperial agents looked out over the city they had commissioned - ghosts of the old colonial oppressors, still lingering in the streets, trapped in white marble sarcophagi.

But Georgetown, with its long history as a major centre for international trade, like much of Malaysia, is also known for its diversity. Branching out from the old colonial quarter, I soon found myself in Little India, walking past streets of Hindu temples. A minute later, I reached China town, where tall purple joss sticks stood smoking in front of ornate pagodas. From there, I passed Armenia street, Love Lane, and Penang Jewish cemetery, strolling by mosques, Buddhist shrines and Christian churches. I even heard of a temple in the south of the city, known as the Temple of the Azure Cloud, where locals worshipped a den of venomous pit vipers and burnt a special type of incense in the hope that the smoke would placate the deadly snakes and keep them from biting.

There was another reason why I found the streets of Georgetown fascinating. As was often the case on my journey, before arriving in Malaysia, I had made a point of searching for a book either written about the country or penned by a Malaysian author. It was in a little bookstore in Bangkok that I had found Tan Twan Eng's *The Gift of Rain*, a novel set in Penang during the years of the Japanese occupation. I had sat down with the book on a beach in Langkawi and read it in one fell swoop, and two days later, as I walked through Georgetown, I was treading both the real city and the fictional map of the old historic town left in my head by the novel. Places that I might have looked upon with indifference took on new meaning as I walked the streets where Eng's characters had lived, fought, and died. There are few better ways to establish a relationship with a place than to read a book set within its limits.

Following the story of a young man of mixed Anglo-Chinese heritage and his relationship with a Japanese diplomat, *The Gift of Rain* is chiefly concerned with the emotional horror that the Second World War inflicted upon the people of Penang. But it is also a study of Malay life as it had been in the pre-war years, just as the last lustre of the empire was fading. And being a book written by a Malaysian, one theme surfaces again and again throughout its chapters, appearing in the midst of even the bleakest events: the Malaysian love of food, and the culinary prowess of Penang's street hawkers.

Scattered throughout Eng's pages are the names of some of the island's most famous dishes, from wan tan mee, to hokkien mee, to char kuey teow. From the moment I arrived on Penang, every stranger I met was eager to recommend places to eat and local specialities, listing many of the dishes named in Eng's novel. I quickly realised that the Malays consider feasting a national past-time, and I had been heavily assured that there was no better place to indulge in that passion than on the streets of Georgetown.

On my first day on Penang, I ate breakfast at Transfer Road, the best roti canai stall in the city. The fresh buttery bread and bowl of fragrant curry took me straight back to the dhabas of India, especially when served alongside a mug of frothy teh tarik - sweet milk tea, blended with condensed milk, poured from a height. At midday, I lunched at Line Clear Nasi Kandar, one of Georgetown's most famous restaurants, which has been serving its famous fish-head curry for over one hundred years. Then, later in the afternoon, as the fierce heat was mounting, I could not deny myself a cup of chendol, a chilled Malay treat made from kidney beans, coconut milk, green rice noodles, shaved ice, and palm sugar, which was rich and deliciously sweet, like honey harvested from a coconut.

But it was not until after dark that Georgetown's most famous hawkers finally emerged and opened their stalls, lighting the city with gas fires and filling its streets with the smell of frying spices. Just like in Eng's novel, I had been told that the best night hawkers were still to be found on Chulia street, in the heart of the old city, where each vendor was known to specialise in a single dish. Impatient and hungry, I arrived there at dusk, just as the hawkers were setting out their stalls. Once in place, the cooks set to work with lightning hands, tossing noodles, stirring sauces, and slicing vegetables with military rhythm. As the evening darkened, no advertising was required, and the hawkers did not once shout for custom. The Chulia street cooks knew how good their food was, and it was not long before pilgrims began to arrive from across the world, queuing for places at little plastic tables, drawn to Penang by the prospect of being able to eat a breath-taking meal for little more than the price of a bus ticket.

The first hawker I came across made char kuey teow, a Malaysian speciality of flat rice noodles with stir-fried shrimps, cockles, egg, bean sprouts, chives, and lap cheong - a sweet red Cantonese sausage. Next to the char kuey teow seller, an old man worked alone on a cart making hokkien mee. He cooked his noodles in a stock made from pig bones and prawn heads, then decorated them with strips of roasted pork, little pink shrimps, and a spoonful of chillies, before crowning each bowl with half a boiled egg. The hokkien mee seller was clearly well known - the queue for his stall alone ran halfway to the ferry port.

Many of Chulia's street hawkers embodied Penang's Chinese heritage, each cook being the custodian of a long tradition stretching back to the days when the first Chinese migrants left their homeland and travelled to Malaysia, bringing their culinary talents with them. But being an island, Penang is also abundant with seafood, and beside the Canton-inspired hawkers were others selling fresh oyster omelettes, boiled half-lobsters, and shiny rows of snapper, laid out on ice, waiting for the grill. Surrounded by so many new opportunities for indulgence, I surrendered entirely to gluttony and went from stall to stall, eating everything I could. The hokkien mee was rich and succulent, the char kuey teow was sweet and delicate, and the oyster omelette sang of the sea. But by far the greatest dish to be found on Chulia street that night was the famous wan tan mee.

Originating in southern China, wan tan mee is a descendant of wonton noodles, the familiar Cantonese dish, often served as a soup. But on its journey to Penang, wan tan mee underwent an evolution, becoming drier, darker, and richer. In its Malay manifestation, wan tan mee consists of egg noodles cooked in oyster sauce, sesame seeds, and oil. The noodles are accompanied by an assortment of ingredients which differ from stall to stall. The hawker that I visited on Chulia street piled his bowls high with mushrooms, water spinach, shrimp dumplings, thin slithers of pork, and little pickled peppers. A perfect harmony of salt, spice, and acidity, it was deeply savoury but tantalizingly sweet, powerfully satisfying yet effeminately delicate, and so delicious that after my first spoonful, I immediately ordered two more bowls.

There was another reason why dining on Chulia street that night was such a pleasure. Beyond the exceptional food, every one of the hawkers wore a wide smile and looked happy in their work. At every table I ate, I was immediately joined by hungry Malays, eager to hear my opinion of their cuisine. This was a place for people brought together by a love of food, and it was also a place which inspired kindness. After finishing my wan tan mee, I looked up to see the ancient hokkien mee hawker waddling across the street, balancing a boiled egg on his spoon, heading to a table where an old lady was just finishing her noodles. Wordlessly, he plopped the egg into her bowl, and without looking up from her dinner, the old lady reached out and gave his hand a tender squeeze in a subtle show of gratitude. As the hawker ambled back through the crowd, the woman lifted the little present to her lips and chewed down upon the egg whilst scrunching her eyes into a wrinkled smile, the very image of bliss.

***

As I sat on a bus to Kuala Lumpur after leaving Penang, I could tell that I was rolling closer to the equator. With every passing mile, the jungle grew thicker, messier, and more clumsy, even as the bus reached the outskirts of the Malaysian capital. In the centre of the city, trees and creepers were draped over the edges of every building, lazily waging war against the skyscrapers, trying in vain to drag the spires to their knees. Up above, far higher than any tree could reach, the twin peaks of the Petronas towers were parcelled in purple clouds - two soaring conductors, calling out to gathering thunderstorms with an enticing lullaby, whispering promises of silver and steel.

That evening in KLCC park, I walked between the feet of some of the world's most iconic skyscrapers, but the towers surrounding me seemed more like apparitions than real buildings, like mirages belonging to the realm of science fiction, but not to the real world. Vast, modern, and impressive, Kuala Lumpur towered above me on all sides, just out of reach. The million-dollar apartments and sixty-storey office blocks made the capital a city to be gawped at, to wander through with wide eyes, but not a place to dwell in. Knowing that I would not stay for long, I sat in KLCC until late, studying the skyline, watching men and women in expensive suits hurry past. The clouds continued to build, and by sundown, the warm, lilac air was saturated with charge. Not long after dark, a deafening storm broke over the city, and as I fled to my hostel, rain began to fall through the black sky, whilst thunder rallied in the distance, echoing between Kuala Lumpur's slender spires.

Two days later, I left for Singapore, the miniature but pristine jewel affixed to the southern tip of the Malay peninsula by two slender bridges. Even compared to Kuala Lumpur, which had felt surreal and inaccessible in its modernity, the immaculate metropolis of Singapore, with its ring of glittering skyscrapers, felt like it had been lifted from another world.

Walking around Singapore's marina, I found myself in a very different Asia from the one I had spent the previous six months travelling across. Far from the wide wastes of Central Asia, or the clutter of India, or the green mountains of Vietnam, I had entered a different continent, separated from the rest of Asia not by geography but by time. Singapore was a city of the future, awe-inspiring in its efficiency, its orderliness, and its wealth. But down by its waterfront, the tiny island-nation also felt clinical and shallow, as if the whole city, if dropped, might smash apart like a glitter-ball and prove to be hollow inside.

Singapore was one of the few places on my journey that I had visited before, and I was glad to find that much of the city was still familiar to me. Walking along Clarke Quay, I passed restaurants selling French wine, Belgian beer, Alaskan crabs, and Australian beef, there to satisfy the expensive international tastes of the colony of office workers milling around the nearby financial district. In the face of rampant globalisation, little Singapore, with its preferential taxes and accommodating government, had opened its arms to the rest of the world and emerged as a major financial centre, but there is a fine line between being a city with a truly global identity, and being a city with no identity at all.

I spent a day wandering around the marina, strolling through the shadows of some of the most expensive real estate on the planet. After nightfall, a riotous lightshow was staged in the centre of the bay, featuring jets of water reaching hundreds of metres into the air and laser beams that bounced off the bellies of the surrounding skyscrapers. Later, behind the Marina Sands Hotel, I stumbled into the Supertree grove, where towering artificial trees, charged by sunlight during the day, glowed electric purple at night-time. Their wide metal canopies were woven with real plants and contained machines that filtered the air, just like real forests. Surrounded by a skyline of concrete and glass, the biomechanical trees looked completely at home - a vision of how the world might one day look if, having lost nature, we are one day forced to rebuild it ourselves.

Singapore was remarkable in its modernity, but as with Kuala Lumpur, I could not help but feel that the whole city was an exhibition, like a model of a metropolis, rather than a real city in which people actually lived. As a visitor, it would have been easy to spend a week trapped inside the manicured bubble, never getting through the city's impenetrable skin. I realised that the only way to learn more about the island-nation would be to sit down with somebody who knew it intimately, and fortunately for me, on just my second day in the city, a Singaporean agreed to take me to dinner.

I had never met Leon before, but we had been introduced by my brother, who had taught Leon to fly light aircraft whilst he was at university in England. He arrived at my hostel in a loud sports car, and alongside his pilot's license, I had also been told that Leon was a fan of speedboats, motorcycles, and anything else that went fast, which can make for a dangerous habit when your home nation is only thirty miles wide.

'Sam?' he called from the window of his sleek coupé. 'Get in. We're going for a ride.'

Inside the car, Leon greeted me with a fraternal air, stretching out his hand with the kind of confidence only found amongst the young and moneyed. He was a natural businessman, built for the boardroom, who split his time between Singapore, Myanmar, and China, overseeing the operations of his father's electronics business. As we sped through the city, he pointed out several properties that he owned, and several others he hoped to buy. Only a few years older than I, our material differences could not have been greater. He was a successful businessman with a growing portfolio, and I was a destitute traveller who had been homeless for nearly a year, but that evening we were just two young men, eager to hear one another's perspective on the world, rendered equals by life's great leveller: the dinner table.

Leon, rightly predicting that I had not yet left the city centre, decided to take me to the East Coast Lagoon Food Village, a collection of hawker stalls on the far edge of the island. We were met there by several of his friends, all of them finance professionals from the city, some of them Singaporean by birth and others Malaysian. The mix of nationalities made for a competitive atmosphere as dishes began arriving at our table. From chicken satay, to sambal stingray, to huge piles of seafood rolls, every dish was fought over by the two factions, each claiming the food to be Singaporean or Malaysian in origin. Timidly, I suggested that the street-food in Penang was surely the best in Southeast Asia, to which the Singaporeans were quick to inform me that the food of a hawker in downtown Singapore was so good that he had been awarded a Michelin star.

We had been eating for a while and were making amicable small talk when something rustled in the grass beside our table. Turning to Leon, I asked if there were any poisonous snakes in Singapore.

'The only venomous thing here is the government,' he said, to a chorus of laughter from all the others.

Intrigued, I pressed a little harder and decided to ask everyone around the table what life was like on the island-nation. The consensus was that living in Singapore was like living behind a smokescreen - a sheltered illusion, in which one always felt safe, but always slightly detached from reality. The media was filtered, the news was censored, society was heavily controlled, and though the country was ostensibly a democracy, the same party always won, triumphing in the last elections with a landslide victory.

'The most ridiculous thing is the newspapers,' said Leon, as he threw me a copy of *The Straits Times*. 'If you want to understand Singapore, a newspaper is all you need. They read like comedies, only making light of trivial stories, partly because the government buries bad news, and partly because Singapore is so dull that there's little bad news to bury.'

Taking the newspaper, I began to read the main stories aloud to Leon's attentive friends:

'One - Subway train travels two hundred metres with door open.'

'Headline news!' someone shouted, amidst loud laughter.

'Two - Man murders boss with meat cleaver after dismissal.'

'The office is the most dangerous place in Singapore,' joked Leon.

'Three - Singapore is first in the world to ground all Boeing 737 Max 8 planes after recent incidents.'

'Great - now we can't even leave the island. We're going to be bubble-wrapped forever,' said Sam, a banker from the city.

All of these young professionals had studied or travelled abroad, so they had seen Singapore from the outside and knew how sheltered an existence they led. Yet despite the media censorship and the sometimes-dubious democracy, they had all chosen to return to the city-state.

'The thing is, however much we complain about the politics of our country, Singapore is still a very pleasant place to live,' said Leon. 'Whenever I go to China or Myanmar, I'm reminded of how lucky we are. Despite its peculiarities, Singapore provides its citizens with safety and comfort, two privileges which many people around the world are denied.'

And besides that, Singapore was Leon's home, and patriotism, being a form of love, does not always adhere to rationality.

Once every savoury dish on the table was finished, I set off alone amongst the hawkers to find something sweet for the group. After searching for a while at the edge of the lagoon, I found a stall piled high with all the fruits of Asia, covered in towering mounds of durians, pitayas, coconuts, and rambutans. And amongst their ranks, half-hidden in the shadows, I discovered a clutch of purple mangosteens.

Ever since my arrival in India, I had been scanning every market I passed in search of a mangosteen, but I had been unable to locate a single one. I was not alone in my frustrations; throughout history, the fruit has been notoriously difficult to find. Queen Victoria, upon learning of delicious mangosteens in the reports of her colonial agents, offered a knighthood and one thousand pounds to any man who could bring one back from the hot corners of her empire. But the fruit, being delicate and a bad traveller, never made it to England, leaving the queen's wish unfulfilled.

Even today, mangosteens can only be found in Southeast Asia, appearing sporadically throughout the year, according to whether the trees are in season or not. Elated at the discovery of such a prize, before I returned to the dinner table, I bought a bag of mangosteens and went to stand alone at the edge of the sea. Taking one of the little purple orbs out of the bag, I split its hide, and one by one, I picked out the little white cloves that lay encased in its pink skin. The sweet, succulent flesh was even better than I remembered.

Looking up from my clandestine dessert, it took a moment for me to appreciate the significance of where I was. In front of me, stippled with the lights of hundreds of container ships, lay the calm, black Straits of Singapore, which meant that after eleven months of travelling, I had finally arrived at the southernmost tip of continental Asia.

Each of the ships out on the water was the remnant of a place, tied to a faraway origin. Gazing out at them, I wondered if any hailed from the ports I had passed on my way. One by one, I guessed the cities from which they had sailed - one from Yangon, another from Mumbai, a third from Istanbul, perhaps even one from as far afield as Santander. There were as many ships on that horizon as there had been days in my journey. A floating fleet of remembrances, standing still on the water, waiting patiently at anchor for the time to come when they would be called into port.

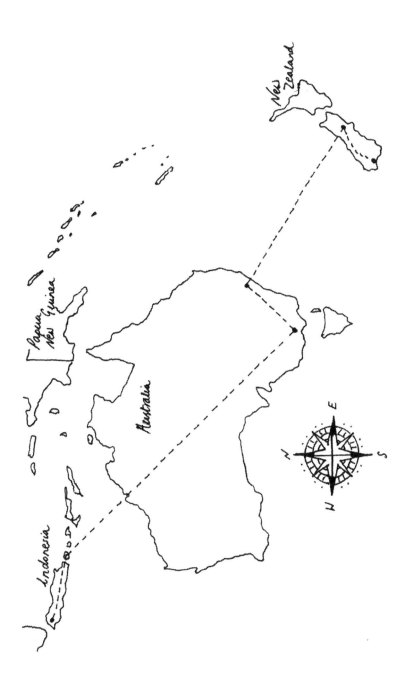

Chapter Nineteen

Then, how the Fire ebbs like Billows—
Touching all the Grass
With a departing—Sapphire—feature—
As a Duchess passed—

- Emily Dickinson, 'How the Old Mountains Drip with Sunset'

There was no red ribbon in the Java Sea as I passed over the equator. Nothing at all to announce the occasion as I slipped out of the northern hemisphere and into its southern counterpart. Ninety minutes later, following a mercifully short flight from Singapore, I landed in Jakarta and stepped out onto the streets of Indonesia's megalithic capital - a city of more than thirty million people, soon expected to overtake Tokyo as the most populous urban area on earth.

In the same time that it took to cover five hundred miles by aeroplane that morning, the motorcycle taxi I hailed at Soekarno-Hatta airport barely managed to crawl from one edge of the Indonesian capital to its centre. Like all megacities, I had predicted Jakarta to be beset with congestion, overcrowding, and pollution, but I also learnt that the city was facing a unique and much more sinister threat. Built atop the swampy delta of the Ciliwung River, ever since its origins, Jakarta has been slowly sinking, and much of the city is forecast to disappear within the next half-century. When my driver stopped outside a hostel and tipped me off his motorcycle into a pool of putrid water, it seemed a foreboding omen.

In recent years, Joko Widodo, the president of Indonesia, has been busy formulating a plan to deal with Jakarta's unusual problem. His proposed solution is to move the entire city from Java to the neighbouring island of Borneo, to a site on the coast of East Kalimantan. An ambitious project, the cost of moving one of the world's largest capitals is expected to exceed thirty-three billion dollars. But at the time of my visit, the plans were not yet finalised, and the new Indonesian capital remained the dream of the nation's president, a man who has been accused of being desperate to secure a grand legacy for himself, irrespective of the cost.

Until the new city is complete, visitors to Indonesia's present capital must contend with an ugly mass of traffic-strangled streets, where every indistinguishable building is stained the same shade of miserable grey. After dropping my bags in a dormitory crawling with cockroaches, I set off to explore the capital on foot, scanning Jakarta's low skyline of dusty offices and apartment blocks as I walked, looking for any sign of open space. The only structure that rose above the dreary cityscape was a tall white minaret, towering above the cavernous dome of the Istiqlal Masjid, the largest mosque in Southeast Asia.

As I walked towards the mosque, I began to notice that beyond the smell of petrol fumes and festering canals, Jakarta wore a distinct perfume. It was a sweet, sumptuous blend of spices and wood-smoke that I had never smelt before. The stubborn scent hung in clouds over the pavement and billowed out from every doorway and window that I passed. Only when I glimpsed shop-owners sat on little wooden stools, drinking coffee and smoking, did I realise that the smell came from kreteks - Indonesian cigarettes, laced with crushed cloves, named after the crackling sound they make as they burn. In Indonesia alone, over six hundred million kreteks are smoked every day, meaning that Jakarta permanently lies under a great cloud of honeyed cigarette smoke, every street smelling of scorched cloves and spices.

After walking for half an hour, I finally turned away from the traffic towards the gates of the Istiqlal Masjid and the dome of its enormous prayer hall. Walking towards the entranceway, I was about to step inside when a wrinkled man dressed in a white robe and black peci (the cap worn by Muslim men across Indonesia) called out and gestured for me to join him on a bench. He had a haggard face, gnarled old hands, and a baleful cough, but like all Indonesians, he wore a welcoming smile, complete with a smouldering kretek resting between his teeth.

'Salaam,' he called. 'Where are you from, my friend?'

'England,' I replied. 'Though I have been travelling for a while.'

'Ah, England. Sit and let me practise my English with you. I am a traveller too. I left home eight years ago, and I haven't been back since. You can call me Budi.'

'Eight years!' I exclaimed, taking a seat on the bench. 'Where have you been on your travels?'

'I have been walking. Just walking. I wake up when the sun shines and sleep in mosques at night. It is a simple life.' With a chuckle, he pointed down at his feet. 'These are my forty-third pair of sandals. I have walked two thousand miles since leaving home.'

'You have walked two thousand miles, just in Indonesia?' I asked, incredulous of the man's claim.

'Do you have any idea how big my country is? There are seventeen thousand islands in Indonesia. One life is not long enough to walk around even half of them.'

'You speak English very well,' I said.

'Indonesians are good with language. We should be - we have over five hundred of our own. You know, if I were to walk in a straight line from one edge of Indonesia to the other, I could keep going for nearly three and a half thousand miles.'

Doing a calculation in my head, I realised that was further than the distance from London to Tehran. Indonesia, I was quickly realising, is a far larger, far more complicated country than many people recognise.

'You have come to see the Masjid?' he asked, pointing his thumb at the enormous temple behind him. 'It's one of the biggest. A quarter of a million people can pray there at once. Did you know that Indonesia has more Muslims than any other country? It is good that you are here. Go look inside. This building is important to my people.'

Budi was still sat smoking by the gates of the mosque when I returned after taking a stroll around the cavernous prayer room.

'Special, isn't it? Istiqlal means Independence. Have you been to Merdeka square yet?' he asked, pointing towards a slim needle of stone rising in the distance. 'In the middle, you'll find another monument to

Indonesian independence, built by President Sukarno. I think you'll also find that impressive.'

After wishing Budi well, I began walking towards Merdeka, wondering what it would be like to do nothing but walk, day after day, for eight consecutive years. Long before I reached the towering monument, I came to the edge of a vast city square, one of the largest in the world, stretching for over half a mile from side to side. In the middle of the wide expanse, a pale obelisk rose into the polluted sky, and in its shadow, several thousand police officers were standing in ranks, shouting and waving riot shields, firing water cannons at flowers for practise. At first, I thought Budi had directed me towards the remnants of a riot, but I would later learn that the police force had gathered in the square that day for training. According to the local news, the drill was in preparation for an upcoming election which was expected to turn ugly. As predicted, two months after my visit, President Joko Widodo was re-elected, and riots broke out across Jakarta, leaving scores of people injured and eight citizens dead.

On my second day in the capital, I visited Jakarta's other famous square, Taman Fatahillah, which lies in the historic north of the city. A far cry from the colossal Merdeka, Fatahillah is a quaint, sedate plaza, flanked by white-brick museums and government buildings, built at the height of the colonial era. It was at the beginning of the fifteenth century that Batavia, as Jakarta was known by its European possessors, came under the control of the Dutch East India Trading Company, and Indonesia did not gain independence until 1949, over three hundred and forty years later. But in the seventy years since, the nation has been busy reclaiming its heritage, and now the small, unassuming square at Fatahillah is one of the few traces that remain of Jakarta's colonial past.

Weaving through flocks of pigeons and crowds of students riding brightly coloured bicycles, I crossed Fatahillah under the midday sun, walked past the famed Café Batavia, and then went searching down the backstreets of the old town for somewhere to have lunch. Eventually, I found a dilapidated restaurant where I sat beneath a faded poster of Mohammed Ali and ordered a plate of nasi goreng - the Indonesian staple of stir-fried rice, meat, and vegetables. I had been nibbling my food for less than a minute when a burly old man pulled up a chair opposite me.

'You are enjoying your meal?' he asked, exhibiting the great talent for starting conversation that is prevalent amongst Indonesians.

'Very much. Will you be eating?' I replied.

'No, no. I have had my lunch already. This is my restaurant,' he said, gesturing to the tables around us. 'Do you like the posters?'

'The posters of Ali? You are a fan?'

'A fan, and a fighter too. My name is Syamsul Harahap, and I am the greatest Sumatran boxer ever to have lived.'

I am no pugilist, but I could tell from Syamsul's scarred face and swollen, arthritic hands that he had made a career out of fighting, and though he was fifty years my senior, I was not about to dispute his claim to fame. His days in the ring might have been over, but it soon became apparent that in his old age, Syamsul had transitioned from the art of combat to the art of storytelling, and with cheeks full of rice, I listened attentively as for the second time in two days another Indonesian decided to share his life's story with me.

'I had polio as a child. I lost most of the movement in my right arm because of it. My uncle had a boxing gym, but I was never allowed to train. Half my family were fighters. Imagine how I felt, only ever able to watch them from the ringside.

'By the time I turned fifteen, I'd had enough of people telling me what I couldn't do. I walked straight into my uncle's gym and started hitting bags. Pah -pah - pah!' he breathed, striking the air as he spoke, raining a concert of shots upon an invisible rival.

'My family told me to stop, but I kept hitting harder and harder. A year later, I was the regional junior champion. A year after that, I was the champion of Sumatra. By 1976, I was representing Indonesia in the Summer Olympics, despite only having one and a half arms.

'But my handicap didn't matter. In the place of my arm, I'd taught myself to have two and a half feet instead. I moved so fast nobody could catch me. In pre-fight medicals, the doctors who looked me over couldn't believe the level I was competing at. Nobody had ever seen an Olympic boxer who could only punch with one hand. I was lightning quick.

'The secret to fighting is to let it come naturally. As a child, I used to watch the buffalo as they cut through fields of grass with their horns. They made it look so effortless. Instead of heavy practise on sandbags in the gym, I used to run out to the forest and punch the leaves off trees. If you twist your fist as you strike, just like a buffalo twists its horns, you can split a blade of grass, or a man's cheek, clean in half.'

Here, Syamsul raised his left hand and landed a gentle punch on my arm, turning his fist as it moved through the air towards me.

'I went all around the world with my boxing, across Asia, Europe, and the US. That's where I learnt my English - in America. I even once beat Tommy 'The Hitman' Hearns whilst he was still an amateur. He went on to be the first boxer in history to win world titles in five different weight divisions, but he couldn't beat Syamsul Harahap from Sumatra.'

'So how did you come to own a restaurant?' I asked.

'I met President Suharto once, just as I was reaching my peak. He asked me what my greatest desire was, and I realised that despite the fame, all I really wanted was to lead an ordinary life.'

After forty years of fighting and commentating, Syamsul had bought himself a little restaurant in the heart of Jakarta and glued fading portraits of boxing legends onto its walls. He said it was a profitable business, but I suspected that the restaurant also provided Syamsul with a convenient excuse to tell his story to any English-speaking tourist that happened to stop for lunch. After all, he had made a career from entertaining. By the end of his tale, my plate of nasi goreng had become the most interesting plate of fried rice I had ever eaten, and Syamsul had gained himself one more fan to add to his following.

As I left the restaurant, I shook his hand, and the old boxer pulled me in close with his one strong arm, before lifting me up into a bear hug with a deep, paternal giggle, and whispering to me:

'The most important thing in life, Sam, is to find your strengths, and once you have, learn how to fight with them.'

***

At seven o'clock in the morning, Jakarta's Gambir station was already a riot of life, filled with a growing crowd of passengers that were fussing, flapping, and collecting in the aimless way that travellers do at major railway stations. Men in brightly patterned batik shirts were waiting in long lines to buy tickets, whilst their wives, clad in plain coloured jilbabs, battled with unruly children. Commuters gobbled breakfasts of fried chicken, doughnuts, and burgers, hurrying on their way across the capital to work. And as with every inch of Jakarta, a cloud of sweet smoke hung in the air, at its thickest above a cigarette vendor who sold packets of kreteks beneath a sign that spelt out a simple message: NEVER QUIT.

I was asleep before my train to Yogyakarta had even left the city, and when I woke, the carriage was surrounded by gleaming jungle. Beyond the window, a wild brigade of trees and creepers bowed before the railway tracks, crowding to within an inch of the train. Occasionally, there were brief breaks in the steaming greenery when I was able to snatch glimpses of the landscape beyond. I saw rice terraces and rolling green hills, glistening rivers and frail wooden villages, and at one point, a cap of cloud encircling its summit, I saw the steep rippled sides of a distant volcano.

The image of the volcano floated before my eyes long after the train had returned to its sheath of jungle. Aside from the innocent pools of gurgling mud in Azerbaijan, I had never seen an active volcano before. I began to wonder if the cloud around its summit might have been smoke and if I had just glimpsed the beginnings of an eruption. Since arriving in Java, I had given little thought to the chain of blazing craters running along the island's spine and spreading out on either side to the far reaches of the Indonesian archipelago. Half-dreaming, as I reclined in my seat, I had visions of lava boiling up over the horizon, of molten stones rocketing across the sky, and of pyroclastic flows running down from the mountain to tear the train from its tracks. I could not imagine what it would be like to live in the little villages that the train passed, forever in the shadow of such menacing neighbours.

Having been told that Yogyakarta was the ancient cultural capital of Java, I arrived in the city at dusk expecting to find an abundance of pristinely preserved palaces and temples. What I discovered instead was a loud, crowded town, centred upon a main boulevard named Malioboro street, where thousands of people were slowly traipsing past a mile-long line of food-stalls selling nasi goreng, beef rendang, and countless sticks of satay chicken. I had been in Indonesia long enough to recognise that the country did not share the same culinary pedigree as some of the other Southeast Asian nations I had visited, but the Indonesians redeem themselves by being some of the best coffee roasters in the world. So despite a mounting sense of disappointment at having traded one drab city for another, I took to the streets of Yogyakarta with some optimism because I had been told that near to the train station, tucked down an alleyway, I would find the best cup of coffee in all of Java.

I knew that the Indonesians were partial to unusual brews because my brother had once brought home a bag of kopi luwak from his own travels to Sumatra. Made from half-digested coffee beans picked out from the droppings of wild palm civets, kopi luwak is one of the rarest coffees in the world. Though the taste had been memorable, I was in no hurry to drink anything that had passed through the digestive tract of a small mammal again. Luckily, the coffee in Yogyakarta was famous for other reasons.

To the north of the station, I came across a row of road-side stalls belching steam and smoke below signs that read 'kopi joss'. Recognising the Indonesian word for coffee, I walked over and joined a crowd of locals sat on the curb-stone. Beneath the sign, the owner of the stall was tending a wood fire and shifting vast cast-iron kettles on and off the flames. Noticing me, he lifted one of the kettles, poured out a measure, and handed me a glass of steaming black liquid. At first sight, it seemed to be just a normal brew - a deep black and richly perfumed draught of Javanese coffee. But as I raised the small glass to my lips, a hand shot out from amongst the crowd and stayed my arm, instructing me to wait. A second later, the owner of the stall returned clasping two lumps of glowing charcoal between a pair of steel tongs, which he plopped into my cup without warning.

Disappearing in a violent cloud of steam, the charcoal sank to the bottom of my glass in a flurry of bubbles, letting out a long, satisfying hiss as it dropped, from which the onomatopoeic name of 'kopi jossssss' derives. As I waited for the coffee to cool, I sniffed at the cloud of steam gathered above it and realised that palm sugar must have been mixed into the brew because lingering above the coffee was the distinctive, irresistible smell of burnt syrup, caramelised by the glowing lump of charcoal that gurgled in the bottom of the glass. When I eventually plucked up the courage to take a sip, the sweet, smoky liquid was hauntingly fragrant and deliciously rich. But fine beans, palm sugar, and glowing charcoal aside, what really made the coffee special was the fact that it was served on the side of a busy Javanese road, amidst a cloud of petrol fumes and kretek smoke, just as the night-creatures of Yogyakarta were emerging onto the city's streets.

Alongside food hawkers, Malioboro street was lined with antique shops, the Indonesians being great collectors of art and ancient things. The little wooden galleries that I walked past after finishing my coffee were filled with remnants of Dutch colonialism, crowded with naval lanterns, diving suits, and shining astrolabes. They were also filled with a vast stock of indigenous artefacts, including Javanese masks, Kalimantan swords, Balinese headdresses, and kris from all over Indonesia. The ornate kris were similar to the slender ceremonial daggers common across Malaysia, with marbled blades, broad hilts, and handles patterned with demons and monsters that shone enticingly in the lamplight: delicate, deadly talismans, believed to bestow bravery upon even the most timid of owners.

As well as antiques, the road-side galleries of Yogyakarta were filled with more recent examples of artwork sourced from across the islands of Indonesia. Subtle differences in style distinguished the pieces, faintly discernible quirks that marked one exhibit as Sumatran, another as Sumbanese, and a third as Balinese. But all the specimens, whatever their provenance, shared the same playful, carnivalesque quality that is the hallmark of Indonesian art. From masks with wide popping eyes and buck teeth to tobacco pipes shaped like dragon-snouts, all of the pieces were enchantingly beautiful, but devilish too, and one particular painting left me spellbound.

It was in a small shop just off Malioboro Street that I fell in love with a black and gold canvas picturing the silhouette of a man sat puffing meditatively on a kretek. When I asked the shopkeeper about its origin, he told me it was painted by a Kalimantan artist, from the Indonesian side of the island of Borneo, using the batik technique. Then, without my asking, the shopkeeper fetched a pot of molten wax from atop a burning flame in one corner of his studio, and after dripping a pattern of wax onto a scrap of canvas, he placed the folded cotton into a bowl of red dye. When the ruby coloured canvas emerged a minute later, the trail of wax remained uncoloured and stood out in stark contrast to the scarlet cloth behind.

'This is batik technique,' smiled the shopkeeper. 'Unique to the islands of Indonesia.'

If I had room in my bag for a two-metre canvas, I might have bought the painting, but I had no space in my luggage at all, a fact which the persistent shopkeeper refused to accept. After sensing that the large painting was a hopeless prospect, he brought out a flurry of other canvases, gradually decreasing in size, desperately hoping for a sale. Like the characters in the art he displayed, the shopkeeper was wily and cunning, fiddling the prices up and down, deviously determined to trick a stranger into relinquishing his money.

In the end, having named the price of every item in his shop, the exasperated man pulled a baby python from out of his breast pocket and tried to sell me that instead. The tiny slumbering serpent was curled into a tight ball, and he insisted that it was an adult and would not grow any larger. Later that night, I learnt from another shopkeeper that pythons on Java have been known to grow up to fifteen metres in length. It seemed that the desperate artist, like a little demon from one of his pictures, was not to be trusted, dealing not only in art but in magic and monsters too.

***

After several days spent exploring Yogyakarta, I took a train to Banyuwangi, a town on the east coast of Java, where I knew I could catch a ferry to Bali. Besides the presence of a port, I was drawn to Banyuwangi for another reason. Ever since glimpsing the smoking mountain on my train from Jakarta to Yogyakarta, I had grown increasingly curious about Java's long chain of volcanoes. When I had asked the owner of my hostel in Yogyakarta how I might learn more about these mysteries, her response had been instant:

'Why don't you go to Banyuwangi? If you want to learn about volcanoes, what better way than to climb inside the crater of one?'

Rising out of the jungle, thirty miles north-west of Banyuwangi, Mount Ijen is one of the most famous volcanoes on the Indonesia archipelago. It is regularly active, but since its last major eruption in 2002, the volcano has been deemed safe enough by locals for groups of tourists to be led down into its crater each day. Determined to see the inside of a volcano, and having heard that Ijen was at its most impressive after dark, I arrived in Banyuwangi and slept through the evening, before waking at midnight to clamber into the back of an old truck alongside a handful of other climbers, all destined for the mountain.

As we careered through the dark jungle, a Balinese man in the passenger seat introduced himself as our guide and passed a box of flimsy gasmasks into the rear of the truck to be shared amongst the passengers.

'Is Ijen dangerous?' a Malaysian tourist asked, whilst I inspected the masks.

'Some people have died,' said the guide, wobbling his head ambiguously. 'All miners though. Eruptions are not a problem. Just the deadly gas that sometimes collects in the crater.'

I would later learn that in the previous few decades, Ijen had claimed dozens of lives, mostly those of sulphur miners working at the rock-face deep in the caldera. The sulphur produced by Ijen is some of the finest in the world, but the same forces that generate the yellow mineral also release clouds of sulphuric dioxide, a highly toxic gas. The masks that the guide had handed to us were thin, cotton specimens, the sort of protection that might have been useful for a house renovation, but not a trek inside an active volcano.

'Will these protect against sulphur dioxide?' I asked.

'No, no,' giggled the guide. 'If big sulphur eruption, everybody die. These just help with the smell.'

After an hour's drive, our truck came to a halt in a flat clearing, walled in on all sides by darkness. This, the guide told us, was the foot of Mount Ijen, and after lighting a dim electric torch, he marched off into the jungle, beckoning for us to follow. It was a two-mile hike to the rim of Ijen's crater, beginning in hot, dense rainforest. But the Balinese guide set a furious pace, and it was not long before we broke above the tree-line and emerged onto the open slopes of the volcano, which were swaddled in thick clouds carrying the faint but unmistakable perfume of sulphur.

As we climbed higher, the rotten smoke from the volcano continued to meld with the night clouds until my eyes and lungs were burning, and alongside the other climbers, I found myself groping for my gas mask. Unfazed, the Balinese guide pressed on, and half an hour later, we reached the rim of the crater itself, nearly three thousand metres above the jungle. To one side, a break in the clouds revealed the silhouettes of other volcanoes standing nearby, just discernible in the moonlight. On our other side, stoppered by darkness and overflowing with rancid mists, a single path led down into the depths of a wide crater.

I was stood beside our guide and was about to ask if we would be walking any further when men began to appear climbing up the side of the crater, drifting out of the shadows with huge baskets of stone resting on their crooked backs. The guide had told me how local boys growing up near Banyuwangi had to choose between the life of a poor rice farmer or going to work on Ijen, collecting sulphur for local factories where the brimstone is used in the manufacture of matches. Mining sulphur inside the volcano paid more than farming, but it was accursed work. Every day the miners risked their lives, toiling amidst noxious fumes and the constant threat of an eruption. To avoid the daytime heat, they worked mostly at night, forced to navigate the steep sides of the crater in pitch darkness because no moonlight ever passes through the clouds of smoke that billow ceaselessly out of the volcano.

Despite the risk, the price that the miners receive for each kilogram of sulphur is only one thousand rupiahs, the equivalent to five English pence, and they are only paid after carrying their quarry two miles down the mountain in one hundred kilogram loads at a time. Stood on the crater's rim, I watched as the men heaved their baskets over the volcano's edge, and I could not comprehend a life spent in such agonising toil. Having reached the path, one miner came towards me and set his load on the ground. He was a tiny man, half my size, dressed in nothing but rags and sandals. Motioning to his basket, he invited me to test its weight. To my shame, I could not lift it even an inch off the ground.

When I asked my guide what the miners did to protect themselves, he explained that they could not afford masks, so in the crater itself, they either continually smoked cigarettes or tied thin cloths around their faces for protection. He said that Ijen miners were lucky to last twenty years on the mountain. Finding one over the age of forty was rare.

To supplement their meagre income, the miners had taken to carving little pieces of sulphur into delicate ornaments to sell to tourists. After catching his breath, the man who had stopped beside me emptied his pockets to reveal a dozen of these sulphur charms, sculpted by his own hand. I bought a little yellow flower from him and had the guide ask how long he had worked on Ijen. Holding up a scaly fist, with fingers bent like claws, the miner explained that he had worked on the volcano for eighteen years. By my guide's reckoning, the man did not have long left.

Once the other tourists arrived at the rim, to my astonishment, our guide announced that we would be descending into the crater. Following his lead, we passed several crude signs that warned against entering the volcano, but one by one we filed down a narrow mountain path, made slippery by an evening of rain, with nothing but electric torches to guide us. Every so often we had to stand aside so that miners climbing in the opposite direction could pass, the laboured sound of their breath echoing up the mountain long before they were visible. For forty minutes, we continued like this, inch by treacherous inch, until we finally reached the bottom of the crater, surrounded by a maelstrom of smoke and darkness. There, spreading wide before us, was the largest acid lake in the world, and beside the lake, climbing up the steep wall of the crater, beautiful and eerie, was the phenomenon which had made the mountain famous: Ijen's blue fire.

Emerging out of a rift in the volcano's thin skin, a ribbon of electric blue flames twisted their way up into the night, fed by deposits of molten sulphur which bubbled out of the ground. Stood at the foot of the burning mountainside, amidst rancid clouds, at first I only caught glimpses of the conflagration. But then a gust of wind emptied the cauldron of smoke, revealing an enormous blaze rippling all the way up one side of the crater - a great cataract of purple fire, rushing upwards into the gloom.

As more of the volcano became visible, I began to notice shapes moving amongst the flames. These, I realised, were the miners at work, busy spraying water onto the molten rock in attempts to condense the burning sulphur which collected in pipes their predecessors had lain. At the bottom of the pipes, by the relative coolness of the acid lake, the sulphur congealed in bright yellow nuggets, where it could be hacked into smaller pieces and loaded into baskets. A life spent prising hot rocks from the mouth of a volcano and carrying them piece by piece down the side of a steep mountain. I could not imagine another existence more akin to living hell.

The miners knew their workplace well, stepping confidently amongst the vents, predicting every flicker of the burning vapour, unperturbed by the danger of their surroundings. From where I stood, close to the sulphur deposits, the acid lake was only a few steps away: dark, ominous, and deadly. I was staring across its waters, trying to discern shapes in the smoke that hung low over its surface, when suddenly a deep rumble sounded on the far side of the volcano. Immediately, I shot my guide a look of concern.

'No worry, my friend. Noise is just landslide. They happen after rain on outside of crater.'

But just as he said these words, the edge of the acid lake began to tremble, and then retreat, forming little waves, before disappearing altogether. I listened carefully, and amidst the snapping flames, I thought I could hear the sound of rushing water. When I turned to look for my guide again, he was running.

Realising that the landslide must have been on the inside of the crater and that its entry into the lake had sent a small tsunami of acid rushing in our direction, my guide had not wasted a second in making his escape. And with one person running, everyone inside the crater, miners and tourists alike, panicked and began a mad scramble up the wall of the volcano, fleeing as fast as they could.

Following suit, I began to rush through the darkness, desperate to reach the crater wall, which was seventy metres in the distance. Then, amongst the screams of the crowd, I heard a miner shout:

'Poison, poison!'

In disturbing the acid lake, the landslide had also released a bubble of sulphur dioxide, which meant that I was fleeing not only a tsunami of acid but also an invisible cloud of toxic gas.

With the volcano bellowing out more smoke than it had all night, I could not find the path out of the crater, and I was left with no choice but to haul myself over the wet rocks, climbing hand over hand up the wall of Ijen. My heart was burning and my lungs were empty, but I did not dare breathe for fear that I might swallow a mouthful of poison. Nearby, I could hear the other climbers and miners, squabbling and pushing past one another, throwing strangers aside in their own bids for safety. After a minute of climbing, I found a woman collapsed on the rocks in front of me. Pulling her back upright, I pushed her on up the rock-face, climbing behind as fast as I could. Ten minutes later, spurred on by pure panic, I reached the rim of the crater and fell onto the ground, retching with exhaustion, with bitter sulphurous tears streaming from my eyes.

By the time I had my breath back, dawn was breaking, and behind me, Ijen had shed its insidious darkness to reveal a vast lake, calm and milky blue. Yellow seams of sulphur ran in rings around the crater, hooping the lake with gold, and trudging up the wall of the volcano, one by one, tourists and miners emerged into the sunlight and collapsed onto the ground, desperately gulping for air.

Feeling that I had succeeded in my aim of becoming better acquainted with the volcanoes of Java, I did not wait to see if Ijen had any other dramas planned for that morning. Setting off alone, I marched back down the mountain, soon reaching the tree-line. Five steps later, I passed a little wooden sign that I had not noticed in the dark. It warned of Javanese leopards in the surrounding area, prone to hunting at dawn. Stopping in my tracks, I considered my options. Strangely, the prospect of being eaten by hungry wildcats did not seem as bad as returning to the dungeon of acid and fire behind me. Having decided my fate, I walked on alone into the jungle, scanning the tree-line for teeth, clutching in my left hand a little yellow blossom cut from the heart of the volcano.

Chapter Twenty

For there is no folly of the beast of the earth which is not infinitely outdone by the madness of men.

- Herman Melville, *Moby Dick*

It takes thirty seconds for a practised deckhand to gut, decapitate, and de-scale an Australian salmon. If the fish are still icy and the deckhand is inexperienced, it takes a little longer. After the four hundredth fish, when the fingers of even the most seasoned fisherman are frozen and bleeding, it takes longer still. On average, each salmon weighs three kilograms, and on my second day in Australia, I found myself stood opposite a three-tonne pile of fish, being watched by an angry captain who bellowed at me with each passing hour, demanding that his bait be ready before sunrise.

After my dramatic night in the crater of Mount Ijen, I had spent a week on the island of Bali, walking amongst Ubud's rice terraces and swimming along surf-swept beaches. I had hoped that I would be able to talk my way onto a sailboat and cross from Indonesia to Australia by way of the Timor Sea, but I soon learnt that few yachts make the crossing, and by the end of my time in Bali, I faced a new and more pressing problem: I had completely run out of money.

Desperate for work, I had just enough funds remaining to pay for a single flight to Australia. Uncertain of where to go, I remembered a friend who had spent some time fishing off the coast of Melbourne. Trawling for prawns, he had told me, was tough but lucrative work. I decided to send him a message, asking if he knew any boats that might be in need of a deckhand. Twenty-fours later, he replied and told me to make my way to a place called Port Welshpool, where I would find a man named Harry Farnwell waiting for me.

During the flight from Bali to Melbourne, I watched a vast, red continent slip past beneath me as the aeroplane leapt from one side of Australia to the other in a matter of hours. I was frustrated at having to resort to air travel again. I would have liked nothing more than to cross Australia by land, but with an empty bank account, I had little choice. Arriving in Melbourne, I boarded a bus heading east, barely even stopping to see the city. Three hours later, after driving into the heart of Victoria's South Gippsland region, the bus came to a halt, and the conductor turned to let me know that we had arrived at Welshpool.

Set amongst rolling green hills, the timber-clad town looked deserted, but nearby there was a small marina with a single sixty-foot fishing vessel named *The Quiet Achiever* moored on its outer pontoon. As I walked closer to the boat, a grizzled fisherman emerged from the wheelhouse and cast me a hostile look. Topless and unshaven, he stood well over six feet in height, and despite his silver hair, he was bound by a frame of thick muscle. Lighting a cigarette, he took a deep drag, spat aggressively onto the deck of his boat, and in a haggard south Australian accent said:

'So you're the Pom, eh? Better come aboard. You're up at midnight to cut the bait.'

'What bait do we use for prawns?' I naively asked.

'Prawns? We ain't fishin' for no prawns, Pom. We're going after sharks. You're gonna see what real fishin' is,' he cackled, throwing his cigarette down at my feet.

Born on Flinders Island - the remote rock that lies halfway between Australia and Tasmania - Harry Farnwell had been a fisherman all of his life. Fifty years of sea-salt and wind-burn had locked his face into a permanent scowl, but a bright madness still burned behind his pale eyes. Though my friend had warned me that he was a tough captain and a hard taskmaster, he had said that Harry was a brilliant fisherman. But nautical prowess aside, as I stepped aboard *The Quiet Achiever*, something about Harry unnerved me. From the minute I shook the captain's hand, I could sense that he was capable of great cruelty.

Inside the smoke-filled wheelhouse, the captain introduced me to his son who was sat in one corner of the cramped galley sharpening a sinister blade.

'This is Jack, the gutter. He's the man who kills everything we bring on board.'

Jack gave me a silent nod, then turned his attention back to his whetstone. Taking a seat beside him, I looked around the squalid wheelhouse, which was covered in filth and grime and heavy with the stink of unwashed men.

'She's a beauty, isn't she, our Quiet Achiever?' grinned Harry. 'You ever been fishin' before, Pom?'

'Not on a boat like this,' I admitted.

'It's a man's business, fishin'. I've been at it all my life. Prawns in the summer, sharks in the winter. Only lost two men in fifty years, which is good goin' for these parts. One over the side and one got caught in a winch. You'll be alright if you do as you're told, Pom.'

'See those two boats that went down in Queensland today, Dad?' said Jack. 'Eight crew lost.'

'Poor bastards,' said Harry. 'More men die fishin' than in any other work in Australia. Bet you didn't know that, Pom?' His wide grin betraying the fact that Harry derived a twisted sense of satisfaction from the grim statistic.

'Anyway, like I said, up at midnight. Our bunks are down there,' he growled, pointing into a dark hole that opened under the wheelhouse.

Before he went down to sleep himself, Harry took a glass, filled it to the brim with bleach, and then reached into his mouth to unclip two rows of false teeth which he dropped into the peroxide.

'Gotta keep em clean,' he mumbled, as he placed a final cigarette between his toothless gums, struck a light, and then climbed down into the dark.

Unsurprisingly, Harry's conversation left me wondering if I had made the right decision by joining his crew. If I had known then what the next two weeks would entail, I would have crept off *The Quiet Achiever* whilst the captain and his son were sleeping, fled back to Melbourne, and never would have set foot in South Gippsland again. But dismissing Harry's comments as an old fisherman's attempts to rattle a greenhorn, I stayed on board, sitting up in the wheelhouse unable to sleep, waiting until midnight, when the captain emerged from his bunk, eyes blazing, and commanded that I start chopping fish.

I had been working on the three-tonne pile of salmon for half an hour when two more men arrived at the pontoon to join me beneath the marina's bright floodlights.

'Pom, this is Cameron and Simon, the rest of the crew,' said Harry. 'We did have another decky, but we had to let him go. Turns out his parole officer didn't like the idea of him being out at sea for two weeks surrounded by sharp knives, so you three will have to pick up the slack.'

Simon and Cameron were both in their early forties, but the deep furrows that ran across their faces made them look much older. As I shook each of their hands, I found myself clutching fists of stone, hardened by decades of work. Cameron's hand, in particular, was a wreck of arthritis and scars, the skin folding in such thick creases that he could barely straighten his fingers. With a crooked back, a jaw set in a permanent gurn, and a face burnt ruby by the sun, his wrecked and misshapen body spoke of a lifetime of hard labour, destined for a premature end.

In the cool night air, we had to work fast to prepare the bait to prevent the fish from defrosting in the morning sun. In between gutting, chopping, and salting the salmon, I chatted to Simon and Cameron and learnt a little about their lives. A handyman by trade, Simon had been to sea once before, setting for crayfish in the warm waters around Darwin, but he had never worked under Harry. Cameron was a plumber by trade, though he had fished on *The Quiet Achiever* before. At one point during the night, whilst the captain was out of earshot, he turned to me and confided:

'That man's a ruthless bastard. You need to watch your back around him. He's got a reputation for using up crew.'

'So why are you here?' I questioned.

'Me? I like the fresh air. And once we slip lines tomorrow, ain't nobody in the world will know where we are for two weeks,' he said, giving me a mischievous wink.

It took us all morning to cut, salt, and load the salmon, and then at midday, another tonne of mackerel arrived requiring the same treatment. Once the bait was loaded, Harry had us clean the deck, tidy the lines, and paint the wheelhouse. We were still working at dusk when he ordered us to fill the hull with sacks of concrete, to be used as extra ballast. We would be fishing in Bass Strait, one of the most violent stretches of ocean on earth, and with the arrival of winter, the captain was expecting rough weather.

The whole day we worked without rest or food, until long after the sun had set. When our duties were finally done, we sat down to a dinner of cold bacon and eggs, sticky with congealed grease. The crew ate in silence in the wheelhouse, surrounded by thick curls of cigarette smoke, as episodes of fishing documentaries played on a small television. Harry laughed at the lifejackets and safety harnesses worn by the Alaskan crab-men on the screen - there was no such protection on his boat, he gloated.

After dinner, the captain turned to the crew and in a very solemn tone, he announced:

'We sail at dawn. Now I'll ask you this only once - ain't nobody brought any bananas on board, have they? Because if I find out you have, I'll drown you myself.'

Puzzled, I shook my head along with the other crew. I would later learn from Cameron that bananas are an object of extreme superstition amongst fishermen across Australia. Harry claimed he had found a banana smuggled onto his boat only once before, and that was in the bag of the deckhand he had lost out at sea. But unlike other captains, Harry's vendetta extended beyond bananas, and he had placed a complete embargo on all fruit and vegetables. Between five men, setting sail for two weeks of fishing, the only nutritious food we had between us was a single pumpkin and sack of old potatoes. The rest of the trip, we would eat nothing but miserly rations of bacon, eggs, biscuits, and fish.

An hour later, one by one, each of us went down into the six-berth bunkhouse to sleep. It was a tight, dark hole, which stank of fish and sweat, with the bunks so close together they were almost touching. Also sleeping in the bunkhouse were Red and Blue, two Australian cattle dogs that roamed freely around the boat, generally causing a nuisance and soiling the deck wherever they pleased.

'Lovely fresh sheets for you boys,' joked Harry, as I peeled back the grubby blankets lying atop my bunk which were damp with mould and grime. Battling the urge to retch, I climbed up onto the festering mattress, closed my eyes, and wondered how I would ever be able to sleep. Little did I know that a fortnight later, bathed in the filth of a thousand dead fish, having gone unwashed for two weeks, I would look upon the squalid bunkhouse as a kind of paradise, it being the only place aboard *The Quiet Achiever* where some semblance of rest, however brief, was ever possible.

***

I was woken at dawn the next day by Harry's thunderous shouts and the sound of his boots stamping the deck six inches above my head. Immediately, we were set to work, receiving orders to fill the freshwater tanks, bring final provisions on board, and secure everything on deck with a labyrinth of ropes and chains. We laboured at a ferocious pace all morning, and within a matter of hours, the boat was ready to sail. When it came to casting off, Harry put on a shirt for the first time in two days, and pulling his pair of teeth out from the glass of bleach, he gave the dentures a shake, fixed them in his mouth, and after lighting a fresh cigarette, issued a grave command:

'Slip the lines, boys. We're going fishin'.'

For twelve hours, we steamed across Bass Strait, heading towards Flinders Island, led by a pod of bottlenose dolphins who steered us past lone albatross drifting atop the waves. The sea was spirited, but not wild, rising in small green mounds, darkened by an overcast sky. In the distance, the coastline of the island gradually became visible - nothing more than a thin edge of grey rock, wracked by white wave-crests. Beyond that rock, all I could see was open ocean and the wide unbroken horizon, dropping down beyond the edge of the world.

But there was little time to study our surroundings because Harry had three thousand hooks which needed baiting with dry chunks of salmon. Shining brightly, each steel barb was bent into a vicious curve, like the sinister grin of a villain, designed to lodge in a shark's mouth and bury deeper into its flesh the more fish struggled. These particular hooks were crafted specifically for gummy sharks, also known as Australian smooth-hounds - the favourite fish of Australian restaurants and our primary catch. On average, gummy sharks grow to just over ten kilograms, but as we were baiting the hooks, Cameron warned me that the salmon might also attract far larger quarry.

The sun had set before we finished baiting, and in the darkness I buried countless hooks into my soft hands, each new wound stinging violently as it became clogged with the salt we used to preserve the salmon. By the time we weighed anchor, my fingers were already in tatters, but before I entered the wheelhouse, Harry grabbed my wrists and poured methylated spirits over my sores, which burnt like acid in every cut.

'Don't squirm, you daft Pom. This is the only thing that will stop your hands going rotten.'

That night, we had just two hours of sleep before it was time to return to work and shoot the line. Stumbling out onto the cold deck at three o'clock in the morning, Cameron, Simon, and I had to unfurl eight miles of rope into the black ocean, clipping on the three thousand baited hooks as we did so. Dragged down by steel weights, the thick line slipped silently into the waves, sinking fast to the bottom. As we clipped the hooks onto the rope, all it would have taken is for one of the silver barbs to have caught on a man's sleeve and he would have been pulled over the edge, dragged down to the depths of Bass Strait, with no hope of ever resurfacing.

As a novice crew, we were slow, and all night Harry stood in the wheelhouse and delivered a tirade of threats and curses, screaming at us to work faster. We were still shooting gear when daylight broke in the east, and even after all the line was in the water, more salmon had to be cut and more hooks baited in preparation for the next morning. It was midday by the time we were allowed to crawl back into our bunks, but by two o'clock in the afternoon, we were awake again and back on deck, making ready to haul in the lines. And when the first buoy was spotted, despite my fatigue, like every other man on board, I felt myself gripped by restless energy, nervously waiting to see what creatures we were about to drag out of the ocean.

To haul the catch onto the boat, one end of the eight-mile line was brought aboard and wrapped around a hydraulic winch, which began to pull the rope onto the deck at lightning speed. As the youngest member of the crew, I was given the job of clipper, meaning that it was my responsibility to lean over the side of the boat and grab the hooks before they hit the guardrail, unclipping them as fast as I could, whilst also throwing any fish we had caught onto the deck. In theory, it was a simple job, but Cameron had warned me that the hooks would come flying out of the water every other second, tangled with slippery sea-weed, often with a monstrous fish attached.

As I stood at the edge of the boat, waiting with eager anticipation, the first few hooks came up empty. But then, close by, I saw a pale grey shape looming underneath the water, rapidly making its way to the surface.

'Get ready Pom! You got a fish!' shouted Harry, just as a twenty-kilogram shark was launched out of the sea. Wrapping my two hands around its rough body, I twisted and threw the shark onto the deck, slipping on a sea urchin as I turned. A second later, I was lying face down atop the struggling fish, listening to the squeak of its writhing flesh underneath my chest, when Jack arrived with a heavy hammer and pushed me away. As the shark flopped and wriggled its way around the deck, it took just a single blow to stun the creature, and then Jack's slender knife did the rest of the work.

In the adrenalin of my first shark, I had failed to notice that five more hooks had already been dragged out of the water and were now caught in a tangle at the edge of the boat. With bloodlust in his eyes, Harry screamed at me to get on my feet and refused to stop the winch for even a second. I ran to the guardrail, and whilst I was unwrapping the line, a hook buried itself into my hand. With no time to think, I ripped the hook out of my palm, threw it to one side, and leant over the rail, just in time to haul another large shark onto the boat. As more fish arrived, Jack worked diligently behind me, and soon the deck was stained red with blood. Everywhere, terrified creatures lay waiting to die as I stumbled over their bodies, slipping on shark guts, throwing fish after fish onto the boat, whilst the captain stood and laughed wildly at the helm, watching through demented eyes.

For the first half-mile of line, we hauled nothing but gummy sharks, to the delight of our greedy captain. But before long, a huge creature appeared in the water, circular in shape, growing bigger and bigger as it rushed towards the surface.

'You got a big ray there, Pom!' said Harry, as he slid a knife across the deck to my feet. 'Don't lose the hook. Just slice the bastard's jaw.'

The ray must have weighed nearly fifty kilograms, but as there was no market for them, it could not be sold and was too big to bring aboard. The easiest way to release it would have been to cut through the thin nylon cord that connected each hook to the main line, but Harry was such a miser he did not want to waste the metal hook. As the massive body of the ray slammed against the side of the boat, the captain kept the hydraulic winch running to keep the fish held aloft, which put immense strain on the line. Then Cameron appeared behind me, and grabbing my waist with his two hands, pushed me forwards, shouting:

'Over you go, Sammy,' and a second later, I was dangling upside down over the edge of the boat, inches away from the ray.

With no other option, I thrust my knife into the creature's mouth and started sawing at its thick jaw, which began weeping red blood into the sea. As I worked, the ray thrashed its tail against the hull, beating a tortured tattoo that echoed through the ocean. Its mouth was built of tough cartilage, and it took thirty seconds for my knife to work through it. When its flesh finally split, the vast fish dropped back into the water and the hook, suddenly relieved of pressure, rocketed upwards, missing my eyes by the breadth of a hair.

'C'mon boys. We need to keep the winch on, or we'll lose the sharks,' bellowed Harry.

Leaving the hooks dangling in the water meant that any sharks we caught were sitting targets for sea lions, which is why the captain insisted on keeping the line moving at all times, irrespective of the danger. On many occasions over the next two weeks, I would find myself caught with a hook in my arm, being dragged towards the hydraulic drum, pleading with Harry to shut off the power. He would ignore my shouts completely, never once pausing the machine. Sometimes I only managed to rip the metal from my hands with inches to spare, and I often wondered if it was this same winch which was responsible for tearing one of Harry's previous deckhands to tatters.

As the day wore on, we continued to haul, dragging up all manner of life from the bottom of the sea. Alongside gummies and rays, we caught carpet feeders, banjo sharks, skates, and flatheads. We hooked blue-throated fairy wrasse, shiny red snapper, and golden hind cod that glowed bright orange in the sunlight. Purple octopus, short-finned eels, and pale pink crabs all appeared over the edge of the boat to be thrown aboard and then kicked down to the end of the deck, where they were quickly forgotten. Aside from sharks, the only other fish which merited attention were gurnets - evil little orange bombs, covered in poisoned barbs, that could be sold for a fair price. I pulled hundreds of gurnets over the side on that first day alone, and inevitably, it was not long before one pricked my finger. In an instant, my whole hand turned to rock, and my fingers began to balloon, whilst Harry, watching and laughing, took a wicked pleasure in my pain.

The gummy sharks we caught varied in size, from babies that were no more than half a metre in length to adults that weighed thirty kilograms or more. The largest creatures in the water seemed to be the rays, but later in the day, just as the pain from my gurnet sting was subsiding, another expansive shadow began to loom under the waves.

This time, rather than throwing me a knife, Harry tossed a grappling hook in my direction.

'Aim for the gills, boy. This one's your paycheck.'

Once again, Cameron appeared behind to grab my waist, and I was soon dangling over the edge of the boat, two metres above the cold sea. But rather than a massive ray, this time I found myself looking into the eyes of a ninety-kilogram tiger shark. Instinct and fear rose to the occasion, and a second later, I had the monster hooked by the gills. Simon rushed forward to help, and with the combined strength of three men, we soon had the three-metre fish on board, much to the delight of Harry who cackled loudly behind us.

'Mind the teeth, boys! She'll bite just as well out of the water!'

'What is that?' I gasped to Cameron, as Jack leapt over and buried his blade into the back of the creature's head.

'A big tiger,' said Cameron.

'Are we allowed to catch them?' I foolishly wondered out loud.

'You shut your fuckin' mouth, Pom,' raged Harry. 'We catch whatever I say we catch.'

'Just keep your head down and get back to work,' whispered Cameron, pulling me away from Harry's murderous stare.

Cameron would later explain to me that the captain was prone to dabbling in the black market, meaning that not all the fish we caught would be sold legitimately. Harry had even told the other deckhands that if we caught a Great White - an endangered species which it was illegal to fish - then its head and fins were to come off, no photographs were to be taken, and it was to go straight into the hold. I knew from the first day I met him that the captain had no respect for his crew, and it was becoming clear that he had no respect for the ocean either. Every fish to Harry was simply a dollar sign and every kill an extra figure in his pay packet. There was no honesty in his work, nothing noble in his profession. He was a mercenary who would have murdered every creature in the ocean if he thought it would have made him an extra dollar.

It took an hour to haul each mile of line, and darkness fell long before we had all the gear back on the boat. Emerging from the black waves, more and more of the sharks we caught were coming up dead, often with only half their carcasses left on the hooks. At first, I thought this was the work of sea lions, but Harry explained that the fish had been eaten by sea lice, tiny nocturnal creatures that feed in frenzies on anything that cannot swim away fast enough. If any of the crew fell into the water, he warned, even if we survived the sharks and the cold, in the end, the sea-lice would tear us to pieces.

Finally, at around ten o'clock at night, all the lines were in, and for the first time in ten hours of unbroken work, I looked at the carnage around me. Because Harry had insisted on hauling so much line, and because he never gave the crew the chance to throw unwanted fish back into the ocean, the deck was covered in the carcasses of animals that could not be sold at market, lying five deep from one side of the boat to the other. If these fish had been unhooked as we caught them, they could have been thrown back into the water and would have survived. But Harry, in his greed, had left them on the deck all day to die in their thousands.

Striding forth with a look of glee on his face, Jack handed me a screwdriver and showed me how to prise the hook out of the mouth of a dead ray. As he knelt down upon the creature's slimy belly, a gasp of air escaped, pouring out of the fish's mouth like a scream. In the end, it was midnight by the time the deck was clear. Only then did I return to my bunk, devastatingly tired, nursing broken hands, and plagued by visions of all I had seen. Too petrified to sleep, I lay awake for two hours, and then it all began all over again.

***

The same hellish routine, of twenty hours of work broken by two brief spells of sleep, went on for fourteen days. Over that time, my hands slowly disintegrated, and my rubber gumboots cut deeper and deeper into my legs, leaving sores that turned yellow and putrid. There was no time to wash, no time to rest, and barely any time to eat or drink. Continuing to hug the barren coast of Flinders Island, we caught many sharks, but the hauls never satisfied Harry. As the captain grew tired and irritable, anger and violence mounted in his eyes, and the crew toiled under constant threats. He made it clear that any man could retire from work, but if they did so, they would be turned out onto the deck, into the howling wind, and given no food or water until we returned to shore. The man was a tyrant, and on the open ocean, miles from land, the crew had little choice but to bend to his despicable will.

Mid-way through the second week, as we rounded the south of Clarke Island, we encountered the roaring forties - the strong westerly winds found between forty and fifty degrees latitude, famous for their violent power. There, the sea really became vicious, soon mounting in five-metre waves that crashed over our prow and swept anything off the deck that was not tied down. But Harry still sent us out, with no lifejackets or harnesses, commanding that we ready the deck for fishing.

On all sides of the boat, white peaks rolled and boiled, piling up along the jagged horizon. Built by the westerly winds, these waves had travelled halfway around the world before reaching Bass Strait, growing into towering walls of water that dwarfed our little fishing boat. For a while, Harry proved his worth, navigating the seascape well and avoiding the largest breakers. But just as we were about to shoot the first line, a rogue swell caught the captain off-guard and hit *The Quiet Achiever* head-on, dragging the boat deep into its watery clutches.

As the wave knocked me off my feet, I reached out and caught hold of the boat's chimney, which shuddered with the impact. Looking around, I saw Cameron sprawling on the floor beside me, caught in a tangle of line. And from far down the deck, clutching the stern guardrail, Simon cast me a look of sheer fear. Only a second earlier, he had been stood by my side, and all that had stopped him from being lost overboard was a small steel pipe, half a metre in height. Even Harry realised that to fish in such weather was suicide, and after calling us all into the wheelhouse with a frustrated shout, he turned his attention to finding a safe anchorage.

Sitting in the stale, smoky room, we were forbidden to go down and sleep, in case the boat rolled over, leaving us stuck in the bunkhouse where we would surely drown. Beneath the wheelhouse table, the two cattle dogs cowered, terrified of the weather. Red, who was especially frightened by the waves, let out a loud whimper with each pitch of the ship. When the dog suddenly stood up and vomited on the floor, the captain turned around and buried his boot as far as he could into Red's ribcage, threatening to throw the cowering creature overboard. Red scampered to the far end of the wheelhouse, and luckily the violent seas kept the captain too preoccupied to inflict any more damage. I realised then that Harry's world was nothing but cruelty, bloodshed, and suffering. There was not one ounce of kindness in his crooked body, and in my journey from one side of the world to the other, I did not meet anyone else half as wretched as that captain. He was rotten to the heart.

The tall seas lasted for a day, but they died down the following afternoon, and we began fishing again. Despite the ceaseless rock of the waves, some days it was easy to forget we were at sea. The universe had boiled down to a tangle of ropes and hooks, soaked in a mire of fish blood, and beyond that, the world had stopped existing. Half-starved, working past the point of exhaustion, past the point of madness, it seemed my time on the boat would never end. Somewhere in the tortured mist of those days, it was my birthday, and when the captain found out, he ordered the rest of the crew to bed and made me clear the deck alone. I turned twenty-three knee-deep in fish guts, wrestling hooks from the mouths of a thousand dead sea-creatures, with my skin falling in sheets from my hands.

One evening, as we were shooting gear, I turned to Cameron and asked how he could stand working for Harry.

'When you've got a criminal record and debts to pay, fishin's the only thing a man can do in these parts,' he replied, a look of deep sadness behind his eyes. 'I've got a young boy to feed back on land. I can't refuse any work I'm offered, however bad.'

But Simon, like me, had seen Harry for all that he was and vowed to never work for the captain again from the moment we returned ashore.

'I'd rather be starving on the street than ever step foot aboard this boat again,' he said, speaking with great hatred.

Nevertheless, both Simon and Cameron worked relentlessly, pouring strength into everything they did. It was not bright, youthful strength, but a desperate kind of power, born from terror and kept alive by dread. It was fear and nothing else that kept the three of us working and gave us the energy to return to the deck each day - fear and a sense of comradeship which deepened as the trip went on. Though we worked often in silence, our jaws locked in tiredness, the small words of reassurance we had for one another in the bleakest moments became sacred to me. Without those two men, I do not know how I would have stomached two days aboard Harry's boat, let alone two long weeks.

By the end of the voyage, after a fortnight at sea, I was delirious with pain and tiredness. Desperately hungry, my clothes were hanging off my body, and festering sores covered my hands and legs. When Harry announced that the hold was full and that we were turning around to steam back into Port Welshpool, I did not even feel happy at the news. It was as if I had forgotten what happiness was, as if its memory had died out on the water.

Unloading the fish from the freezing hold took eight hours, with half of the catch going straight to market, and another half going into the back of dark trucks to be sold illegally to local restaurants. Harry watched over it all, greed glinting in his eyes. When I dropped a fish into the water because my frozen hands refused to work, he turned and gave a furious shout:

'You do that again and I'll sail back out and feed you to the sharks myself, you stupid fuckin' Pom.'

I had gone to Welshpool expecting to fish with Harry for several months, hoping I would save money and perhaps even write a little whilst on his boat. In the end, the minute the haul was unloaded and our duties were done, I turned my back on that man, and I hope that I will never have to set eyes on him again.

As Simon lived nearby, he insisted on taking me home and said that I could rest in his farmhouse for as long as I needed. When his fiancée opened the door, she shed tears at the sight of us. I showered, ate, and then collapsed onto the bed in Simon's guestroom, where I slept like the dead for two days.

A month later, I received my wage from Harry. The captain paid me a total of eight hundred dollars for two weeks of work. Counting up the hours I spent on deck to reach an hourly rate, I realised that I had been paid just over one pound for every hour of labour. Reluctantly, I called Harry to ask why my pay was so low. Just hearing his voice again made me tremble with anger, but as soon as he realised it was me on the end of the phone, he hung up like a coward.

As awful as the fishing trip was, I learnt a lot from Harry Farnwell. He taught me something of how bleak life may be, about how worthless, cruel, and pitiful a man's existence can become if neglected and allowed to decay. For people like him, life was something to be suffered and endured; there was no place in his world for happiness. He was bred in hardship, and so felt compelled to breed hardship in others. I will always be grateful for the two weeks I spent aboard his boat because afterwards, life's little trials seemed far less testing in comparison. In the end, all I felt for Harry was pity. Whereas I was able to return to my life and to happiness, Harry knew no other way. He will live out the rest of his life a miserable and angry man, slowly rotting in his fetid bunkhouse, alone on the freezing waters of Bass Strait, utterly numb to the melancholy beauty of the vast ocean around him.

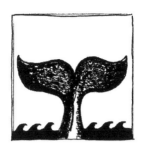

Chapter Twenty-One

I could tell you of the heartbreak, hatred blind,
I could tell you of crimes that shape mankind,
Of brutal wrongs and deeds malign,
Of rape and murder, son of mine;
But I'll tell instead of brave and fine,
When lives of black and white entwine.
And men in brotherhood combine -
This would I tell you, son of mine.

    - Oodgeroo Noonuccal, 'Son of Mine'

It was a warm, sunlit day when I stepped out of Flinders Street station into Melbourne's city centre. Opposite the blue copper roof of the Edwardian terminus, the triple spires of St Paul's Cathedral looked down upon Federation Square, which was littered with tourists dawdling in the autumn afternoon. A line of city-workers shuffled past in front of me, stepping lightly over the tram-tracks, rushing on towards Princes Bridge and the brown Yarra River which curled away to the right, snaking between the feet of a cluster of skyscrapers. Crossing the road to the Young and Jackson pub, I stood outside under the sun for a while, studying the faces of people as they walked past. After the frigid waters of Bass strait, few cities on my journey had looked so beautiful.

On my bus out of Welshpool, I remembered that Rick, the Tasmanian photographer that I met in Kyrgyzstan, used to live in Melbourne. Wondering if he had returned from Central Asia, I decided to give him a call. Rick told me that he was back in the city, working in an Italian kitchen, and he promised that if I could make it to his restaurant by evening, then there would be a hearty dinner waiting for me. That phone call was the best belated birthday gift that I could have wished for.

For an hour, I walked around Melbourne's heart, passing down wide leafy avenues that were lined with glass towers and old Victorian buildings, the colonial relics making the city seem far older than I had expected it to be. When the time came for me to head towards Rick's restaurant, I took a tram in the direction of Fitzroy North and swapped the city for the suburbs. Leaving the business district behind, the tram slipped between rows of trim Edwardian terraces, shuttling through neighbourhoods cluttered with vintage bars and independent shops. To find the restaurant, all Rick had told me was to look out for a crooked yellow wall, with the name *Good Times* written in large letters at its summit.

I first heard the lively music that was playing inside the restaurant from half a street away. A loud album of African jazz was spilling out of its doors, whilst bathed in the candle-lit glow of the restaurant's windows, a long line of people stood waiting for tables. As I came closer, wriggling my way through the crowd, I saw a sign above the door that warned of the resident possum, liable to steal any food left unattended. It is a special kind of restaurant that can advertise the presence of a tenant marsupial and still attract hundreds of customers each night.

Good Times was housed within a thin slither of a building, crammed with odd furniture, wobbling tables, and towering candelabra, dripping in white wax. Covering the walls, I recognised some of Rick's photographs, which stood beside the murals of local artists and pictures drawn on the butcher's paper that lined every table, there to encourage creative patrons to doodle whilst waiting for their food. Brimming with people from end to end, the restaurant was busier than any I had ever seen. Amongst the customers, a tiny crew of cooks, waitresses, and barmen were running across the tiles at ferocious speed, spurred on by the deafening music. In the distance, dancing between a clutter of pots and pans, I spotted Rick, beer in hand, just as he caught my eye across the crowd and smiled, waving me excitedly inside.

'Good to see you, Sammy!' he shouted from the kitchen, padding his damp brow with a towel. 'You know how this fishing boat didn't work out...well, our dishy didn't turn up tonight, so how'd you like some work?'

Before I even had a chance to consider, Rick had clapped me around the shoulder, thrown an apron over my head, and steered me into the dish-room, where a colossal heap of dirty plates lay waiting. I had never worked in a restaurant before, had no clue how to operate the sinister-looking dishwasher, and I was unsure how my wrecked hands would cope with the scalding water. But eager for a glimpse of the frantic inner workings of a restaurant like *Good Times*, I agreed, and Rick disappeared as quickly as he came, leaving me alone in the hot little room with three hundred bowls to clean.

Five minutes later, a casual young man appeared in the doorway carrying a negroni.

'Sam, right? I'm Sean, the manager - good to meet you, buddy. I hear you've had a bit of a rough time on a boat, eh? Thought you could do with a drink,' he said with a smile, before placing the cocktail on the ledge in front of me and dashing off back to the bar.

Half an hour later, I had barely made any progress on the pyramid of dirty crockery when Sean re-appeared and deposited another negroni.

'Thirsty work, eh? Just thought it best to keep you hydrated.'

And every half hour throughout the night, without fail, Sean returned to check on me, always leaving another negroni behind when he went. It did not take me long to understand why the staff of *Good Times*, despite the overwhelming stress, were all running around the restaurant with wide smiles on their faces.

Buoyed by the prospect of working for decent human beings, and with an endless supply of potent spirits working its way through my body, I began scrubbing with fervour. By eleven o'clock, every pot in the kitchen was clean, and I was rewarded for my efforts with a healthy envelope of cash, a bottle of wine, and three bowls of puttanesca. Once all the customers had left, the music was changed to something slower, and then the staff congregated outside on the street, where they began steadily drinking the liquor shelves dry.

'You're a pretty quick dishy,' said Sean, raising his glass to mine under the glow of a streetlight. 'Our current man is always late. I think tonight might just be the final straw. How'd you like a permanent job?' Flattered, I immediately agreed and was welcomed into the fold, receiving handshakes, hugs, and congratulations from all of the staff, as well as from a few strangers lingering outside, hoping for a free drink. 'Sammy,' said Rick from across the table. 'Now that you're working here, looks like you need somewhere to live. You can stay with me as long as you like, but my friend Kyle here has got space at his place if you're interested?'

Kyle, one of the other chefs, looked across and explained:

'This restaurant has a history of taking in waifs and strays, and my house has become something of a hostel for those we pick up. I've got a spare bed in my living room. You're welcome to crash as long as you need, buddy.'

In the space of a few hours, Rick had not only found me a job, but also a home, and a whole host of new friends to go with it. For that evening alone, I will be indebted to him forever.

***

Kyle lived at 189 Nicholson Street, a dilapidated timber building at the end of the tram line in the northern suburb of Coburg. As we were strolling to his house late after my first night in the restaurant, he turned to me and said:

'Just so you know, my two housemates - Hank and Andrew - they can be a little eccentric at times.'

When I pushed open the door to my new room at one o'clock in the morning, I found the two men sprawled across the living room sofa. Hank, wearing nothing but a fur-coat and a top hat, was tattooing a picture of a banana onto his leg, whilst Andrew, three sheets to the wind, was busy sculpting a human face out of a ball of clay. I knew then that my time in Melbourne would be interesting.

'G'day mate!' shouted Hank, parodying his own accent. 'Glad to see you've brought us some new company, Kyle.'

'Welcome aboard buddy,' slurred Andrew from the corner. 'How'd you like a beer?'

During the week, Andrew and Hank held down respectable jobs, whilst Kyle was training to be an accountant. Monday to Friday, they were three upstanding Australian citizens, living a quiet life in the suburbs. But as soon as the weekend arrived, they ran riot, disappearing for days at a time, stumbling back on Sunday evenings to narrate their adventures. Their energy was infectious, and they immediately welcomed me with open arms into their strange, affectionate, dysfunctional little family.

As in Hanoi, after many months of travelling, I found that I quickly slipped into a new domestic routine in Coburg. During the weekdays, I rode the tram to the city centre and wrote in the State Library of Victoria - a grand, old building that reminded me of my university. In the evenings, when I was not needed in the restaurant, I went with Rick to galleries and concerts, swapping stories about the places we had been since our parting in Bishkek. From Kyrgyzstan, he had continued westwards across Central Asia, as far as Iran, photographing as he went, returning to Australia with a catalogue of images that captured the hallmarks of life in Central Asia.

When Rick auctioned his pictures during a two-night exhibition, his work deservedly fetched a fair price. He, in turn, was a generous patron of other artists, regularly attending concerts and buying the pictures, books, and records of his friends. Melbourne, I came to realise, was full of writers, singers, painters, and photographers who all supported one another. It was as if the city had been founded by a community of artists who had silently agreed to fund each other's creativity, friends buying work from friends, enabling each other to go on living beautiful lives, without anyone ever needing to starve themselves for their art.

Several of Rick's pictures hung on the walls of the restaurant, and *Good Times* itself was a crucible of creative talent. Bryce, the owner, was an avant-garde designer and architect. Sean was a video producer, whilst Kurt, the grumpy cook, ran his own record label. There were three beautiful waitresses, Hannah, Chloe, and Sophie - actresses, scholars, and philosophers each. And then there was Micah, barman and resident poet, who spoke in the prettiest sentences I had ever heard.

The restaurant was always busy; people were drawn to its delirium. The staff worked incredibly hard, but they always had a negroni stashed somewhere discreetly, from which they took subtle sips throughout their shift. If it wasn't a negroni, then it was wine, and if not wine then whisky. Whatever the drink, the restaurant was making so much money that Bryce was happy for us to empty its fridges each night. Once service was over, we would sit and talk for hours about the world, tripping restlessly from topic to topic, draining dozens of bottles of wine. I spoke most often to Rick, almost always about photography and books. I remember one night, when we were trading book recommendations, I mentioned to him that I had just finished reading Bruce Chatwin's *Songlines*.

'It's a pretty book, sure, but he got it completely wrong,' he said, rolling a thin cigarette. 'If you really want to learn about the Aboriginal way of life, stop reading books by Englishmen. You should take a look at Bruce Pascoe's *Dark Emu*. It's the most important book ever to come out of Australia.'

Trusting Rick's judgement, the next morning, I sat down with a copy of *Dark Emu* in the Victoria State Library. The contrast with *Songlines* was profound. Chatwin, a famed British explorer, used his book to argue that Aboriginal Australians have always been nomadic hunter-gatherers, predisposed to a lifetime of movement. But Bruce Pascoe, an indigenous Australian writer with Bunurong, Tasmanian, and Yuin heritage, counters Chatwin's claims by proving that before the arrival of Europeans, many Aboriginal Australians were settled in permanent agricultural communities. Whereas Chatwin cites the notion of going 'walkabout' - the Aboriginal Australian practice of leaving home and entering the wilderness - as evidence of nomadism, Pascoe argues that in order to go walkabout, someone must have a place to go walkabout from - a home to leave behind.

In *Dark Emu*, Pascoe points to reports written by early European explorers which describe Aboriginal Australians living in permanent settlements, managing arable land, tending fish farms, and engaging in sophisticated agricultural practices. In light of these reports, he questions how the myth that Aboriginal Australians were purely nomadic ever arose. The answer is a sad one. For the early European settlers, it was easier to justify their colonial actions by claiming that they were helping to civilise primitive natives who had no close ties to the land. The existence of permanent native settlements threatened the colonial agenda, so they were quietly forgotten, whilst the rest of the world was sold the myth that Aboriginal Australians were inherently nomadic. Pascoe's book is a crucial step towards combating that myth and re-writing Australian history.

Reading *Dark Emu* in the State Library inspired me to do a little research of my own. To reach the city that morning, I had walked along the Merri Creek trail, a peaceful waterway that rises thirty miles north of Melbourne and runs south towards the city, brushing Nicholson Street on its way. I wondered if the trail, which seemed abundant with life, had ever been home to an Aboriginal community. It did not take me long to discover that before the arrival of Europeans, the Merri Creek had been home to the Wurundjeri-willam clan, a community of Aboriginal Australians who used the creek to hunt for fish, fowl, eels, and shellfish. The close relationship between the Wurundjeri-willam people and the Merri Creek was itself a perfect illustration of Pascoe's argument that native Australians were not inherently nomadic but were closely tied to the land, often living in permanent settlements, intelligently using natural resources to support their communities.

But I also discovered that not long after the arrival of European settlers, the Merri Creek played host to one of the most significant events in Australian history. It was on the banks of the creek that Batman's Treaty was signed by John Batman (Melbourne's founding father) and a group of Wurundjeri elders in 1835. As a contract which agreed to the sale of land in exchange for gifts and commodities, Batman's treaty was the only written deal ever struck between European settlers and Aboriginal Australians. The very existence of the treaty was an admission that the land belonged to the native people, and that if Europeans were to occupy it, then compensation needed to be paid. But as soon as he heard of the contract, Richard Bourke, the Governor of New South Wales at the time, immediately declared the treaty void on the grounds that the government did not recognise Aboriginal Australians to have any claim to land that was the sole property of the British crown. The treaty signed on the banks of the Merri Creek was the closest that Aboriginal Australians ever came to having their land-rights officially recognised by British agents, only for it be snatched away before the rest of the world even had time to consider its validity.

I was still reflecting on European land-snatching when I reached Coburg after walking back home along the trail. Opening the door to 189 Nicholson Street, I strolled into the living room deep in thought, only to find that my bed was occupied by a stranger. Beneath a sea of blankets and pillows, all I could make out was a shock of black hair and the faint contours of a sleeping body. Reluctant to disturb the intruder, I quickly retreated to the kitchen.

'There's someone in my bed?' I said, finding Kyle studying at the table.

Barely looking up from his work, Kyle casually replied:

'Ah, yeah, about that. I forgot that a few weeks ago I promised someone else they could crash here for a while too. You might have to take the living room sofa for a while if that's alright? I'm sure you two will get along.'

An hour later, I was still sat in the kitchen, trying to come to terms with the idea of having a new house-mate, when a young woman walked into the room. Stifling a yawn and straightening her dishevelled hair, she sat sleepily down beside me, barely noticing my presence. With dark curls falling down to her shoulders, and deep golden eyes, her prettiness took me by surprise, and all that I managed by way of greeting was a meek hello.

'Good morning,' she replied, despite it being six in the evening, speaking in a soft, lilting voice, thickly accented with French. It was the same voice that had called to me twelve months before over the French ferry speakers of the *Pont-Aven*, warning of my motorcycle's oil spill. Except this time, rather than sentiments of doom, it seemed to promise happier prospects.

'Would you like some wine?' she said, pulling a bottle of claret out of her suitcase that she had carried all the way from France. I'd barely taken two sips from my glass when she stood up, grabbed me by the hand, and led me towards the front door.

'Come, I need you to help me steal something,' she said. 'I'm cooking dinner tonight.'

Outside, the Frenchwoman walked slowly along the road, scanning houses and gardens, whilst I followed, silent and bemused.

'I'm sure I saw some on my way down here,' she muttered thoughtfully. 'I'm Eva, by the way. Looks like we're roommates now. Keep an eye out for a moment, will you?' Then, after beaming a curious smile, she vaulted over a fence and disappeared into our neighbour's garden, emerging a moment later with a bunch of rosemary clutched in her hand.

Eva had been in Melbourne for two months, studying at the university as part of an exchange programme based in Bordeaux. She still had half a semester left, and in need of a place to stay, a friend had put her in touch with Kyle. Maddeningly clever, she barely wasted any time studying, and she spent most of her days jolting around the city, enjoying herself with friends, working twice a week for two families who paid her exorbitant sums of money to cook them French recipes for dinner. She was furious in the kitchen and dangerous to be around if things were not going her way, but her first night in Coburg she cooked a wonderful feast for Hank, Kyle, Andrew, and I, beginning with a baked camembert, topped with stolen rosemary.

That night, with my fears about a disagreeable new roommate allayed, I lay on the sofa as Eva sat atop my old bed and we talked for hours, each rushing to fit our whole life into words. As she spoke, Eva stumbled often, slipping back into French, and then tripping through butchered English, her frustrated mistakes leaving us heaving with laughter. It had been a very long time since I had spoken with anyone the way that I did with her that night. By the early hours of the morning, we were still talking, and my eyes had just begun to close when Eva sat up and asked:

'Sam, how much of this city have you actually seen? Beyond *Good Times* and the library? You talk so much about the rest of the world, but you hardly ever mention Melbourne.'

'Well, the creek is lovely...' I mumbled, realising that the answer was not very much at all.

'Hmmm,' she said, lying back down, plotting in her sleep.

***

When I woke the next day, Eva was already dressed and sat waiting expectantly on the edge of her bed.

'Come, winter is on its way, and its time you saw some more of Melbourne whilst the sun is still shining,' she said, throwing a pair of shoes at my head and marching out of the door.

Though we had been in the city for the same amount of time, I knew only a fraction of Melbourne compared to Eva. Overnight, she had decided to prove to me that there was more to the city than just libraries and restaurants, and she set to her task with zeal. On that first day alone, we roamed far from Coburg, lounging in Melbourne's manicured parks and visiting hidden streets that I would never have known existed. From Albert Lake in the south, we walked to Victoria market to buy our lunch, which we ate in the Botanical Gardens beneath the last hot sun of autumn. Whilst it was still light, we marched northwards to Royal Park to join thousands of people sat in the grass, sipping wine and enjoying the fantasy of a second summer. Then, after sundown, we pranced amongst the streets of Fitzroy, leaping from bar to bar late into the night. On our way home, beside an abandoned car park, Eva led me up a flight of iron stairs to a hidden rooftop. From its summit, we could see the shape of the entire city, each of its towers draped in purple clouds, stretching high into a lilac sky. I had seen more of a Melbourne in a single day with Eva than I had in the previous four weeks combined, and my guide was only just getting started.

When the winter rains arrived late the following week, they did little to thwart Eva's plans. Together, we continued to explore, racing back and forth on Melbourne's trams, watching the carriages kick up electric sparks as they glided along the damp tracks. We visited every café, surveyed every park, and tried every unlocked door in the city, seized by a mad desire to see it all, both knowing that our days in Melbourne were numbered. When we had exhausted the centre, we ventured further afield, wandering down to St Kilda to watch tiny penguins returning to their roosts amongst the rocks at sunset. Further from the city, we visited Mornington Peninsula, the green claw of land that curls round one edge of Port Phillip Bay, where we stumbled across animal sanctuaries, with fields full of kangaroos, wallabies, and wombats. We drank wine at a dozen different vineyards, foraged in forests for wild mushrooms, and when the cold rains were at their most malicious, we ran screaming into the steaming lagoons of Mornington's hot springs, sheltering in the boiling baths for hours whilst rivers of frozen rain poured down on us from above.

Without my realising, days slipped into weeks, and weeks into months, as Eva and I began to spend almost every second of our spare time with one another. We joked often about the strange way that we had been thrown together, living alongside Hank, Kyle, and Andrew. Every weekend, when I came home from the restaurant, and when Eva returned from the city, we never knew what madness we would encounter in our kitchen, or how many strangers we would find sprawled outside in the garden. Every second in that house was a carnival, and we passed a wonderful, bewildering, contented time there. Every morning when we woke, without fail, Eva had thought of another place for us to visit. For a while, I believed that she had an inexhaustible list of ideas, enough to keep us in Melbourne for years whilst we mapped every inch of the city. But then one day in late May, she took me by surprise when she turned to me and said:

'Sam, we have seen everything there is to see in Melbourne. I have only one more place to take you.'

That evening, an hour before dusk, Eva led me to the summit of Mount Dandenong, a small mountain on the edge of the Great Dividing Range, thirty miles to the east of Melbourne. As we walked together up above the tree-line, kookaburras were flying home to their nests, just as possums were emerging from their dens to hunt. In the forest, the air was fresh and light, scented with pine needles and sweetened by the cold. When we finally emerged at the top of the mountain, a clutter of silver towers was just visible in the distance - a spectral city, wrapped up in clouds, delicately floating above the flatlands below.

'Do you like it?' asked Eva, turning to face me, framing the city above her shoulder.

'The city looks like something from another world,' I said, mesmerised by the view.

Being able to look down and inspect millions of lives in a single gaze reminded me of standing atop the Lotte tower in Hanoi. Just as in Vietnam, I found looking down upon a city that had been my home for two months to be a potent catalyst for reflection. I did not doubt that Melbourne had been kind to me. I had known great happiness there. But amongst the perfumed pines of Dandenong, I rediscovered an old, familiar calm, and that evening, high above the city, as Eva and I stood and watched a blazing sunset, I realised that the time had come for me to move once again.

***

There were many sad farewells when I left Melbourne. First, I said goodbye to everyone at *Good Times*, thanking them for friendship and for enough negronis to last a lifetime. Next, I went to visit Rick, who was himself leaving the city, bound for France, where he planned to spend his summer in a vineyard. Lastly, on the eve of my departure, I sat down at the dinner table of 189 Nicholson Street to eat a monstrous feast and drink a case of wine with Kyle, Hank, and Andrew, howling with laughter until long after the sun had risen. But as I sat on the plane to Sydney, I was glad that I had at least managed to delay one goodbye, because in the seat beside me, gazing down at a string of golden beaches clinging to Australia's eastern edge, sat Eva, having been persuaded to spend three more days with me before it finally came time to part.

In the end, Eva had finished her studies at Melbourne University just as I had begun to grow restless in the city. A week after her final exam, she was due to meet friends in Sydney to begin a long drive up the east coast to Cairns, from where she would fly onwards to Vietnam. Though I had hoped to continue from Melbourne overland, the prospect of spending a little longer with her was enough for me to abandon my plans and book two flights to Sydney. Besides, by that stage in my journey, I had come to realise that broken plans are often far more memorable than ones which are successfully kept.

After landing at Sydney airport, Eva and I took a taxi to The Rocks, the outcrop of land where European settlers first landed in Sydney Cove over three centuries earlier. As we wandered amongst the Victorian laneways searching for a room, we passed back and forth beneath the colossal shadow of Sydney Harbour Bridge. After a long time spent walking in the shade, we emerged at the edge of the glittering harbour and followed the waterline around, past old docks and warehouses which had been transformed into decadent restaurants and hotels for Sydney's sparkling elite. The vast bridge behind us took up so much sky that I was transfixed by its presence, but when we arrived at the water's edge, Eva pulled me around to look across the silver waves of the harbour. Standing close by, the white carapace of the opera house rested on its promontory like a huge fossil cast in concrete – the still image of a giant creature, trapped in stone millennia ago, scuttling slowly towards the water.

After dropping our bags in a cramped apartment, we strolled from The Rocks to Circular Quay, the bustling port nestled between the harbour bridge and the opera house, flanked by the tall glass towers of Sydney's business district. Looking up, the view surrounding the quay was impressive, but my eyes were drawn downwards to a curiosity that appeared beneath my feet. Running around the port, gold medallions had been built into the ground, collectively forming Sydney's 'Writer's Walk' - a path of script, set down in metal, recounting famous words written about Sydney and celebrating the lives of Australia's most prominent literary figures.

Amongst the names written on the floor, there were many I recognised. Literary heavyweights like Robert Louis Stevenson, Joseph Conrad, and Mark Twain all had their place, each having written pretty sentences extolling the virtues of Sydney and describing with relish the wild buccaneering that once went on in the city's ports. But amongst the plaques, only one medallion was dedicated to an indigenous poet, inscribed with the words of Oodgeroo Noonuccal, the first Aboriginal Australian to ever publish a book of verse. The writing on Noonuccal's plaque was very different to that of her white European counterparts, alluding to the struggles of Aboriginal Australians at the hands of the same men who only a few paces away were documented praising Australia's loveliness. As with the recent appreciation of Bruce Pascoe's work, Noonuccal's place on the Writer's Walk was well deserved, but the fact that her medallion stood alone amongst sixty others was a telling reminder that Australia still has far to go before Aboriginal heritage, culture, art, and history achieves the recognition it deserves.

Meanwhile, the tales of pirates and mariners as told by the old European storytellers were a far cry from modern Sydney. Gone were the wild inns and the debauched hotels of Stevenson's day - all that remained was a crisp, corporate metropolis, home to an endless stream of suited citizens dashing back and forth between their offices. Eva and I spent all afternoon wandering beneath the bright sunshine, happy for the warmer weather, but unable to draw our thoughts away from the life we had left behind in Melbourne. Compared to Australia's second city, Sydney seemed vain and shallow, too business-like to be admired. Our hearts had already been given to cold, damp Melbourne, with its rough edges and its bohemian charm, which had been loveable even in wintertime.

But Sydney also had its moments. That night, Eva and I shared a bottle of wine on the roof of the Glenmore Hotel with the harbour bridge blotting out the sky behind us. From anywhere in The Rocks, the bridge can be seen stretching across the water, curling its humped back upwards like a prostrate giant waking from a century-long sleep. Sat beneath its shadow, we watched little human figures climbing up its thick pylons to wave for photographs at the summit. To our other side, a vast cruise-ship was anchored in Circular Quay, hiding the rest of the harbour from sight. But a minute after we sat down, the ship let out three short blasts, weighed anchor, and sailed out of Port Jackson Bay. In the space where the vessel had been, the opera house was revealed, its curving sides glowing pink in the dusk, mirroring the rose-gold waves that gave chase to the ship and followed its vast stern out to the edge of the harbour.

Having been told that the coast surrounding Sydney is some of the prettiest in the world, Eva and I set out the next day walking from Bondi beach southwards to Coogee. The path that we followed lived up to its reputation, vaulting above pristine beaches, bright blue lidos, and quiet little coves dotted with wooden boats bobbing on the tide. We passed street after street of lavish homes, some with wooden jetties leading down to the water that looked unfathomably expensive, and I laughed with Eva, remembering a quote from the Writer's Walk by the Australian playwright David Williamson which had read:

'No one in Sydney ever wastes time debating the meaning of life - it's getting yourself a water frontage. People devote a lifetime to the quest.'

Walking on, we soon passed Waverley cemetery, adorned with the stone sepulchres of old colonialists that faced out towards the same ocean which had carried those early settlers to Australia from their faraway homes. We walked for hours and hours, following the coastline southwards as the sun inched its way down the sky. By evening-time, we were just rounding the final headland to Coogee when I turned to look at Eva, and at that same instant, over her shoulder, miles in the distance, I saw the black silhouette of a breaching humpback whale leap clear out of the ocean and crash back into the Tasman Sea amidst a billow of spray.

'Eva! Look!' I cried, pointing out at the water, but she turned too late to see the whale.

For half an hour afterwards, we sat on the rocks, whilst Eva scanned the ocean, desperate to see a whale, but no other humpbacks appeared.

'That's the saddest thing,' she said, as we turned to make our way back to the city. 'I've never seen a whale before. It would have been the most perfect way to remember Sydney.'

I did not tell her then, but in another instance of exquisite coincidence, as Eva uttered those words on the headland at Coogee, hidden in my pocket were two tickets for a whale watching tour, setting sail the following day - a surprise that I had planned to mark the end of our time together in Australia.

***

Early the next morning, after a rushed breakfast at Darling Harbour, I pulled a confused Eva onto a boat which slipped out of Port Jackson Bay onto a glittering sea. It was a crystal-clear morning, thick with the fresh smell of sea-salt, and from the prow of the boat, we could see for miles into the distance.

'I thought you said you never wanted to step foot on an Australian boat again?' teased Eva, still unclear as to why we were heading out to sea.

'I did say that, but I think an exception can be made for today. When else will we have the chance to see one of those,' I said, pointing to a plume of spray which had been thrown up into the air from a pod of humpbacks that were swimming just beyond the entrance to the harbour.

Every year, thirty-five thousand humpback whales swim past Sydney on their way from Antarctica to their breeding grounds in the Great Barrier Reef. Purely by chance, we had arrived in the city at the peak of the migration, which meant that a minute after spotting the first whales, we saw a second pod, sending more spray up into the air, the plumes of seawater melting into rainbows underneath the morning sun. After that pod came another, and then another and another, until the whole ocean seemed to be teeming with humpbacks, and it was half an hour before a speechless Eva could utter a single sentence.

The whales were curious creatures, swimming so close to the boat that I could count the barnacles on their old, crinkled heads. Their massive bodies would loom beneath the surface as they followed the boat for a while, and then suddenly their vast white chins would break through the waves, revealing cavernous mouths full of glinting baleen. A few were particularly playful, dancing for the boat, flourishing their tails and rolling over, saluting with their flippers before they disappeared back down to deeper seas.

There were so many whales in the water that it was difficult to believe that humans nearly hunted the humpback to extinction. Sydney itself was once a major whaling hub, sending out ships which slaughtered the creatures in their thousands. Nowadays, hunting whales is prohibited by Australian law, and the docile giants return to Sydney in greater numbers every year. Majestic and untroubled, the whales seemed relaxed as they played amongst the waves, not a trace of fear or ill-feeling remaining, despite the fact that humpbacks can live up to eighty years, meaning that some of the creatures were old enough to remember the days of whaling, which did not officially cease in Australia until the late 1970s.

Back on the open ocean, I found that I was also able to let bitter memories fade. It felt good to reclaim the sea, to root some happiness there after the time I had spent on the cold waters of Bass Strait. As we steamed up and down the coast, a few sailing boats slipped out of the harbour behind us, racing on a fresh morning breeze, bookending the distant city with sailcloth. Suddenly, the ocean was the only place in the world that I wanted to be. I thought about diving into the water, climbing up onto one of those little yachts and begging the owner to let me borrow it for a while. I would turn the helm, pick up Eva, and sail northwards up the coast. We would stop at Brisbane, Cairns, and the Whitsundays, letting the whales guide us all the way to the Great Barrier Reef. Then we would break eastwards and cross the pacific, weighing anchor at every island between Australia and the Galapagos, going on through the Panama canal to dance around the Caribbean for a while, before crossing the Atlantic, stopping at Madeira and the Azores, and then finally returning home to Plymouth. If only it were as easy as a sentence. It seemed a very fine idea for a book.

Chapter Twenty-Two

Though I am old with wandering
Through hollow lands and hilly lands,
I will find out where she has gone,
And kiss her lips and take her hands;
And walk among long dappled grass,
And pluck till time and times are done,
The silver apples of the moon,
The golden apples of the sun.

- W.B. Yeats, 'The Song of Wandering Aengus'

I could see pigeons roosting on the cracked rafters of Christchurch cathedral as I walked through the city's streets. One side of the wrecked temple stood exposed to the bitter wind - an ugly maw torn open in 2011 when a devastating earthquake levelled half the city. Below the cathedral's crumbling walls, a crowd of drunks were sprawled on the cold ground, dressed in tatters, fighting with one another and begging pedestrians for money. Though it had been eight years since the earthquake, Christchurch was still only a shadow of its former self. Many parts of the city were yet to be repaired, and the parts which had been fixed looked clinical and faceless. It was a sad town, beleaguered by winter and ruin.

When my flight from Sydney had begun its descent towards New Zealand's South Island, I had glimpsed the snow-tipped peaks of the Southern Alps through the aeroplane window. They were the first white mountains I had seen on my journey since the Tian Shan of Central Asia, and as soon as I saw them, I felt a longing for the wilderness. Having travelled nearly halfway around the world, I did not want my journey to end in faded, grey cities. So after just a single day in Christchurch, I rented a little car, filled it with enough dried and tinned food to last for two weeks, and then I left the city for the mountains.

Christchurch, though miserable, was mercifully small, and I had not been driving for long when the concreted streets gave way to fields of green grass, home to herds of dairy cattle and flocks of thick-coated sheep. It meant everything just to be moving again, to be alone and surrounded by unknown country, rich with freedom. The straight, empty roads were immaculate, and I raced south with my foot pressed to the floor. For as far as I could see, flat yellow fields stretched away to the horizon. Even after an hour of driving, I was still surrounded by the same grassy plains, and I had just begun to wonder if I had taken a wrong turn out of Christchurch when the road started to climb and the white crown of Mount Hutt appeared in the distance, just past the town of Windwhistle, where the flatlands of Canterbury crash against the feet of the Southern Alps.

In my mind, the edge of those mountains marked a border with the wilderness. Once I entered the alps, it would be weeks until I would have a warm bed to sleep in again. By the roadside beyond Windwhistle, the white peaks possessed an old, noble beauty, but also an air of menace. Ancient and dispassionate, their frost-flecked summits cast an ominous shadow across the road. With no other cars nearby and no houses in sight, the slither of asphalt stretching into the distance was the only evidence of mankind's presence in the landscape. Crossing into the mountains felt like I was entering another world, one where few intruders went unnoticed.

The barrenness of the landscape was partly due to the fact that of all the large nations on earth, New Zealand was one of the last to be inhabited by man. It was not until the thirteenth century that the Māori crossed the Pacific from Polynesia and arrived on the islands that they named Aotearoa, meaning 'land of the long white cloud'. From the beginning, the relationship between the land and its settlers was strained, and within little more than a century, the Māori had wreaked havoc on New Zealand's fragile ecosystem. In just one hundred years, the entire native population of moa - a giant ancestor of the kiwi - had been hunted to extinction, fire had burnt away half the native forest, and the rats and dogs that arrived on Polynesian ships had decimated local wildlife. After the Polynesians came the Europeans, who reaped their own destruction by prospecting for gold and introducing foreign livestock. Though the history of mankind's presence in New Zealand is short compared to other parts of the world, the effect of human habitation on the islands has been profound, and as I drove deeper into the alps, with the landscape rolling past my windows, I felt as if the mountains were turning their backs on me, scowling over their white shoulders with disdain at the presence of another human liable to disrupt their pristine territory.

From Windwhistle, I continued south-eastwards, following the spine of the alps as they stretched diagonally across the country. Eventually, I passed the wind-whipped waves of Lake Tekapo, and driving onwards, I soon reached the shore of Lake Pukaki, where the water was blue and inviting but bitingly cold. Its cloudy colour reminded me of the little pieces of frosted glass that wash up on beaches after decades at sea - soft in appearance, but with a cool, crystalline heart. Leaving the car, I walked along the shore and cast my eyes across the lake, listening to the surrounding mountains as they creaked and murmured beneath sheets of shuffling ice.

Winter in the South Island clips the days short at both ends, and soon the surrounding landscape began to fade into darkness. After parking between two trees, I crawled into my car and wrapped a sleeping bag around myself that I had bought from a store in Christchurch. In my rush to leave the city, I had paid little attention to my shopping. The sleeping bag, I realised, was made for a child, and after wriggling inside, I found it barely reached to my waist. Shivering in the cold, I closed my eyes and listened to the lullaby of icebergs drifting across the lake, whilst the wind rustled through the trees and left kisses of frost upon their barren branches.

I woke in the middle of the night to find that the inside of my car was lined with ice and a deep cold had fastened to my bones. Knowing that only a clear night could be so cold, and half-worried that the blood in my legs had frozen solid, I unravelled my sleeping bag and stepped out from the car to walk down to the shore of the lake, hoping to bring some semblance of warmth back into my body.

By the water's edge, I found a smooth boulder and sat for a while, staring up at a sky ruptured with silver. The thousands of tiny stars looked very fragile up above, each mighty constellation reduced to mere rubble and dust after millennia of wheeling back and forth across the night sky. Diminutive alone, together the stars formed a pale belt of crystal, running parallel to the mountains, strung above the silvered peaks. Too cold to sleep, and no warmer in the car, I sat there for a long time, until the glow of daylight broke behind me, and I watched as one by one the string of stars faded away, the belt of crystal disappearing like the damp mark of an ocean tide, slowly drying to nothing in the early hours of the morning.

At the first lick of sunlight, I lay a frozen banana on the bonnet of my car to thaw for breakfast. I had nothing to drink - my water had all turned to ice - but the returning sun did eventually still my shivering body. I had known the South Island would be cold, but I had not expected such extremes. Overnight, winter seemed to have trebled in size, and the peaks of the alps which were merely frosted with snow when I went to bed were blanketed with white when the sun finally rose. Even the waves of Lake Pukaki seemed to move more slowly, the water thick and sluggish, each crest only a few degrees away from hardening into a curl of crystallised ice.

As I drove away from my make-shift campsite, I pointed my car towards the stony heart of the alps, searching for one peak in particular. To my right, Pukaki glowed milky blue, whilst ahead of me, the white curtain of the mountains gradually drew apart. Of all the jagged summits rising behind the lake, one was touched with more sunlight than all the others. Standing at over three thousand seven hundred metres, Aoraki, also known as Mount Cook, is the tallest mountain in New Zealand. After the freezing night, deep snow had muffled its triple pointed peak, softening Aoraki's edges and blunting the mountain's horns, making it look less menacing. But only a few days before, a storm had rolled down from its summit, washing away footbridges and reducing the Hooker Valley below to rubble, rendering the walking trail that I had hoped to follow to the mountain's base impassable.

With the Hooker Valley trail closed to visitors, I decided to hike to the top of Sealy Tarns, a mountain track running up the opposite side of the valley. Devastatingly tired, I had barely slept or eaten, but fed by sunshine and fresh air, my legs felt electric on the mountain. Striding fast, it was not long before I passed above the tree-line, where for the first time since Central Asia I felt the crunch of snow underfoot. Remembering the simple joy of feeling alive inside my own body, I bounded up the trail, amazed at the power of my feeble limbs. Up and up I went, a hot heart thumping in my chest, as sheets of snow and ice melted all around me, the mountain slowly turning to droplets beneath my feet. Everywhere, signs warning of avalanches were staked into the ground, advising hikers to stay below the snowline, but I pressed on, not believing that such a lovely morning could be dangerous.

The view from the top of the trail was staggering, sweeping across Mount Cook, Mueller Lake, Hooker Valley, and all the way down to Pukaki in the distance. The blue water of the lakes, the white cloak of the mountains, and the golden grasses of the hills formed a trilogy of colours that for me would come to symbolise the South Island in winter. Standing above the snowline, I wondered what the Māori must have thought of those three colours - blue, white, and gold - when they arrived in New Zealand from their temperate islands in the middle of the Pacific. I had read that the Polynesians, having never experienced such a cold climate before, attempted to comprehend the strange new land in which they found themselves by relating it to their ancestral home. Hence the Māori word for snow came to be *huka*, meaning sea-foam. Faced with an alien world, the only way the Māori could come to terms with something as inexplicable as snow was to imagine that it was ice-cold sea-spray, cast up onto the mountains by a monstrous wave. Reframing the world in more familiar terms is an enduring human habit; we are creatures conditioned for metaphor. And as I looked up at the peaks surrounding the lake - shards of rock and ice rising up out of heaped whiteness - I could imagine how the storm-swept mountainside of a few days before might have resembled a bleak, tempestuous sea.

After another cold night sleeping by the shore of Lake Pukaki, I drove to Wanaka along the icy Lindis Pass. My tenacious car flew down the mountain roads, twice sliding sideways on frozen asphalt, leaving me staring with horror down the sides of steep precipices. At one point, as I rounded a bend, I glimpsed two cars twisted into a wreck of rubber and steel, left to rot on the roadside. Despite the countless warning signs, I could understand why accidents were so common. Surrounded by such staggering scenery, it was a constant battle to stop my eyes from wandering off the road, however lethal the corners.

The next day, after another treacherous drive, I spent an afternoon wandering around Queenstown, trawling past billboards advertising sky-dives, bungee-jumps, and helicopter tours. Established one hundred and fifty years earlier by a community of Scots drawn to the Southern Alps by the discovery of gold in the Arrow River, in recent years, Queenstown has become a playground for New Zealand's rich. The resort town's setting on the shore of Lake Wakatipu is undeniably impressive, but surrounded by holidaymakers in designer jackets, on their way to decadent restaurants after a day on the ski-slopes, Queenstown left me feeling fantastically poor. So after a night camped on the outskirts of the town, I left the next morning, following a road named the devil's staircase which carried me out of Otago and down into the Southland region.

The mountainous route, deserving of its name, wriggled along the shore of Wakatipu until the lake's southern tip, where it broke eastwards and flattened, rolling into warmer country where the snow on the mountains grew a little thinner. By midday, I reached Te Anau, a small settlement on the edge of Lake Manapouri, where the snow disappeared altogether. Glad to take a break from driving, I carried my lunch down to the shoreline and sat looking out across the water. On the opposite side of the lake, a wall of dark green mountains stood wrapped in mist and rain, and after comparing their impenetrable flanks to the squiggles on my map, I realised that I had reached the boundary with Fiordland.

Despite its name, Fiordland is not a Scandinavian province but a remote region in the south-east of New Zealand, where the southern alps step down into the Tasman Sea. Wild and inaccessible, it is known for its shifting beauty, its sheer cliffs, and its cavernous lakes, deep enough to swallow entire mountains. Half sunken in the sea, the region's weather is capricious at the best of times, and only one road leads into the interior, carrying tourists to Milford Sound. Unfortunately, whilst I was in Queenstown, I learnt that recent snows had rendered the route impassable for cars without snow chains. I wanted badly to drive into the fjords, to commandeer a boat and sail between the drowning mountains, but with only a feeble automatic car, I had to settle for a picnic on the edge of Lake Manapouri, where I spent an hour watching mists drift across Fiordland's impenetrable boundary, imagining all the lost worlds that lay trapped behind the mountains, wrapped up in frozen forests and walls of stone.

Returning to the road, as I drove southwards that afternoon, the mountains gradually faded, their tall peaks slowly dwindling in size. By evening, they had disappeared altogether, and the landscape of grey rock and ice changed back into rolling green hills and farmland reminiscent of Canterbury. That night, for the first time since leaving Christchurch, it was warm enough for me to sit in my car and scribble in the dark without my fingers seizing up with cold. And when I stepped outside at midnight, a southerly breeze was blowing, carrying with it the scent of the ocean.

***

The day after coming down from the mountains, I arrived in Bluff, the southernmost town in mainland New Zealand. A provincial scrap of land at the very tip of the South Island, Bluff is home to just one thousand permanent residents. The very name, Bluff, makes it sound less like an inhabited place and more like a barren stretch of coastline, as if it were little more than an insignificant spur of rock dangling between New Zealand's toes. As an inconsequential little fishery, the town is unapologetically charmless and quite unused to tourists, which made it the perfect place for me to spend the night before my final journey to Slope Point.

Driving into Bluff, I felt like I was moving back through history, and by the time I reached the town centre, the world seemed to have reversed half a century. Bluff's dreary streets were full of crumbling shops, old hotels, and dusty victuallers, where ships' supplies lay piled behind cracked windows, nestled amongst maritime antiques. All along the banks of the estuary, decrepit vessels leaned on their sides - old relics which had been left to rust on a falling tide. After parking my car by the harbour, I set out on foot, but the town seemed deserted. The only noise to break the silence of the streets was the crunch of my footsteps which crackled loudly as I walked, my feet slipping atop thousands of huge white shells that were scattered across every inch of the road.

Amongst connoisseurs, the white oysters of Bluff, grown in the freezing waters of Foveaux Strait, are revered as some of the finest molluscs in the world. Every year in May, at the annual Bluff Oyster festival, pilgrims arrive from across New Zealand to gorge on vast hauls of the shellfish, plucked fresh from the sea. Though the season is short, over ten million oysters are caught every year, and the discarded shells are cast onto the streets of Bluff, where they lie in mounds a metre deep. As I walked into the town, most streets I passed were lined with the shiny white plates, and several buildings sported giant murals of molluscs, proudly painted by the residents of Bluff onto the walls of their homes.

Though the oyster festival attracts many visitors, it lasts for just a few days each year, and as I crunched down the empty streets, I felt like I was the first outsider to step foot in Bluff for a very long time. In part, that prospect worried me because after more than a week spent sleeping in my car, I was desperate to find a shower and a bed. But the thought of being the only visitor to Bluff for months was also thrilling. In a place so devoid of reasons to visit, just arriving in Bluff had seemed like an extraordinary act, and I strode into the town feeling like a modern-day explorer discovering a lost world. For lone travellers in search of unique experiences, there are few better places to visit than a forgotten fishing town at the far edge of the earth, especially in wintertime.

As enamoured as I was with Bluff, I still needed somewhere to stay. After ten minutes of trudging around, I was just beginning to lose hope when I arrived in front of a gaudy old building, coloured bright orange, with a sign above the street announcing *Bluff Lodge*. Below the sign, a piece of yellowed paper was nailed to the door. It informed visitors that the lodge was open for business, but as the owner was out for the day, prospective guests were invited to step inside and make themselves comfortable. Unnervingly, the scrap of paper carried a date from three weeks before.

As I pushed against the front door, it creaked open to reveal a musty hallway. Stepping inside and trying more wooden doors, I walked into a warren of rooms, all of them filled with empty beds, heavy with the scent of mothballs. I called out to see if anybody was home, but the sprawling house was empty. Eerily quiet and deathly still, it felt like an old Victorian boarding house had been frozen in time. But when I eventually found a drab kitchen, there was food in the cupboards and wine on the table, which I took as a sign that the lodge had not been entirely abandoned. Dropping my bags in the corner of a dusty dormitory, I found a bathroom tucked beneath the stairs, and after ten frozen days, I threw myself beneath a gloriously hot shower. Half an hour later, when I emerged from the bathroom amidst billows of steam, the lodge was still empty. Desperate to meet some residents of Bluff, I gulped down a hot meal and then stepped outside, just as evening was falling.

I had walked no more than fifty paces from Bluff Lodge when I found myself outside the Eagle Hotel, peering through a clouded window at a saloon lit with golden light. Propped up against the bar, a few haggard drinkers stood beside jugs of pale lager, mumbling beneath faded pictures of fishing vessels. From the outside, it was easy to imagine that the same characters had been drinking at the same bar undisturbed for decades. It was another little fragment from the past, trapped in time, mummified by the cold Bluff air. Intrigued, I pushed through the peeling swing doors and stepped into the soft amber glow within.

The moment I sat at the bar, the landlord placed a jug of Speight's ale before me and held out his hand.

'The name's Geoff, and if you're to sit at my bar, then you'll have to shake my hand first. I'm afraid there's no other way,' he said, smiling congenially.

Dutifully, I shook his hand, then took out my notebook and began scribbling as Geoff walked away to refill the jug of another customer. A minute later, the landlord returned.

'Thirty years and I've never seen a man sit down and write at this bar,' he said, through narrowed eyes. 'What is it you write about?'

'Bluff,' I said, simply.

'Bluff?!' he shouted, eliciting a giggle from a few other men. 'I'm afraid that might not make for a very good book.'

'It seems an interesting town to me,' I replied.

'You reckon? We don't have many visitors who say that, but I guess it's special in its own way.'

'What type of visitors do you get?' I asked.

'Well, apart from the oyster festival, the only strangers we get are fishermen. Most are from Asia these days, stopping off on their way to the Southern Ocean. There's a Chinese crew upstairs as we speak,' he said, pointing his thumb to the ceiling.

'Tell him about the ghost ship, Geoff,' croaked an old man from across the room.

'He's only just got here,' replied the landlord. 'We don't want to scare the lad. But perhaps we'll tell him anyway.'

'The ghost ship?' I asked, setting down my pencil.

'Two years ago, a Korean fishing boat docked at Bluff in spring. When the harbourmaster went aboard to carry out an inspection, he found a dead man lying in the galley. The captain said he had died in an accident out at sea. It was international waters, but being the closest nation, New Zealand was obliged to investigate. When an officer went down to the harbour the next day, the crew had vanished. They still hadn't been found went the boat slipped its moorings a week later and sailed away, with the harbourmaster swearing that he hadn't seen anyone step back on board. For months afterwards, residents in Bluff claimed to have seen members of the crew roaming near the town, looking hungry and wild.'

'The fishing is tough here?' I asked.

'All depends on who you go out with,' chuckled Geoff. 'I tried my hand once. Can't say I'm in any rush to do it again.'

'I'll drink to that,' I said, clinking my glass against his.

'By the way, if you haven't already, don't leave town without trying some of our oysters. Best in the world, aren't they boys?' he beamed, looking around at a gaggle of drinkers who nodded their approval.

Over the next hour, accompanied by another jug of Speight's, I was gradually introduced to every one of the locals in the bar. They took a great interest in me, puzzled as to why anyone would choose to visit Bluff for pleasure. Most were in the oyster business, either fishermen, boat-builders, or exporters. Mariners are superstitious folk at the best of times, but especially when they live on the edge of the map and earn their living in the South Seas. Collectively, the men of the Eagle Hotel possessed a limitless inventory of stories, mostly involving shipwrecks and strange encounters on the ocean. After a while, I told them of my own time on a fishing boat, which won me a handshake from every man. But when I revealed that I hoped to reach Slope Point the next day, I was met with blank faces. Not one of them had ever heard of such a place, despite the fact it only lay thirty miles to the east. Many had never been so far from Bluff, at least not by land. And when I left the bar later that evening, whilst every man wished me luck, one grizzled old sailor took my hand as I made for the door and said:

'Good luck to you lad, but I'd bet my life that Bluff is the southern tip of New Zealand. Sixty years in these parts and I've never heard of a place named Slope Point. You might find that what you're searching for doesn't exist.'

I was still ruminating on the sailor's warning as I pushed open the door of Bluff Lodge a minute later. Like earlier, I was expecting the lodge to be empty, but this time, as I entered the hallway, I could hear voices coming from upstairs. Treading softly to the top floor, I opened the door of the sitting room and stumbled inside, unintentionally giving two old ladies the fright of their lives.

Sat in their hiking socks with a bottle of red wine resting between them, the two women leapt to their feet as soon as I opened the door. With a look of panic on their faces, they each turned to a shelf behind them and grabbed a handful of books, brandishing them like weapons. Sensing that the women were about to launch a battery of novels at my head, I held up my hands and explained that I was not there to murder them, but was simply hoping to sleep in the dormitory downstairs.

'Oh, we are sorry, dear. We don't get many visitors this time of the year, and you took us quite by surprise,' said one of the women, setting her book down with a sigh of relief. 'I'm Kay, and this is Lois. Here, let me take your jacket.'

Once over their initial fright, the two white-haired women began fussing over me like a pair of old grandmothers, folding my coat, offering me a drink, and brushing my shoulders with old, arthritic hands.

'We're so quiet during the winter that I'm about to head away for a few months, leaving Lois in charge till August,' said Kay, the owner of the lodge.

'Yes, I'm just the winter steward,' smiled Lois, as she uncorked a second bottle of wine.

'How old is this place?' I asked, taking a seat beside them.

'Well, a very long time ago, long before Kay bought the place, it used to be a Post Office,' said Lois. 'I remember staying here just after it had been converted into a hotel. Back then it was owned by a one-legged Irishman named Patrick who lived with a three-legged dog and a cat with all its appendages.'

'Yes and I bought it from poor Paddy ten years ago,' continued Kay. 'It's a quiet little hotel, but we get the odd fisherman coming and going, and a few naturalists on their way to Stewart Island.'

'What will you do here all winter?' I asked Lois, as Kay padded to the kitchen, searching for some whisky.

'Well, I'm a traveller like you. I've been to London many times, though I've never actually visited the place,' she said, giving me a wink and tapping the cover of the book spread across her lap.

'Life has few greater pleasures for me than reading, so whilst my eyes still work, I think I'll spend my winter here amongst these books. And when I read, I always keep an atlas beside me, so in a way, I can leave Bluff whenever I want.'

Lois had never travelled beyond New Zealand, but after just a few minutes of conversation, I could tell that the seventy-six-year-old had seen more of the world than I had. As we drank wine and spoke of our favourite books, she told me that she liked to read anything that took her to a far-away place, the more remote, the better. Later in the evening, I would describe my journey to her and name some of the places I had visited. Whether Italy, India, or Singapore, she knew the sights, the smells, and the character of every country I listed. Describing them back to me, it was as if she had lived for months in each one, despite never having been abroad in her life. Later that night, whilst Kay was softly snoring under the influence of the whisky, Lois turned to me and admitted:

'My only regret in life is never having seen a whale. I've spent the last twenty years living in Nelson, where sightings are common, but I've still never seen one. That's another reason why I've come down to Bluff. A whole winter spent staring out of this window at the ocean, and surely I'm bound to get a sighting, don't you think?'

'I'm sure you will,' I said, not having the heart to tell her about my time with the humpbacks in Sydney only a few weeks before.

Silently, Lois turned in her chair to face the harbour, and she was still gazing out at the moonlit waves when I went to bed a little later. She mumbled a distracted goodnight as I stood up to leave the room, but her eyes remained fixed on the ocean. As I closed the door, she remained perfectly still, and it was easy to imagine her sitting there all winter, alone in the cold lodge, swaddled in musty blankets, looking up from her book between sips of wine to stare through the frosted window, desperately searching for blue flukes on the horizon.

***

Kay must have forgotten that the lodge had a visitor because when she stumbled into the dormitory the next morning, the sight of my sleeping body caused her to let out a small scream and arm herself with a bedside lamp, ready to fight off the unexpected intruder. She was still apologising for her mistake half an hour later as she stood on the doorstep and waved me goodbye. Stood beside her was Lois, who made me promise to post one of my books to her, explaining that there were still some places she was yet to visit.

On my way out of Bluff, I stopped at Fowler's fishmongers and collected six white oysters, the largest I had ever seen. They were to complement a loaf of bread and a bottle of wine that had been tucked in the boot of my car since Christchurch. With all the makings for a fine lunch, all I had to do was find a suitable setting. I could think of no better place than the Antipodes.

As I pointed the car eastwards and tracked along the coast, my mind went back to Brome's play and the slim volume that had inspired my journey. When I first formed my travel plans in my university library, I had revelled in visions of strange lands and improbable places. Over the past fifteen months, there was no doubt that I had encountered incredible new worlds that were more diverse than I ever could have imagined, but along the way, I also encountered many glimmers of home. One of travel's greatest gifts is the way it can refashion the familiar in new and unexpected ways, and by doing so, make even the most mundane elements of our lives seem novel, even sacred. And as I drove east over the rolling hills of Southland, through a landscape of green fields smoothed by sunshine, I could not help but smile to myself because I had never expected that the Antipodes would look so much like home.

I followed the road in the direction of Slope Point as far as I could, until it came to an end near the mouth of an estuary which bled out into a shallow lagoon, bordered by green cliffs and hidden from the ocean by a sweeping sandbar. Stepping out of my car, I could hear a constant battery of white rollers breaking in the distance, but from behind the cliffs, the sea was invisible. A portion of the road continued up the hillside in front of me, but it was a muddy, uneven track that I knew would be too difficult for my car. So packing the oysters and wine in my bag, I put on my boots and started walking, thinking to myself that it was a fitting tribute to Brome's protagonist, Peregrine, to be completing the last stretch of my journey on foot.

Hauling myself up the muddy trail, I emerged hot and breathless at the top of a hill that rolled down to the cliffs in the distance. It was a calm, balmy day, but the handful of trees scattered across the gently sloping fields spoke of harsher winters. Sculpted by gales blowing from the south, every plant was bent sideways, as if fleeing from the ocean, twisted and contorted into wild angles by the wind. Just to look at those trees was to hear the shriek of their branches in the fury of a midwinter storm. At one place, a clump of conifers had been planted to the south of an old house, to protect against the weather, but over the years, the small thicket had closed around the home like a tight fist of green fingers, clutching at the crumbling walls. All that remained of the homestead was a ramshackle ruin, a remote outpost abandoned by its builders, left to be carried away, stone by stone, on the unrelenting breeze.

Following a faded trail, I walked down the hill in the direction of the ocean, completely alone in the landscape. Growing larger in the distance, I could see a small white lantern standing at the edge of the land, glinting against a dark swell. As I neared the lantern, the grass beneath my feet turned to dirt, and then the dirt turned to stone as I stepped onto the exposed rock of the sea-cliffs. A few steps later, the ground grew damp with spray, and then it suddenly fell away to a ribbon of shattered rocks far below, veined with white sea-foam. The metal lantern rose beside me, a compass emblazoned on its side, and nearby a little yellow sign carried a simple message:

Slope Point
Lat 46 40min 40 sec SOUTH
Long 169 00min 11 sec EAST

After more than four hundred days and over thirteen thousand miles of journeying, I had finally arrived at the southernmost point of New Zealand's South Island - the closest I could get to the Antipodes of my home.

Walking on weak legs, I shuffled out to the edge of the cliff, turning my face into the fine spray flying up onto the land, watching as thick tassels of kelp washed against the rocks below. I thought of the day, fifteen months before, when I had stood atop the cliff-top at Santander with the Atlantic at my back. I had worried then about how much earth was before me, about how much of the world I had to cross. Now, all that lay ahead was the open ocean, desolate and bleak, and beyond that, invisible in the distance, the howling ice-wastes of Antarctica cowered beneath an unbreakable winter.

I was glad that I was alone. Since leaving home, I had tried not to covet any portion of the world, but that afternoon, I wanted the cliff-top at Slope Point all to myself. As I sat down with my back resting upon the lantern and my feet dangling over the edge of the world, I felt profoundly happy, but I also sensed that my journey was still not quite complete.

Memories, if revisited too often, are worn smooth over time. Whilst travelling, I tried always to look towards the future, and I often denied myself time for reflection, out of fear that living too much in the past might have caused my remembrances to lose some of their lustre. But I always knew my memories were there in my head, perfectly preserved, all the more potent because untouched, waiting for the right moment to be revisited.

As I sat on the cliff-top overlooking the Southern Ocean, for the first time in a long time, I unshackled my memory and let it run back along the full course of my journey. Moving slowly at first, it lingered in New Zealand, gradually gathering speed as it roamed over Australia, rolled across Asia, and then vaulted towards Europe with astonishing ease. One by one, each of the four hundred days that had passed since I left Somerset pirouetted into my head and arranged themselves in a single, glittering cord of memory, wound around the earth from one side to the other. Fixed in place by every landscape, face, fear, hope, and joy that I had encountered along the way, the chain of memories unfurled, pristine and flawless, all the way from Slope Point to home - a journey which ended as it had begun, within the borders of my mind, where it will reside for a lifetime.

Acknowledgements

On my journey to the Antipodes, I was offered help and hospitality from nameless strangers more times than I can remember, and the kindnesses that I received are too many to number. In sixteen months of travelling, most of what I saw led me to believe that the world is a much more benevolent place than many paint it to be. If your name is not featured below, it is not out of a lack of gratitude, but simply because the multitude of gifts that I received outweighs my errant memory. I am deeply grateful to everyone who played a part.

In particular, I would like to thank my parents and grandparents for their continued support, in all its forms, for all my wayward adventures, both geographic and literary. In many ways, travel is the most selfish of human endeavours, and I understand how difficult it must be to watch a loved one disappear to the other side of the world for an unknown period of time. I hope this book offers some compensation for the anxiety that I caused. I would also like to thank my brother for inspiring me to travel from a young age. At least some portion of blame must lie with him.

For helping prepare me for my journey, I would like to thank Tracy from Taunton School of Motorcycling, as well as the team of mechanics at GV bikes. Some of the things you taught me quite literally saved my life. I would also like to thank the team at Optimus Education for their support and boundless enthusiasm ahead of my departure.

I would like to thank Emma and Charles for their generous hospitality, and thanks must also go to Jen, Steve, Tom, Tish, and Greg for having me aboard the *Antares*, a venture only made possible by Jackie and Dave, to whom I am also grateful.

I would like to thank John, Irvin, Pepita, and Keith, all of whom feature in this book, for their wisdom, tuition, and stories. It was also a pleasure to spend part of my journey with Marine, Eddy, Athalia, Gunnar, Freddy, Cody, and everyone else who was forced to wait for five days at the ferry port in Baku. Mentions must also be given to Maxime, Elve, Alex, Peter, and Claudia for their help and company at various stages along the wild roads of Central Asia.

I am particularly grateful to Jake for visiting me in Greece, and to Emma, Tom, and Alex for visiting me in Georgia. After months alone on the road, your company provided some much needed respite. Likewise, thanks must also go to Harry, Ashiba, Joss, Deej, and Eleyna. It was a privilege to share a portion of my journey with each of you.

From old friends to new, I would like to thank Bertie for his companionship across Central Asia and beyond, and for his continuing willingness to sit with me and reminisce about our travels in the various pubs of Somerset. Jan, I hope, already knows how grateful I am to him for his friendship, guidance, and company. Without my dependable Dutchman, I would never have crossed Central Asia by motorcycle, and for that, I shall remain indebted to him forever.

I would like to thank Ismail for taking me into his family and showing me a side of India few get to see. Likewise, I would like to thank all the people that I spoke to in Myanmar for offering their perspective on troubling topics. I am also grateful to Leon and his friends in Singapore for their impeccable hospitality and for their honesty.

Thanks must also go to Steven, Ivan, Dom, Justine, Tim, and Jack for making me so welcome and providing a home for me in Hanoi. Though I grumbled often about the teaching and the weather, I look back upon my time in Vietnam's capital with profound fondness, largely due to having spent it with you all. I am also grateful to Miss Quyen and all the teaching staff of Doan Thi Diem Greenfield School.

A special thanks must go to Rick for piecing me back together whilst in Melbourne after my dreadful time on the fishing boat. You worked tirelessly to find me a home, a job, and a whole new company of friends, and I cannot express how badly your kindness was needed. Thank you also to everyone at *Good Times* for your friendship and for treating me from the beginning as one of your own.

I would also like to thank Hank, Kyle, and Andrew for everything they did for me in Coburg. Beyond providing me with a home, you all made me feel incredibly welcome in Melbourne, and a part of me will always miss my little life in Australia.

The reason that I look back upon Australia with such fondness is also largely due to one other person, and I would like to thank Eva for her support and companionship both during my journey and afterwards. Without you, so much of Australia would have remained unknown, something which the writer in me will always be grateful for. Added to that, more than anyone else, you had to deal with all the frustrations and anxieties that came with my attempts to write this book. Your patience was infinite. I hope it was justified.

Finally, thank you to everyone who has picked up this book. In a world crowded with distractions, the fact you have all forfeited some portion of your lives to read my pages means more than you can ever know.

Printed in Great Britain
by Amazon

46380529R00192